The Persistence of Orientalism

Middle East Studies Beyond Dominant Paradigms
Peter Gran, *Series Editor*

For a full list of titles in this series,
visit https://press.syr.edu/supressbook-series
/middle-east-studies-beyond-dominant-paradigms/.

The Persistence of Orientalism

Anglo-American Historians and Modern Egypt

Peter Gran

Syracuse University Press

∞ The paper used in this publication meets the minimum requirements
of the American National Standard for Information Sciences—Permanence of Paper
for Printed Library Materials, ANSI Z39.48-1992.

For a listing of books published and distributed by Syracuse University Press,
visit https://press.syr.edu.

ISBN: 978-0-8156-3697-7 (hardcover)
978-0-8156-3698-4 (paperback)
978-0-8156-5508-4 (e-book)

Library of Congress Cataloging-in-Publication Data
Names: Gran, Peter, 1941– author.
Title: The persistence of orientalism : Anglo-American historians
and modern Egypt / Peter Gran.
Description: First edition. | Syracuse : Syracuse University Press, 2020. |
Series: Middle East studies beyond dominant paradigms | Includes bibliographical references
and index. | Summary: ""The Persistence of Orientalism" is a study of Anglo-American
historiography of modern Egypt, which emphasizes the work done by other professional
historians, especially Edward Said"—Provided by publisher.
Identifiers: LCCN 2020008444 (print) | LCCN 2020008445 (ebook) |
ISBN 9780815636977 (hardcover) | ISBN 9780815636984 (paperback) |
ISBN 9780815655084 (ebook)
Subjects: LCSH: Egypt—Historiography. | Orientalism.
Classification: LCC DT76.7 .G73 2020 (print) | LCC DT76.7 (ebook) |
DDC 962.05072/41—dc23
LC record available at https://lccn.loc.gov/2020008444
LC ebook record available at https://lccn.loc.gov/2020008445

Manufactured in the United States of America

Contents

Preface

This work is a contribution to the study of Anglo-American history writing about modern Egypt. The emphasis is on the American side. The subject is not a developed one. At this point, what one can find are a few bibliographical tools for students studying Egypt and a certain amount of incidental commentary on methodologies and archives. The present work attempts an overview concentrating on the history of the dominant paradigm found in scholarship on Egypt from the era of the professionalization of the university until now—that is, from roughly the 1890s onward.

My goal in writing this is twofold: first, to write a trade book useful for colleagues, and, second, to write a book drawing scholars in other fields into the study of some of the main issues that I am raising here in the belief that such work would be mutually beneficial. Thus, I begin the book with two introductory statements—this opening chapter, which is addressed to the wider audience, and then the one that follows, which is for the more narrow audience of specialized readers.

This chapter raises three broad issues, which Egyptian studies, among other fields, confronts and proposes a way to deal with from the narrow vantage point of this field. The first of these concerns the question of periodization of modern professional knowledge in the United States; the second concerns the contemporary identity of Orientalism and, in particular, its relationship to the study of modern Egypt; and the third concerns the apparent close connection between the dominant paradigm found in the study of modern Egypt and the dominant formulation of American identity found in American studies and in American life in general.

The Periodization of Modern Professional Knowledge

The history of American knowledge production and its periodization is of concern to many scholars, not just those in this field. What we know is that learned societies and professional groups date back to the early years of the nineteenth century. The professionalization of the university, which is sometimes associated with the birth of modern knowledge in a more general sense, is usually dated from the period of the late nineteenth into the early twentieth century. My hypothesis is that changes on the level of the university in this period forced the various fields in the university system—large and small—into a new format, the one with which we are familiar today. Some might see these matters quite differently—that professionalization was more a matter of serendipity. There are new fields and old fields. Still, I would contend that professionalization as an ideology and set of practices seems to have arisen at a particular time and that it redefined old fields as well as new fields.

Another hypothesis concerns the importance of the prehistory of modern professional knowledge to our understanding of what developed thereafter. In the case at hand, the outcome of various struggles in the late nineteenth century around race, class, gender, and region, as we shall see shortly, very much affected how the field would develop thereafter.

Whether such findings have a wider applicability is hard to judge. Studies of the professionalization of knowledge that I encountered were not concerned with the prehistory of the various fields as much as they were with the activities of the scholars engaged in creating professional organizations and programs. While perfectly understandable, this conventional view of professionalization tends to ignore questions of power and of political economy and perhaps rather too quickly assumes that some sort of radical change had taken place in civil society, which may or may not have been the case. This is not to suggest that the role of the government is ignored, but, rather, that it is downplayed. The conventional view is that the government played a part when professional organizations sought to obtain accreditation, but then and only then. The big emphasis in the scholarship on professionalization is on how professionalization largely took place in civil society. The field of Egyptian studies suggests the relation between professionalization and the state may have been quite a bit more than that all along and that the priorities of the government very likely influenced the choices scholars made.

In dealing with these matters, it is no doubt useful to make some quick reference to the familiar narrative of the victory of the East Coast in the sectional conflict in the election of 1896, and the entry thereupon of America into a new phase that we term the "Rise to Globalism." In this familiar narrative, it is assumed that the victory of the East Coast coincided with the victory of the eastern white male elite. How this victory came about is less clear. In any case, following this victory government policy tilted toward imperialism in the Middle East, and this in turn resulted in a need for the kind of knowledge that would be useful for such a venture, other kinds of knowledge and expertise being marginalized. Thus emerged the modern fields of Middle East and Egyptian studies.

From immersing oneself in this material before 1890 and then thereafter, the context starts to become clear. Since the middle of the nineteenth century, the American contact with modern Egypt had been the one that was fostered by the Protestant missionaries. There was no other body of American expertise comparable to theirs. To the East Coast elite, who themselves came from Protestant backgrounds, the missionaries, however, were too involved with people in Egypt to be of use, so they forged a de facto alliance with British imperialists and began to rely on their writers and expertise concerning Egypt. What gets overlooked are the works of two eminent Presbyterian missionaries: Andrew Watson, author of *The American Mission in Egypt, 1854–1896* (Pittsburgh, 1898), and his son Charles R. Watson, author of *Egypt and the Christian Crusade* (Philadelphia, 1907). Both of their books presented a narrative account of politics in Egypt along with detailed information about the activities of American schools and other institutions in which the missionaries were involved. Both saw Egypt as Pharaonic as opposed to empire building. This may explain why one finds that the East Coast establishment turned to the work of the British proconsul in Egypt, Evelyn Baring, Lord Cromer's *Modern Egypt* (1908), making it their founding work. This led to the unexpected development of the subject becoming an Anglo-American field as opposed to a simply American one.

When American knowledge became professionalized and thus modern but was then dominated by works such as Lord Cromer's, I had to make a choice. I decided to emphasize the work Americans took to be authoritative. Someone else in my position might have taken the subject differently and begun their account after World War II, when America became the leading center of its own knowledge production. However, having begun as I did with the issue of the dominant paradigm and its evolution, the post–World War II period would have been much too late. Still, all this raises the question as to whether other fields in American academia had similar experiences in this period, one in which a preexisting intellectual community was appreciated in a token sense, but professional scholarship was reshaped and proceeded on another basis.

The Contemporary Identity of Orientalism and Its Critique

This book's argument may also be seen as a part of the "critique of Orientalism"; however, at this point the phrase "critique of Orientalism" is rather loose and in need of further elaboration.

There are at least two different but overlapping usages of the idea of "the Orient" and, by extension, of "Orientalism" and the "critique of Orientalism." There is an older Orient associated with the colonial and early state-building period. In this older Orient, medieval studies dominated modern studies and philology dominated history. Then there is the Orient of today, which is more concerned with economic development and political stability. Scholars often simply gather data. One of the findings presented here is that there has been a common thread running through the literature of the field, old and new, as the metanarrative of the field has not changed moving from colonialism to postcolonialism.

The literary critic Edward Said claimed that Orientalism was a discipline resting on the relationship of colonizer to colonized. It produced a set of images that served the needs of colonialism. From this, Said reached his rather controversial conclusion that knowledge produced and framed in terms of an Orient was tainted knowledge. And he reached that conclusion in a way that made the point all the more controversial, basing his argument as he did on an examination of the main literary commentary and travel accounts of the British and French empires as opposed to the work found in scholarship. Of course, he had his reasons for proceeding in the way that he did. He believed (correctly so, in my view) that the idea of the Orient was widely embedded in Western culture and therefore not one to be understood simply from the works of specialists. Following the publication of his book came the predictable counterattack from Orientalists who held that their work was done in a scientific spirit, and that Said—given his training in French and English literature— was not qualified to say anything about it one way or another. To some degree, these points were valid, but they ignored the main issue that Said was trying to raise, which concerned the rather spurious nature of the very idea of an Orient. Said, it must be said, took a rather dismissive view of critics in the United States and the United Kingdom, and perhaps rightly so. Less easy to dismiss, however, was the criticism Said encountered in the Middle East itself by some who pointed out that many of the influential figures of the past century that one would call "Orientalists" were themselves Middle Easterners and, with only a few exceptions, not a part of European imperialism in any sense. Most of these individuals taught in Middle Eastern universities, a few in European and American universities. This called into question Said's correlation between colonialism and Orientalism.

Said died in 2003, and during the later years of his life he was not disposed to deal with such criticisms and his critics were not disposed to deal with the more radical implications of what he had written, perhaps because even some of his supporters believed that there was in some sense an Orient. As this book will show, what developed in

American scholarship on Egypt and on the Middle East was a selective use of the Saidian heritage by the generation coming into the field after 1980, virtually all of whom considered themselves to be critics of Orientalism from a postcolonial perspective and followers of Edward Said.

However, it is useful to recall that not everyone finds it persuasive to tie Oriental studies so closely to colonialism as the Saidians have tended to do. If one studies the British officials of the era of Cromer and beyond who wrote the books that shaped the field, one finds that their actual background was classics. Their education in classics was useful, as it allowed them to compare what they were doing to what the Greeks and Romans had done earlier; their view of history was one of the rise and fall of empires. While this would overlap with some of the East-West discourse of Orientalism, it was more of a cyclical view of world history than a dialectical unfolding as one finds in the idea of the rise of the West and the stagnation of the Orient commonly associated with Orientalism and, of course, with Hegel. On this point, one might note as well that there is some divergence between the United States and the UK; for the most part, the Americans were closer to the Germans and to Hegel than were the British imperialist scholars.

And, while, of course, some Orientalists did serve as colonial civil servants, the center of gravity of Orientalism from the nineteenth century into the twentieth century was Germany, not England. It was the German study of religion that gave rise to higher criticism, comparative Semitics, the development of philology, and modern Oriental studies. It seems pointless to gainsay these achievements, as is often done these days. The Saidian tradition, in my view, went astray conflating colonialism and Orientalism, and in dismissing this scholarly work in toto.

Where Said was more to the point was in his attack on the idea of an Orient. There is no such place as an Orient or a West. There is no such thing as an Oriental despotism. What exists are countries with their dynamics of ruler and ruled. What scholars have assumed, however, in the case of Egypt, is that there was an Oriental despot: someone who created a system in which he had total power.

This power resulted from control of the irrigation system on which the agriculture depended. It would follow that such a system would be a static one; the only change possible would be change coming from the outside—for example, Napoleon. As the later chapters show, this is a weak part of the logic of the dominant paradigm. It defies common sense, and it flies in the face of a considerable body of empirical evidence to the contrary, but there are reasons why it survives, as we shall see.

The Dominant Paradigm of Modern Egypt and of American Identity in American Studies

A third major finding of the book is that the Oriental despotism approach to the interpretation of Egypt survives because it plays an essential role in the narrative associated with American identity, the narrative in which America was founded by Pilgrims coming to a new world.

I realize that I enter here into some controversies. I am asserting that there is a main structure of American identity and that the interests of state are tied up in it. For others, the hypothesis may be difficult to accept, at least without the longer, more nuanced account found in the book. Why would not one expect there to have been a rupture with the Puritan past by this point? How can one use the term "national identity" in an age marked by hybridized versions of American identity (e.g., Chinese American, African American)?

To conclude this section, let us turn now to consider a few examples of how identity issues impact the study of Egypt. An obvious place to begin might be pointing to the idea of the rise of the West, meaning that the common heritage was one coming out of Greece, Rome, and the Bible. Of these the Bible is the most important part of heritage, and the book in the Old Testament entitled "Exodus" is one of the most important parts of the Bible. Exodus tells the story of how Moses led his people out of Pharaonic Egypt to the chosen land. The image of Egypt portrayed in Exodus is one of a static system run by a Pharaoh. Given the centrality of this story to Anglo-American culture, is it to be wondered that few would take the time to consider what its impact might be on the study of Egypt?

As with the discussion of periodizing modern knowledge production, so with the critique of Orientalism, and so too with the subject of the influence of American identity on scholarship, one can find no one arbiter or center of gravity to guide one's research. As a result, a specialist in one of a number of fields may not only understand a book of this sort but be able to offer suggestions and insights about what might logically come next that would not occur to those of us who work on modern Egyptian history. At the same time, it might not occur to those outside of Egyptian studies how detrimental this biblical story is to modern Egyptian society and to the study of it.

Acknowledgments

I would like to thank my department for nominating me for a sabbatical leave for the year 2015–16, which permitted me to write this book. I would also like to thank colleagues at Temple University who have encouraged this project from the beginning, particularly Teshale Tibebu, whose *Hegel and the Third World* (Syracuse University Press, 2011) was inspirational.

The Middle East Center of the University of Pennsylvania has supported my research for many years; it is a pleasure to thank it. Co-teaching a course with Robert Vitalis on the history of Middle East studies was of great value to me. I want to thank Bob for helping me question how the subject had been put together. Also from UPenn, Heather Sharkey gave me useful references, as did Eve Troutt Powell. The interlibrary loan departments of that university and Temple University have been indispensable.

Colleagues in the Middle East Studies Association (MESA) and in the American Research Center in Egypt (ARCE), too numerous to mention individually, have played a role in this book, and I am grateful to them.

Ali Ahmida of the University of New England and I have been in regular dialogue about historiography, and especially about Libya. Rifaʻat Abouʼl Haj, whose critical insights over the years have been of great help, also very much deserves my thanks.

Equally, I would like to thank the Egyptian Society for Historical Studies, here paying tribute in particular to the late Raʼuf ʻAbbas, with whom I was privileged to be able to discuss Egyptian historiography for many years.

I have also received a good deal of help from Assem al-Dissuqi, especially during the time of the translation of his work into English. In addition, I want to thank 'Ali Barakat, Sayyid 'Ashmawi, and Emad Abu Ghazi for sharing their insights.

Nelly Hanna opened many doors for me in Egypt through the annual American University in Cairo (AUC) Conference and by nominating me for the distinguished Cleveland Bayard Dodge lectureship at AUC, as well as through her own trailblazing writing, unique in shedding light on the seventeenth century and on Egypt's early modern economic history more generally. It seems unlikely that this book could have been written without her support of my work and without the research she herself carried out over the past years.

I would also like to thank Mehrzad Borujerdi for the chance to rethink the historiography of al-Tahtawi's life, and Joseph Lowry and Devin Stewart for a chance to rethink that of Hasan al-'Attar.

As this book is the fruit of many years of thought about the paradigm dominating the study of modern Egypt, I should also thank the group that sponsored and published the *British Review of Middle East Studies* in the 1970s, in particular the late Roger Owen and Talal Asad, who played a leading role in those days. It was there that I made some initial attempts to understand how the field was the way it was.

In more recent times, Mahmood Mamdani has encouraged me to reflect on the problems of Eurocentrism in Egyptian studies from my experience. He published an essay on that subject that as it turned out became the takeoff point for this book.

In the 1980s and 1990s, following the cultural turn, what was meant by the "critical understanding of history" changed in the academy. In the process, there was a certain disruption of the traditional studies of different nations in favor of the global and local. I personally happened to have missed the turn, but over time I have benefited from some of the thinking it produced. Conversations with Timothy Mitchell were helpful, as was his work on the state of area studies in the university.

Osamah Khalil persuaded me to push ahead and complete the work, and Tanner Howard commented on it editorially. Mohammad

Ebad Athar of Syracuse University selected the entries for the glossary section. This book would not have come to fruition without my copyeditor, Emily Shelton, and the dedicated team at Syracuse University Press, in particular Peggy Solic, Kay Steinmetz, Nora Luey, Meghan Cafarelli, Fred Wellner, and Lisa Kuerbis.

My wife, Judith Gran, has encouraged me in my work over this past half century. For the past thirty years, her struggles in the area of disability rights have been a source of inspiration to me. To her this work is dedicated.

The Persistence of Orientalism

Introduction

This book offers an interpretation of the history of Anglo-American studies of modern Egypt, based on a reading of scholarly works written over the past century. My hope is to contribute to the history of knowledge production in Middle East studies and other related fields.

As this chapter reveals, the book began simply from the observation that this was a field about which little had been written—a field that had had few debates, but more than its share of lore. My sense was that probably the two points were related.

I approached the subject with rather conventional assumptions, which, as the work progressed, I discovered were not all that sustainable. Among them was that, in a scientific sense, the field began after World War II, following the creation of institutions such as the Middle East centers, and that what came before was a body of colonial and missionary writings that might on occasion be of some interest but were not scientific, with the exception of the early work by the French savants at the time of the Napoleonic conquest. What I discovered undermined my confidence in those assumptions to a considerable degree. What I found was that it was British colonial writings on Egypt that provided the framework for much of what was written before today; it was missionary writing on Islam, some of which was American, that provided the foundation for the contemporary Anglo-American study of Islamic society. The two together in effect gave substance to the paradigm of Egypt as an Oriental despotism, the paradigm that continues to underlie modern scholarship. For this and other reasons, I wound up beginning the work at an earlier period than expected, looking at the actual nature of the American field—again, contrary to expectations—as Anglo-American, rather than as strictly American.[1]

This chapter defines what is meant by "the main paradigm," or orthodox approach, to the study of modern Egypt, noting how a kind of colonial paradigm known as Oriental despotism has managed for whatever reasons to live on as the field's orthodoxy, doing so even in the era of postcolonialism, but how the origins of the paradigm predated the well-known colonial period of the nineteenth century, leading to the need for yet another hypothesis that long-term cultural factors associated with heritage and identity, not just short-term ones of a colonial or postcolonial nature, were contributing to its persistence as well.

As a work of interpretation, this book is unusual in that it does not seek out and challenge other interpretations. Those interpretations do exist, but they are associated with Middle East studies as a whole. This book is simply about Egypt. There are analogous problems in the study of other countries in the Middle East, but they are different. I also preferred not to base what I was writing on the institutional development of the field in Egypt after World War II, since the issue of the dominant paradigm was resolved much earlier, and I did not want to set up a straw man to attack. My priority was to try to understand how this field evolved. Nearly everyone in a field such as history would agree that there is a context within which knowledge is being produced. Quarreling with the odd work that would claim otherwise scarcely seemed productive.

What is noticeable is the unchanging nature of the dominant paradigm in studies of Egyptian history over a long period of time. Historiography, like history, usually reveals change over time; here, for whatever reasons, changes were minimal. I tried to come up with explanations largely of a short-term nature, assuming that the field's dependence from the beginning on government and foundation money would have some bearing on the matter. Had this worked out, as I had hoped, it would have allowed for a materialist analysis, challenging a more free-will line of interpretation rooted in the idea of the sovereignty of scholarly choice.

However, on closer scrutiny, it became apparent that while the government did fund the field, it was interested in empire more than in supporting the Oriental despotism paradigm. Not content to drop the matter there, I also tried to link the history of the field to oil, and to argue that the government supported oil companies, and that Middle East studies mostly came out of that context. However, that assumption was not borne out either.

This was made clear to me from reading about the Suez Canal. I had thought that the Suez Canal was how oil came to Europe; therefore, the defense of the Suez by the British government and the American government was the defense of British or, later on, of American oil. But historians have found that the Suez Canal was more the lifeline to India, and that India was the jewel of the empire. Empire came first. Then, in the postcolonial period, the Suez Canal was a part of the world economy and not simply the world oil economy. Control of the Suez was once again an expression of power.

I also knew that the paradigm had roots in Egypt and not simply in the Anglo-American context. The Egyptian royal family and segments of the large landowning class (i.e., groups with close ties to the United Kingdom) were strong supporters of the Oriental despotism paradigm, perhaps as a way to maintain hierarchy in Egypt. This raised the question of whether the Egyptian ruling class could therefore be said to be a factor in the maintenance of this paradigm in Anglo-American scholarship in conjunction with the other factors that have been mentioned. This issue I did not pursue.

Finally, as a work of interpretation, this book does not provide the kind of bibliographical dimension that the field most certainly needs, nor does it offer the kind of evaluative statements sometimes found in handbooks pointing to the superiority of some books over others. Such work would also be useful, but it would be a different kind of enterprise.

Here, what the reader will find is reference to work categorized in one of three ways: books that have an iconic status because they were foundational; books that may be said to represent different types of work as the field evolved; and, finally, samples of what is today a very large and diverse field. A handbook or an annotated bibliography would not approach the material this way. Rather, it would tend to be more hierarchical.

The Orthodox Approach:
The Paradigm of Oriental Despotism

The Oriental paradigm assumes that there is an enormous gap between ruler and ruled, that Cairo is the center of power, that little or no power exists on the provincial level, and that the provinces are simply out there and essentially interchangeable. The ruler, in effect, is an autocrat more so than rulers in other countries. The population at large is understood to be powerless, not unlike the peasantry of biblical times, and civil society is perceived to be weak. Property rights and legal rights are believed to be less secure than is the case in other forms of government, and the country by its nature is assumed to be static. When change occurs, it comes from the outside. Since this happens only occasionally, Egypt has been assumed to be in decline, asleep, or simply stagnant throughout much of its history.

As my own thinking on the subject evolved, I came to think that countries are not stagnant, but scholarship sometimes is. When scholarship stagnates, sometimes the main sign is a single approach being taken to a subject; normally, a field would encourage conflicting models of interpretation. In the case under discussion, however, this is not what one typically finds. In place of conflicting models of interpretation, one finds differences of opinion among colonial writers, nationalists, Islamists, leftists, modernization theorists, and, more recently, postcolonialists, all of whom share the Oriental despotism paradigm as their model. In recent times, this may be coming under criticism, but there is still no new paradigm to be found.

To proceed, some further discussion of Oriental despotism is obviously called for, given not just its centrality, but its odd and uncertain genealogy, as well as the unexplained fact that, while familiar to some, the term remains unfamiliar to many. What seems to be the case is that, for whatever reason, the term is well known to sociologists, who deal with models of society. Its equivalent, *al-mustabidd al-sharqi*, is a familiar term in Egyptian Arabic, as is *despotisme Oriental* in French, but it is not familiar in Anglo-American studies of modern Egypt.

How the concept of Oriental despotism arose in modern thought, who was influenced by it, how they were influenced, and how the paradigm got applied to Egypt, or even what difference earlier usages might have made to the age of modern professional scholarship, all remain questions for which there is no systematically worked-out set of answers. We have some writings from the age of exploration and from the Enlightenment era, and we have some writings reflecting the influence of biblical archaeology and the classics. While these works are all helpful, they suggest that all that is known with certainty is something about particular moments in the history of the usage of the term.

In the context of the European mercantile ascendancy of the early modern period, Jean-Baptiste Tavernier, a French specialist on India, wrote books beginning in 1676 showing that Mughal India was an example of an Oriental despotism. His work established the term, which was later extended to include China. As for Egypt, long before *La Description de l'Égypte (1809–1822)*, European travelers and merchants seemed to be preparing the ground to apply the term to Egypt; they no longer wrote about "Great Cairo." Cairo had become one of the centers of "Turkish misrule." By "misrule," what they meant was that Egypt was no longer a disciplined centralized state in the way it was under the earlier Mamluks or the Pharaohs—that is, the kind of state that would have welcomed foreign merchants.

And, indeed, the observations about the relative lack of centralization are not entirely inaccurate. In early modern times, Egypt was only a centralized state in a formal sense. At least until the conquest of Upper Egypt by 'Ali Bey al-Kabir in the 1760s, Jirjah, the capital city, was not predictably controlled by Cairo at all. In addition, the Western Desert and the Sinai Peninsula had a considerable degree of autonomy from Cairo, as did regions controlled by rural notables or tribes throughout much of the rest of the country.

Nonetheless, the idea of the Oriental despot, once floated, took on a life of its own in European thought. No less a figure than

Montesquieu was one of its popularizers: in his *Persian Letters* (1721). While, of course, some suspected he was writing in a cautious way about French absolutism, and not about Persia at all, for our purposes, this is secondary; what is important is that he was using the concept, thereby enabling its circulation and lending it credibility.

What is also important, however, is that in the eighteenth century the utility of the concept was disputed by at least one writer who was also a part of the Enlightenment project: Abraham-Hyacinthe Anquetil-Duperron (1731–1805), a French Orientalist who believed in the broad similarity of the world's different peoples. He was the author of the well-known *Legislation Orientale* (1778), a work that disputed whether property was less secure in the Orient than it was in the West. His observation was that Middle East Islamic law and South Asian custom served to safeguard property, making it as safe as it was in the West. In his view, the extravagant claims that various Asian rulers may have made to European travelers about their ownership of everything were on the same level as those of Louis XIV, the so-called Sun King. In combining philological evidence with his own personal experience, Anquetil-Duperron struck at several core assumptions of the Oriental despotism paradigm.[2] This is a significant point when one comes to evaluate the work of the savants of Napoleon, all of whom took the idea of Oriental despotism for granted.

We do not know for sure how this idea entered Egyptian thought, nor how it found acceptance there, as it did sometime in the nineteenth century. Given that the concept was not in use in early modern Egypt, it is plausible that one version or another must have come about through contacts with the Europeans or the Ottomans, perhaps in the Muhammad 'Ali period or later.[3] What is certain is that al-Jabarti's history—the main Egyptian source for the early nineteenth century—does not demonstrate familiarity with it.

Moreover, when one turns to a consideration of the nineteenth century, one finds several competing formulations of the concept. The savants adopted one of them in their *Description de l'Égypte*, one stressing Oriental despotism as ancient civilization. Published in Paris in the years leading up to the invasion of Algeria, it aligned the ideas

of Orient and civilization, civilization being what France used to justify its colonialism.

Given the book's fame, one might have thought its formulation of
the concept of Oriental despotism would have become the standard
one. However, when considering the influence of this work outside of
France—as, for example, in the UK—uncertainty arises. In the UK,
we find that the British civil servants assumed Oriental despotism to
be a political arrangement, like the one described by Herodotus. For
the British, the overriding concern was maintaining their empire as
the Greeks and Romans had maintained theirs.[4] The issue of civilization was only a part of the background. Then we also have two other
understandings of the concept: that of the Egyptian royal family, for
whom the idea of an Oriental despot made their dreams of greater
and greater power seem more and more normal, and that of the British and American missionaries, for whom the concern with Pharaonic
Egypt derived from a preoccupation with the story of Exodus in the
Old Testament.

As noted earlier, the founding work of the Anglo-American field
was Lord Cromer's *Modern Egypt* (1908), a book in the tradition of
both British imperialism and the Bible, reinforcing the image of Egypt
found in Herodotus as well as Exodus.[5] In the next chapter, Cromer's
book will be discussed at greater length, but suffice here to note that,
while it had its critics as well as its admirers, no one criticized Cromer
for assuming that despotism and centralism were somehow elements
of Egypt's true nature. Criticisms, such as there were, tended to be
simply political. One might recall here the work of the Anglo-Irish
writer Wilfred Scawen Blunt and the Anglo-Russian writer Theodor
Rothstein.[6] It is from their work we learn that Britain's actual interests in occupying Egypt had more to do with Anglo-German bank
and investor interests than with Egypt's well-being, despite what was
claimed.

One might therefore ask: Were there critics of the paradigm of
Oriental despotism anywhere and, if so, who were they? Casting the
net widely leads to the discovery of a limited critique of the idea of
Oriental despotism by Russian and Chinese Marxists dating back to

the early twentieth century, which, oddly enough, did not survive. We might assume that the Oriental despotism paradigm, like other aspects of liberal theory, ought to have been seen by Marxist theorists as incompatible with a class-conflict dialectical approach and therefore rejected; after all, not only was the paradigm based on the idea of elite and mass and not class, but it had no theory of change. Add to this the fact that the two most influential writers on Oriental despotism in the twentieth century were both from the liberal tradition: Max Weber produced some of the most important insights about the paradigm, and Karl Wittfogel was the best known of all writers on the subject. Yet so apparently uncontroversial was this paradigm, no major writer in the Marxist tradition has bothered to try to produce a sustained refutation. The typical Marxist engagement has simply changed the name from "Oriental despotism" to "Asiatic mode of production" (AMP). Those unsympathetic to AMP have argued that the country in question was feudal, not AMP, but even the feudalist interpretation does not question the assumption of centralism.

We know that in the late 1920s, the heyday of his influence, Stalin opposed the AMP paradigm, believing that Asian countries were feudal, not Oriental. In that period, he had Mikhail Pokrovsky, a leading historian and party official, punish historians who deviated from the party line by supporting the AMP. This still leaves the question of why AMP was so important in the Soviet Union to such a large number of scholars, and why this is still the case. Perhaps one way of understanding the survival of AMP theory both in the Stalinist period and then in the years beyond—which might have some bearing on Egypt as well—would involve a class analysis of the Communist Party, to come to terms with where it stood on the question. And, while it has not to my knowledge been attempted in any systematic way there or anywhere else, it would be logical that as one moved up the party hierarchy in terms of power and wealth, the AMP would seem more and more plausible. After all, the paradigm was something of a defense of the land system. During the Cultural Revolution (1928–32), Stalin's base was the "New Man" (i.e., the new Soviet proletarian), and it was at this point that his opposition to AMP was most apparent. The

Communist Party as a whole, however, was not unified around the Cultural Revolution, the New Man, or the attack on AMP.

Divisions among Egyptian communists on the question of AMP seem to run along class lines as well. Those who came into communism from the working class tended to see Egypt as feudal.[7] Those taking that approach argued that the class war would overcome "Egyptian feudalism." A classic text along those lines was written by Shuhdi 'Atiyyah al-Shafi'i (born 1912; died in prison from torture in 1960). In his *Tatawwur al-haraka al-wataniya al-Misriya, 1882–1956*, al-Shafi'i sought to demonstrate that the progressive anti-imperialist struggle in Egyptian history had always been the one led by the masses. In the 1940s, al-Shafi'i was known for his opposition to Henri Curiel over the strategy the party should pursue, practice (or strategy) being tied to theory. Coming from an elite background, Curiel prioritized the struggle against imperialism and supported a popular front approach led by intellectuals, believing that that set of alliances to the working class should be the basis of the party. This got him thrown out of the party for several years.

A number of writers in later years followed al-Shafi'i with histories of the trade union movement. However, their methodology was no longer that of dialectical materialism, but that of Oriental despotism. There would be labor history, but labor history would be trade union history, and trade union history would be one theme among others in Egyptian history that came to the fore during strikes. Here one thinks of labor historians, such as Amin 'Izz al-Din, who compiled heavily documented books on the history of the Egyptian trade union movement.[8]

The problem Amin 'Izz al-Din and other labor historians faced was that, even as early as the 1970s, Egypt was beginning to de-industrialize, and the salience of a trade union–centered narrative as an approach to labor was declining. What was needed was a more broadscale approach, one that would deal with the great majority of workers, most of whom were not unionized. This became the project of two leading historians, Ra'uf 'Abbas Hamid and 'Asim al-Disuqi, from the late 1960s until the 1998 publication of *Kibar al-mullak wa-l-fallahun fi Misr, 1837–1952* (The Large Landlord Class and the Peasants in Egypt, 1837–1952).[9] This work presented a history of Egypt that shows that the growth of private land ownership created a small class of large landowners and a huge mass of rural workers and that over time, the latter found themselves in an increasingly hopeless situation. This work, along with that of 'Ali Barakat, has been considered the major challenge to the Oriental despotism paradigm until now.

Anglo-American scholars have also long followed the debates in Egypt on the subject of the working class. In 1987, Princeton University Press published *Workers on the Nile*. Its authors, Joel Beinin and Zachary Lockman, both had deep ties to Egyptian leftist circles and unusual access to sources.[10] Their work was similar in many respects to the Egyptian works I have identified, methodically tracing the struggles of the trade unions.

Apart from scholarship that directly challenges the Oriental despotism paradigm, of which there is very little, there is, however, work of an empirical nature that poses an indirect challenge by showing the vitality of provincial towns; the importance of rural power, commerce, guilds, and Sufi orders; and the role of informal strikes and protests.

More challenges, however, come from studies in the field of Egyptology and medieval Egypt. These studies suggest that over the past few thousand years only intermittently was there an important centralized state, so that overall the irrigation system depended on—and continues to depend on—regional decision makers and the self-interest of the peasantry to maintain the flow of the agreed-on allocation of water through the myriad side canals and ditches. The Oriental despotism model postulates, to the contrary, that placing peasants under the direct command of a central authority was the only way a ruler could manage the Nile River, which explains why Egypt was supposed to always have been a country with a centralized bureaucracy.

If the Egyptological and medieval Islamic bases of the paradigm are no longer in place, how secure then is the Oriental despotism model for modern Egyptian studies? Of course, in modern times, the state does dominate decision making, and it controls the major canals, but, as in the past, the system still depends on the peasantry to actually use the water to produce agricultural products; agricultural production is not that centralized. In sum, it would seem impossible, given these findings, to uphold the idea of Egypt as having an unchanging nature.[11]

The Historical Context of Scholarly Production

The field of Anglo-American studies of modern Egypt appears to have emerged as a subfield of colonial policy studies, religious studies, archaeology, and, subsequently, Middle East studies. Not surprisingly, there is not much written about this; there is very little written about the history of subfields. That point noted, it nonetheless appears that the history of the field can be traced through three distinct periods. The first period, which saw the founding of the field, ran from the late nineteenth century into the interwar period. The second period extended from the 1930s to the 1970s, during which the field adjusted to the Development Revolution, the Cold War, and the coming of Egyptian independence. The third period, from the 1970s to the present, saw the field adjust to the effects of globalization and American neocolonialism.

1890s–1930s: The Founding Period

This period coincided with the heyday of colonialism and with the professionalization of higher education, the combination of which exerted a considerable influence on the way many fields of knowledge were organized or reorganized. For example, biblical archaeology gave way to professional archaeology, the term "Near East" gave way to "Middle East," and new norms came to govern the production of knowledge. In this process, Egypt eventually became a subfield in American Middle East studies, all the while remaining Anglo-American in orientation. These developments did not arise organically out of the existing university culture, but were shaped by larger forces.[12]

The historian Osamah Khalil has summed up in his recent book what took place in this period in the following way.[13] The year 1919 witnessed the birth of the colonial Middle East following the Paris

Peace Conference of that year. From 1919 onward, the study of Egypt was a subfield in that context.[14] Had modern Anglo-American Middle East studies been set up fifty years earlier, it seems unlikely Egypt would have been a subfield. The strategic needs of the mid-nineteenth century were those of the India Office; this would have led to the field being defined around Egypt and the Suez Canal. However, following the Paris Peace Conference, the main strategic interest of the UK became that of the control of the Middle East oil fields and of Palestine.[15] Egypt appears to have become a subfield on that basis.

To understand the geopolitics of that era, one has to keep in mind both the broader imperial vision and the actions of the decision makers involved in oil politics, as, for example, those of Winston Churchill. It was Churchill who made the basic decision to transform the British navy from one that burned coal to one that used oil, to the considerable benefit of the Anglo-Iranian Oil Company. Slightly later, in his capacity as colonial secretary in charge of Near Eastern affairs, it was he who decided to limit the size of the Palestine Mandate by creating the Kingdom of Jordan. While this has been discussed in numerous works, it is odd that we find so few attempts outside of political journalism to explore the possibility of a connection between Churchill's work on behalf of the fleet and the Anglo-Iranian Oil Company and his commitment to Zionism. This might make clear what the British really meant at a certain time by the term "Middle East." Imperial power required keeping the control of oil out of German hands. (Incidentally, this was quite a profitable activity.)

Still, even if the birth of what we now simply call the "Middle East" followed from oil, it did not follow that officials in the UK would all necessarily write their books on that basis or separate Egypt from the Arab world as a way to divide and rule. But that is what they did.[16] It is also important to keep in mind as an explanation that most of those who wrote about Egypt were civil servants, and thus a part of the bureaucratic organization of the British government, and therefore also pursuing the imperial project.

From an American scholar's perspective, it is significant that, from the beginning of the twentieth century onward, the field was not so much American as Anglo-American, and that American scholars entered a field established in the UK to serve the needs of imperialism.[17] At the same time, one might want to keep in mind that the United States, like the UK, had an imperialist tradition that, while much smaller in scale, was growing fairly rapidly. Following the Spanish-American War of 1898, a number of prominent Americans, including Theodore Roosevelt and Alfred Mahan, began to express interest in building a navy on the scale of a leading imperial power, one reason being that at that point the United States had colonies of its own and an interest in how colonies could best be ruled. Here Egypt emerged once again.[18] It seemed to be a model colony, thanks to Lord Cromer.[19]

But there was more to Anglo-Americanism than simply the utility of Cromer's model for governing a few islands now under American control. There was also the fact that the proimperialist trend in the United States was still a minor one compared to the isolationist trend, which opposed imperialism. It seemed almost inevitable, therefore, that US imperialists who were looking beyond the Caribbean would have to search abroad for allies to strengthen their position at home. Those Americans interested in a more imperialist policy toward Egypt or the Middle East more generally seemed to have found their allies in Britain, not among their generally more isolationist countrymen.

As America was becoming an imperialist power internationally, internally one of the main trends taking place was that of professionalization. The two phenomena, I am hypothesizing, sometimes overlapped, although, of course, each progressed according to its own trajectory. To test this hypothesis of an overlap, let us take a closer look at the professionalization of knowledge in the United States in the years leading up to World War I. At that point, professionalization involved three different communities: those immediately engaged in forming the professional organizations, sometimes in a university context, sometimes not; those in the government concerned with cultural policy and who were in a position to extend or withhold official blessing and funding; and those who came to be characterized as amateurs or provincials, who lost out as professionalization progressed and who in some instances might have stood in opposition to the choices being made. Looking at professionalization in this way, it appears to be not just an intellectual phenomenon, but also a bureaucratic, a political, and sometimes an imperial one, one that resulted in the modern structures of various different academic fields and in the process put pressure on scholars across the board to adopt certain new norms.[20] It is equally apparent that professionalization was an uneven process; not all the same features are found in every field. Sometimes one can observe what appears to be the emergence of clearly delineated fields with their professional organizations, and sometimes not. In the case at hand, long before the age of professionalization, scholars already knew what was meant by "modern Egypt," but they had not made it a particular specialty, as the concern of the missionaries was the Muslim world as a whole, and the British Empire's was the Suez and India. Later, when Middle East studies emerged, the primary concerns were control of the oil fields and the disposition of Palestine. Through all these years, the study of modern Egypt continued to evolve, but, as I noted before, it often remained spread across fields adjacent to it. When these fields professionalized, so, too, I am assuming, did the study of modern Egypt.

Yet another aspect of professionalization concerns its prehistory. At the end of the nineteenth century, when the professionalization of knowledge and of the university supposedly crystallized, there was no one event or clear marker to which one can point that would symbolize that development. In fact, it is difficult to separate this late nineteenth-century moment of crystallization from earlier events in American history, the outcomes of which were significant for the orientation adopted thereafter in various fields. What I have in mind here is Egyptian studies, but doubtless the point would apply to others as well.

In the years following the Civil War, the state was weakened by the trauma of what had just occurred and too divided to forge a social contract with society. In this context, the ruling groups found themselves challenged by gender, race, class, and sectional issues. Famously (or infamously), it fell back on its powers of coercion in agreeing to Jim Crow legislation, in perpetrating the Haymarket Massacre against workers, and in thwarting the attempts of women to gain the vote. Unable to forge a social contract, the state attempted to rely on short-term alliances to sustain its prestige. One might recall the staging of international fairs, the expression of interest in major sports events, the exploitation of the new mass media, and the selective and conditional recognition of professional organizations.

This was a period marked by coercion and violence. Of concern here, of course, was the violence taking place in higher education, often associated with professionalization itself. In the various battles fought in academia, women, African Americans, and even the upholders of the biblical worldview of the core culture generally lost out to a white male elite on the East Coast that was either secular or somewhat inclined to higher criticism. Had the outcomes of these battles been different, the dominant paradigms in a number of fields, including the one of concern here, might have been different.

As regards gender, for example, the result of the various conflicts in the years following the Civil War created some fields essentially for women, while reserving other, often more prestigious ones, such as university teaching, for white men. From the mid-nineteenth century of Seneca Falls onward, feminist women fought to enter into these domains from which they had been excluded. The arguments men often used to maintain their positions of privilege were, ironically enough, drawn from the Bible, a work they considered best left for men to interpret. At the end of the nineteenth century, however, this, too, was contested. Bible studies became an arena not only of sectional and racial conflict but of gender conflict as well. In the 1890s, the patriarchal control of biblical interpretation was challenged by the famous American radical Elizabeth Cady Stanton, who in *The Woman's Bible* (1895–98) expressed doubts about the accuracy of the King James Version, as so few women appeared in it, as well as about the blatant patriarchalism of the portrayal of Moses and Exodus, for some of the same reasons. In the stories about Moses, Stanton showed, there were no women except when Moses confronted problems; then, quite implausibly, there were women. This amounted to an attack on what would be the orthodoxy of professional history and archaeology as regards Egypt—in effect, an attack on the Oriental despotism model. Had Stanton's attack carried the day, our understanding of the figure of Moses might have undergone a major revision, and the field of Egyptian studies might have developed with quite different assumptions. Stanton, however, did not prevail, despite the logical nature of her arguments. And indeed it was not until the 1970s and 1980s, with the state once again weakened, that Egyptology and Egyptian studies were once again forced to allow gender issues to make some headway, along with which came a renewed criticism of the Oriental despotism model.

In the years following Stanton's setback, the gender struggle continued and, in doing so, continued to face many obstacles. Among them was the fact that the history professors decided which sources to consider and which to ignore. In the UK, a similar battle was waged, but the amateur historians, as they were called, held on; there, being an amateur was not something so easily dismissed. Still, in both cases one could claim that the professionalization of Anglo-American writing on Egypt resulted in the perpetuation of patriarchy, and that this situation continued for decades.

Yet even a brief look at the existing material suggests that some of what women wrote may have made men dismiss their work for its viewpoint and not simply because its authors were amateurs. One finds among the authors upper-class Anglo-American white women who lived in Egypt, some of whose commentary suggested that they were not comfortable with the dichotomies of the Oriental despotism paradigm. These books do not appear in the bibliographies of standard books, but a few have nonetheless managed to survive. One suspects there would have been more such books, but that some of these women may have felt constraints for personal, political, or commercial reasons, given what publishing houses would accept. I pursued very briefly the possibility that there might be unpublished materials out there, and I found that the World Cat search program lists hundreds of unpublished materials linking Americans and Egypt, some of whose identified authors are clearly women, waiting for a new generation of researchers.[21]

Looking at the women who had direct contact with Egypt—missionaries aside—we find that some of these women were the spouses of colonial civil servants and therefore close to what was going on officially, but some were more independent. While none that we know of were systematic commentators or critics like today's academics, some had much to say and revealed their skepticism about the prevailing orthodoxies. As the contemporary literary critic Billie Melman suggests, given the intimate relation between Orientalism and patriarchalism, some kind of feminist critique of Orientalism should scarcely be surprising.[22] Indeed this seems like a fair inference, as one finds in more than one Anglo-American work expressions of solidarity with Middle Eastern women, a solidarity obviously at odds with the East-West binary of the more masculinist version of Orientalism. In the American case, at least, according to Deborah Manley, an author who has collected some of their writings, it is apparent that some women writers were free to travel and to have contacts with women in Egypt, thereby gaining an exposure to the routines of daily life that their male counterparts did not have.[23]

Paradoxically, many of these travel accounts date from the late nineteenth and early twentieth centuries, the very period during which the prestige of colonialism and of the Oriental despotism paradigm was at its highest point.[24] This is a conundrum of a sort. The main resolution appears to point to what Anglo-American women and men shared in common: race and class consciousness. It seems fair to hypothesize that Anglo-American women of the middle and upper classes thought in terms of race and class as well as gender, and that it was their whiteness and their wealth that led them to accept imperialism and some of its intellectual baggage, even if their personal experiences made them doubt some aspects of it. In her dissertation, Melissa Lee Miller dramatizes the centrality of race in recounting a passage from Lady Duff Gordon's *Letters from 1862 to 1869*, where the famous traveler recalled receiving a slave girl as a present from the American consul (in Asyut?), observing how black she was, and how disagreeable.[25]

It also seems reasonable to suppose that Anglo-American women were in contact with educated Egyptian women, and that this might have been a way by which a critique of Orientalism was transmitted. Who these people were is a matter still to be studied. One possible example might be Ella Russell Torrey (b. 1925), a woman from the Philadelphia area who worked as an editor on *Al-Misri* newspaper in Cairo in the 1940s and subsequently as a close aide to Eleanor Roosevelt. Without further study of the lives and writings of such individuals, the hypothesis suggested here of Egyptian influence on Anglo-American women is not one that can be pursued; this would be a project for an AUC research team with access to the alumni records.[26]

In any case, those who would pursue such a subject will be in debt to the historian Lisa Pollard for her article on the scholarship by and about early feminists in Egypt itself, an article drawing to our attention the importance of the pioneering 1945 study by Doria Shafiq and Ibrahim ʻAbduh, *The Development of the Women's Awakening between the Time of Mohammed ʻAli and That of King Faruq*. Who, one wonders, were the first Americans to read this book? In later years, of course, Doria Shafiq became a familiar name from the monograph on her life by the anthropologist Cynthia Nelson and from the work of the historian Margot Badran.[27]

Events leading to professionalization were a factor not only in the maintenance of gender relations but also in racial relations. Questions of the day of a race-related nature that demanded a resolution included whether Africa had a history and, if so, whether Egypt was a part of it or a part of Europe. The debates around these questions take us back a number of decades before the birth of the modern university system. After the North won the Civil War and abolished slavery, African Americans attempted to get the white American cultural establishment to acknowledge the African origins of the United States as it acknowledged the European ones. Egypt was a crucial part of the discussion: Euro-Americans had a connection to Egypt through the Bible, and Egypt was in Africa. The state, professional historians, and archaeologists, however, did not allow this line of thought to be legitimated. Egyptian studies thus arose as a part of a racial paradigm, one that separated Egypt from Africa and left Africa a continent disconnected from the narrative of history prior to the arrival of the Europeans. From the nineteenth century onward, until the rise of Afro-Asiatic linguistics in recent times, Egypt was dissociated from Africa in the academy through its characterization as Hamitic.

In the opinion of various writers from the nineteenth century to today, some black, some white, if the study of Egypt were done in a purely scientific spirit, one might well reach the opposite conclusion, and, if that were the case, it might help mainstream African Americans into American culture by confronting Jim Crow racism. How the academy would situate Egypt was thus obviously important; it was not some remote matter about which few had time to investigate.

A particularly well-known figure in this campaign was Martin Delany (1812–85), an African American abolitionist, writer, and physician, and perhaps the best known of those who challenged the attempts to Europeanize Egypt. Based on the available archaeological record, Delany asserted the African basis of Egypt.[28] Delany was ignored just as Stanton was, and Egyptian studies emerged as racist and sexist. It was not until recent years, with the state once again weakened, that writers have begun to take another look at Egypt's African roots.

Besides the conflicts around gender and race, the prehistory of professionalization saw other conflicts as well, most important for our purposes that of sectionalism. In 1896, sectional conflict reached a high point during the presidential race, in which William McKinley ran supporting the gold standard, backed by voters on the East and West Coasts, as well as the more export-oriented farm bloc of the Upper Midwest, against the bimetallist platform of William Jennings Bryan and his supporters in the core culture. McKinley won but was assassinated shortly thereafter.

Among the issues separating the two regions of the country was the orientation of US foreign policy. After 1896, the internationalist East Coast pushed the country into war and into imperialism and away from the isolationist policies favored by the populist trend, which was dominant in the core culture. In the lead-up to the US entry into World War I, it was the Woodrow Wilson and Colonel House side of the US power structure (i.e., the East Coast imperialist one), and not the William Jennings Bryan side, that stood for US entrance into the war. Bryan, for his part, opposed not only the war but US colonialism as well. He was even a critic of Lord Cromer's policies in Egypt, which, as mentioned earlier, had gained considerable popularity since the United States had become a colonial power.[29]

To succeed in mobilizing public opinion in order to get the country into the war, it was necessary for one side or the other to control public opinion, knowledge, and culture, and to do so across sectional lines. This proved difficult. In fields such as American history, the cost of writing books was low, and the state had limited leverage over the professors. The state showed little interest in such fields, much to the frustration of the American Historical Association. The opposite pertained, however, to fields where the cost of writing books was high, as in Egyptian studies, where scholars had to depend on the government and a few foundations to cover their research costs. There, real control could be exercised. Even today, fellowships in such areas carry with them the provision that the research objective should include the production of research useful for policy.

1940s–1970s: Egyptian Studies and the Rise of an Independent Egypt

In the period between the 1940s and the 1970s, a number of important developments took place. Some of these influenced Anglo-American scholarship over the long run, while others were more specific to that period. For example, as we will see in the next chapter, when Egypt gained its independence in 1954, its historians began to explore the country's internal dynamics, and in the long run this affected the trajectory of history writing not only in Egypt but in Anglo-American studies of Egypt as well. In the short term, it was the Development Revolution launched to combat Soviet expansion that led to a new stage in scholarship. This we also take up in the chapter that follows, leaving for the discussion here the most important aspect of the period: the gradual breakdown of Anglo-Americanism, which had been a major feature of the field up to that point.

For a long time, the Anglo-American relationship was so strong it could overcome conflicts. As the twentieth century progressed, however, this was less and less the case. Following World War I, the relationship, especially in regard to the control of oil fields, became increasingly fraught; by World War II, it was one of an open rivalry, which was apparent even in the context of wartime cooperation and came to a head sometime between World War II and the Suez War. During World War II, the Middle East Supply Center in Cairo, which was originally Anglo-American, became increasingly American. In fact, the longer the war dragged on, the more the United States asserted its growing power. It was the length of the war, some claim, that gave the United States the chance to push its way into Egypt and into other areas of British influence in the Middle East, doing so by using the Lend-Lease Agreement as a form of leverage. Following this line of interpretation, the Lend-Lease Agreement not only gained the United States the upper hand in Egypt, but improved American trade conditions, oil transport conditions, and much else besides throughout the Middle East in areas controlled by Great Britain. A few years later, at the time of the Suez War, the United States unilaterally chose not to intervene. The result was a disaster for the UK.[30] It was also a blow from which Anglo-Americanism did not quickly recover.

After Suez, America began to dominate the production of Anglophone scholarship on Egypt. From that point on, while the British contribution to scholarship continued to be respected in the United States, American students no longer went back as far as Cromer in their reading; they read Albert Hourani, H. A. R. Gibb, and other contemporary UK academics instead. It appears that, from then on, American scholars no longer seemed so concerned with the earlier history of their field. They would spend time in London because it had an archive, but then they would also go to Cairo for the same reason. The framework was one of modernization and one of the United States and Egypt. It was less and less Anglo-American.

This raises the question of why the British accepted Anglo-Americanism for so long and did not break with it when they were clearly getting the worst of the relationship. Perhaps it was a matter of necessity. As early as World War I, Britain lacked better options. Given the rising power of Germany and of Japan, the British Empire was overextended. It needed the backing of the United States, and that need sustained the relationship.

Earlier, the situation was different. In the late nineteenth century, the two countries both had an interest in Middle East oil, but they were not yet competing against one another for control of it; Middle East oil was British. At that point, the two countries generally agreed with each other on oil-related matters, so third parties such as France and Italy were to be kept out and national oil company claims denied. The basis of what I am calling this shared interest appears to date back to the founding of the Anglo-American Oil Company in London in 1888, and the fraught nature of the relationship appears to date back to the San Remo Oil Agreement of 1920, an agreement whereby Britain kept the United States out of Mesopotamia, leading the United States to create Aramco.

While one can scarcely deny the importance of the struggle for oil on the level of geopolitics, its importance as a factor in Anglo-American scholarship on Egypt in later years is difficult to assess. The Suez War was a geopolitical nightmare, yet it was ten or more years later that one finds some indication that scholars seemed to be attaching more importance to their own national scholarly organizations than had earlier been the case, when the field was more solidly Anglo-American. Eventually British scholars fell back on the resources of Oxbridge, SOAS University of London, Chatham House, and the British Council, which had been founded in Cairo in 1938. US scholars fell back on the American University in Cairo, founded in 1919, the American Research Center in Egypt (1948), and the Fulbright program in Cairo (1949).

Still later, new organizations appeared, and they too were nationally oriented. In 1966, the Middle East Studies Associations (MESA), an American organization, was founded, and the British Society for Middle Eastern Studies (BRISME) was founded in 1973. The British-Egyptian Society began in 1990. In a different kind of book, some deeper scrutiny of these organizations would be in order, but here these developments do not detain us, as their appearance had only a limited impact on the dominant paradigm.

In this same period, from the 1930s to the 1970s, professionalization continued to develop, and with it came improvements in terms of what would be considered appropriate research procedures. One might recall that, in the earlier times, scholars looted not only works from antiquity, but books, manuscripts, and documents as they saw fit, doing so literally or through nonattribution of sources. Later, following professional norms, MESA came out in favor of more ethical scholarly behavior on the part of scholars going to the Middle East.

To sum up, over the past century, it appears that the British and American governments sought to have the field develop in a way useful to their respective policy needs. For the better part of the last century, Anglo-Americanism fulfilled that need, until interimperialist rivalries and the competition for the control of oil got in the way.

1970–Present: The Era of Globalization

With the arrival of globalization came a new set of dynamics. Much of the commentary stresses the return of finance capitalism; other features draw attention as well. Understood in its political, economic, and historical context, globalization appears as an experiment by various rulers who hoped to raise the rate of profit by returning to the political economy of the nineteenth century, thereby eliminating the costs associated with the social contract. What made this particularly enticing was the prospect of appropriating the wealth that had been accumulated by the middle classes. Not surprisingly, the attempt to restore what amounts to classical liberalism gave rise once again to the struggles around gender, race, class, and region that we associate with the nineteenth century. There were, of course, a few differences. As globalization progressed, the American government handled the challenges more adroitly than it had earlier. Through a series of experiments, it hit on playing gender against class and race, which has worked now since the 1980s. As we shall see in the next chapter, it is this set of dynamics that underlies the contemporary development of academia and its various fields, including the study of Egypt.

To pursue the subject more precisely, this section begins by look-ing first (1) at the alliances of the state, then (2) at the consequences of the Nietzschean challenge in the university, which was another feature of the period, concluding with (3) long-term factors, as short-term historical analysis does not suffice.

The Changing Alliances of the State Leading to a Linkage with the Pro-fessional Woman.[31] The maintenance of hegemony typically requires alliances to play off race, class, gender, and region so as to divide and rule. In the case of the United States in the era of the social contract (1930s–70s), the state, especially during the Great Depression, built up the working class until segments of it turned toward communism. This led to repression and to a decade or so of support for civil rights and African American studies. When racial issues led to radicalization in the late 1960s, repression was exercised once again, and the state turned from African Americans to professional women and feminism. Women's rights began to advance despite opposition from the Chris-tian right and challenges posed by third-wave feminists. This set of alliances has lasted until now, or at least until the very recent rise of Donald Trump.

Over these decades, shows of support by the media, business elites, and politicians for the rights of women had an immediate impact in academia. There was a growth in the number of women who became professors and seemingly as a direct result the beginnings of a chal-lenge to the Oriental despotism model.

The Rise of a Nietzschean Challenge to Hegel in University Culture: A Challenge to the Oriental Despotism Paradigm? Nietzschean anar-chism or antihistory was a major force in Anglo-American society and culture of the late nineteenth century. While, for some, it was a form of oppositional discourse, this was not always the case. Some-times, the state, too, had an interest in Nietzschean thought, given its need to dismiss middle-class claims based on history, law, science, and morality. Even after the late nineteenth century and the rise of the middle classes, Nietzscheism continued to exist in one or another corner of the university. It always seemed to be a tradition waiting in the wings if Hegelianism faltered, and, as it turned out, in the post-1970 period of Anglo-American history Hegelianism faltered. At that point, the ruling class set out to expropriate the wealth of the middle classes, and the university was the bastion of the middle class. Anarchism was a way to disrupt university culture. By the 1980s, struggles between the Hegelians and the Nietzscheans were a conspicuous part of academic life, an unanticipated consequence of which was the beginning of a challenge to the idea of an Orient in works such as those of Edward Said.

This was new ground. Over the preceding 150 or more years (and many would say until now), the wider academic context has always been one defined by the Hegelian organization of knowledge and by the Hegelian model of world history, a model composed of the rise of the West, the stagnation of the Orient, and the existence of peoples without history. Throughout this period, it appears that Hegel's philosophy addressed the needs of the state and the middle class. Its view of the human future, after all, was an optimistic one. And, despite its obvious Eurocentrism, most historians embraced it because Hegel was the only important philosopher to acknowledge that history was not just a matter of background details but a way of knowing; in other words, history was a discipline. In more recent times, given the disillusionment with nation building, the shocks of World War I and World War II, and the dislocation of the middle classes caused by neoliberal policies, some of this long-term support for Hegel has begun to weaken. For many, the rationale for shifting from Hegel's worldview to some latter-day variant of Nietzscheism such as postmodernism arose out of the belief that a rupture had occurred and that Hegel was no longer relevant. Many college textbooks today assume that with the rise of AI, the breakdown of the Soviet Union, and the wider diffusion of democracy, a new world has dawned. In any case, with the rise of China it was no longer so clear how to deploy Hegel's foundational idea of the rise of the West.

It was, perhaps, not surprising that the traditional male professoriate in the post-1970 period, especially the historians, were among the last to acknowledge that their model was out of date. Even today, a large majority are probably still Hegelians. So it was that with the rise of Japan, many found themselves in denial of that fact. They tried to maintain that even during the great sell-off by Reagan the Japanese were simply good learners; it wasn't that America, the symbol of the West, was declining. However, with the rising power of China, India, and other Asian countries, it became clearer and clearer that Asia had become the world center of production, and that the old idea of the West versus the East or Asia had to give way. The West was no longer necessarily the most advanced or the most geared to the future.

There were still other developments as well, which also had their effect on the Hegelian culture of the university. Following the collapse of the Soviet Union, there was a brief interlude of "end of history" euphoria in which it seemed that the West was once again its mythic self; globalization was simply the latest chapter of its rise. This brief interlude, however, was soon interrupted by the realization that Russia, whether as an imperial power or simply as a country, was still what it long had been: a powerful antagonistic rival. Now one had to confront the fact that the United States had become just another country fighting for its own interests, and that historians no longer had a metanarrative for their discipline. Historians of imperialism experimented with cyclical history, proclaiming the idea of an American Century, while others turned to nostalgia and wrote about the Greatest Generation, and still others experimented with polycentrism. What is essential to keep in mind is that through all of this the idea of the Orient lingered on. East Asia might not have been an Orient any longer, but the Middle East was.

Under these changed conditions, a number of Anglo-American scholars (among them some feminists) turned from Hegel to Nietzsche. This was a major intellectual development. In recent years, as a result, the academy has witnessed a series of critiques of Hegel's ideas about history and modernity. Where Hegel believed the modern age to be universal but Western in inflection, Nietzsche believed that the modern age was inauthentic, especially in the Euro-American context compared to the Islamic one, which was premodern and thus still authentic.[32] Perhaps, this suggested, one should take another look at the power of women in medieval Europe.

As the Nietzschean current grew stronger, some scholars in that tradition came to think they should be studying countries as civilizations, as Michel Foucault did in Iran, that civilization was in some sense a paradigm, and that civilizational discourse might be more explanatory than was the narrative of the nation-state coming down from Hegel. After all, the very idea of a nation-state was a part of Western discourse, and, therefore, for countries such as those in the Orient, it would be inauthentic and not surprisingly unfulfilling. Edward Said was the best-known heir to the Nietzschean tradition in Middle East studies. Said's *Orientalism* (1979) has been an immensely influential work, and scholars in Middle East women's studies make extensive use of his writings.[33]

To sum up, a study of the context of the late nineteenth-century and early twentieth-century period, the interwar period, and the more recent period of globalization, taken together, provides some understanding of the context of Anglo-American studies of modern Egypt. What is also clear, however, is that this approach does not explain why one finds no real change in the paradigm of Oriental despotism or why this is not even a matter of scholarly concern.

Why, Then, Do We Still Find the Oriental Despotism Paradigm in the Study of Egypt? Here it becomes clear that while the short-term historical context explains some aspects of Anglo-American scholarship on Egypt, it does not explain the persistence of the Oriental despotism paradigm. Following Edward Said's *Orientalism*, it would have been logical to suppose that the paradigm was built into Hegel's idea of the Orient, that one could explain its persistence on that basis, and, by extension, that it would die out with the rise of postcolonial discourse and the critique of Hegel. However, as the foregoing has indicated and the next chapter will spell out, a generation of postcolonial scholars has been criticizing Orientalism and even Hegel, and yet one finds the Oriental despotism model still in place. To explain this, we need to unpack what we mean by "historical context." This section hypothesizes that in this case the historical context includes some parts of heritage from the remote past that are still alive, and in fact are still important, and for this reason have to be included in our understanding of the idea of Oriental despotism.

In adopting such a hypothesis, one might then suppose that in Anglo-American studies of Egypt a body of writing appears to be being written on two levels. One level, which is susceptible to a conventional short-term analysis, is the one we have been discussing up to this point. There is also another level, one that is not susceptible to this type of analysis and that requires adjusting one's approach. If before the concern was with ordinary cause and effect, at this point one relies heavily on inferences drawn from the long-term role of Egypt in Anglo-American culture and identity.

An examination of this second level leads to the idea that what the specialist in Egypt is engaged in over and above the production of knowledge is the maintenance of the Anglo-American self or American identity, that the continuing dominance of the Oriental despotism paradigm can probably be better understood from a consideration of American identity issues than from a short-term cause-and-effect type of science. While this may sound like an invocation of Egyptian exceptionalism, it is not, although it seems fair to claim that few other scholars need to confront this landscape of their own identity as a part of their daily work. Still, one might wonder why if what is going on is a struggle to maintain identity it is not more visible as such. The apparent reason is that this struggle is embedded in the assumptions we normally make about who we are as Westerners. There is no reason why a scholar would make them a part of his or her text.

Two examples illustrating this second level must suffice. Each takes up one aspect of what I am terming the "maintenance of identity"; taken together, they offer an explanation for why the Oriental despotism paradigm persists for the study of Egypt. Both of them relate to scholarly production in this field and, of course, to other fields as well, although perhaps to a lesser extent. The first of the two examples concerns the role heritage plays in normalizing the idea of hierarchy, while the second is tied more specifically to the particular role Egypt plays in our identity and heritage.

The question of what sustains the idea of the normality of hierarchy in historical works is a complex and fascinating one, with many aspects. My interest here is to point to one small part of this subject: the role of childhood socialization and the use of heritage in inculcating the acceptance of hierarchy among historians.

What is under consideration here is the question of what explains scholars' deference to the various global ruling classes' formulations of what is normal and authentic in their respective countries: Why is deference to such authority such a conspicuous part of historical scholarship? Why, given that historians are urged to doubt their sources and to question a reliance on elites, does most historical work nonetheless tend to adopt the view of a king, landlord, or bureaucrat?

A history book reflects not just an author's graduate education and subsequent research but his or her earlier socialization. This is my hypothesis. We are God's children, or we are in the hands of some other authority figures, and, for a child, these ideas are reassuring. In those years, we learn to obey and to show deference. In later years, out of a habit of deference, scholars are prepared to accept a certain definition of what is to be studied and from what sources. Deference to hierarchy, be it an academic or a political hierarchy, continues throughout one's career.

Were this a purely neutral matter, it would not be buried but open for discussion, along with other parts of a historian's formation. However, the acceptance of hierarchy in this sense is not neutral any more than are ideas about race or gender, or about Egypt as an Oriental despotism.[34]

The second example is chosen to show the implications of accepting hierarchy, Western identity, and Egypt as Oriental despotism. Here one needs to recall the important connection of the story of Moses and of the flight from Egypt to the birth of the West and, by extension, to ourselves as Westerners. Here the hypothesis is that, if one tampers with that story, a great deal of what follows or is related to it becomes less certain.

Still, one might wonder how this comes down to us today. When Europeans came to the New World, did they not try to rid themselves of a great deal of the baggage of the past? The answer would have to be that they did, but then they found they could not function without parts of it, among which are the core elements of the story of Moses. The Anglo-American of later years, like any other human being, cannot imagine his or her ancestors as mass murderers who killed Indians and enslaved Africans. The alternative, which the cultural heritage provides, is to understand one's ancestors and, by extension, oneself as being from the chosen people (i.e., Westerners, pioneers, pilgrims, evangelists, settlers, or modernizers), from among those who spread the word of God and civilization and represented the rise of the West, as Moses did, and in the process sometimes witnessed collateral damage and widespread killing, as Moses did. One's assurance is based on that fact.

At the same time, there is a difference between God's decision to drown the Egyptian army in the Red Sea and the decision of one's ancestors to murder and rob people. Killing is sinful. In retrospect, it is clear at least for some that these foundational acts that took place in North America and in other parts of the British Empire were of an essentially criminal nature and, presumably, as a consequence, have had a lasting impact on the Anglo-American psyche, which makes it troubling for many to think about their forebears. Add to this the fact that the conquest of North America or of the British Empire was not that long ago. In the nineteenth century, the past was not yet past; what was happening to First Americans, slaves, and colonial subjects was still happening. By the early twentieth century, more time had elapsed. Anglo-Americans had come to believe that by virtue of being Western they were racially and culturally superior. By this point the idea of Egypt as Oriental despotism was locked in place.

As the twentieth century progressed, however, there were some signs of change. Questions began to arise about what had happened in earlier times. Was the damage done to people in North America simply collateral, or was there some level of intent? Evidence suggests that civilized societies were demolished and civilized people enslaved, and if that was the case how could the myth of Exodus fulfill its promise that our ancestors were the chosen people of God and thus absolved from responsibility? Some Americans, at least, no longer could believe that slavery was an ordinary part of anyone's history or that the First Americans just died from diseases. Thus, it was perhaps a natural desire on the part of many to cling to the myth of Moses escaping from the Oriental despotism in Egypt, as there was nothing else to cling to.

In such matters, academia has been heavily involved. Large groups of scholars specialize in the study of American cultural themes and American myths, and for them the myth of Exodus is a major concern. One such group terms what it studies "American character literature," the British analogue to which studies Englishness. Another group of scholars is more specifically concerned with racial myths in American history; its work is called "whiteness theory."[35] Not surprisingly, these groups have been criticized by mainstream historians and social scientists even for interrogating American identity.

In addition, these critics do not share many views in common. For the character-studies tradition, there has to be a West, there has to be a "Rise of the West," and, by extension, there has to be a nonwhite Orient that was left behind. In a few places in that Orient, there may have been a golden age, but the main point is that thereafter, in all non-Western places, there was nothing but stagnation and hopelessness until the coming of God's chosen people—that is, Westerners. Exodus explains this, and it also explains and justifies one's being a Westerner, the flight to the New World, and the creation of the United States and the British Empire. Finally, it justifies the various invasions of Egypt that took place in later times to help Egypt return to its authentic self.[36] Here, one thinks of Napoleon or Cromer. Certain truths go beyond history.

For the whiteness theory/ethnicity school theorists, Americans have many ethnicities and many heritages. What they share is the culture of science. If a paradigm such as Oriental despotism persists today, it does so because it is scientific, not because of settler colonialism or racism in some previous century. Science tells us America is postracial; it elected Barack Obama, an African American, as president.

The most logical way to understand American identity is to postulate that (for the past few generations, at least) the country has been a complicated construction of different ethnic groups, much more complicated than it was in the seventeenth or eighteenth centuries. If the Exodus story plays a role in national identity today—and this is a second critique of the American character school—Anglo-Saxonism or Anglo-Saxon heritage alone cannot explain it, because the country has become multiethnic due to being made up of newly arrived groups.[37] Identity today is now more commonly a matter of hybridization (e.g., African American).

The ethnicity school also has its critics. Can one seriously argue on the basis of election results that America or Britain has become postracial? How would one explain the highly racialized controversies over immigration and incarceration? Until change on those fronts takes place, it seems reasonable to many that we still need to retain some focus on race-based politics and on the founding myths that justify race in the first place. For ethnicity theorists, this is not the case at all. To them, the most important form of social solidarity is ethnicity and not race or class. Ethnicity theorists see Anglo-Saxons as an example of one such ethnic group, but only one of many.

Scholars in whiteness studies have a more historical sociological perspective; they see Anglo-Saxonism more as an orientation toward class and power than as a matter of cultural inheritance, an orientation that some individuals find themselves born into but not necessarily wanting to be associated with, while others, coming from other backgrounds, make efforts to assimilate into and embrace. The term for this is "whitening." Whitening explains why today's American accepts the idea of Exodus, and why there is not some diversity of founding myths matching the diversity of ethnic groups. Were the situation otherwise, the Oriental despotism myth would in all likelihood have been pushed aside a generation or more ago as other formulations of American identity emerged, but this never happened.

To sum up, this chapter has portrayed the context within which Anglo-American studies of Egypt were produced.[38] It favored short-term factors, linking the development of the field to US foreign policy in Egypt and turning to a long-term structural analysis only when the former proved to be inadequate. The short-term analysis seemed to be most incisive in studying the field when it was small and close to the government policies of the day. As the number of scholars entering the field increased, the ranks became more diverse, and the scholarship became more academic, something else was needed. The conclusion was that the scholarship of Anglo-Americans working in Egyptian studies should be seen as less and less tied to the elite's imperialism and more and more tied to the maintenance of American identity, which in turn meant holding the Oriental despotism in place.[39]

This is a somber note on which to end. It is not intended to be. Other countries have had some success coming to terms with their past through efforts at peace and reconciliation. Perhaps this lies in the American future; one might hope so. In the short term, choices scholars make will play some role. A new generation of students in the field might arise that would deal with this ambience in a new and more creative way.

Chapter 1 examines the scholarly endeavors of the three main periods already identified. It thus begins with the late nineteenth-century to the early twentieth-century period. During this time, the most influential works on modern Egypt in the United States and the UK were found to be mainly those of British colonial officials. The chapter proceeds to take up the following era, extending from the late interwar period up to the 1970s, which was marked by the entrance of the middle classes into the academic world. This was the one in which the center of knowledge production shifted from the UK to the United States, and from philology to history and data gathering. Finally, the chapter takes up the third period, which began in the 1970s and continues to the present day. This is the period in which the Oriental despotism paradigm begins to come under attack from postcolonial discourse.

Chapter 2 takes up the orthodox narrative of modern and contemporary Egyptian history following the Oriental despotism model, demonstrating how it is put together on the level of factual detail via a close reading of a canonical work published by Cambridge University Press on modern Egypt, and of a major Egyptian work of reflection on the meaning of 1798 looked at after two hundred years. The rationale for the inclusion of the Cambridge volume over others is that it offers a synthesis that the postcolonial scholarship does not; the rationale for the inclusion of an Egyptian volume is that what we mean in recent years by Anglo-American increasingly includes Egyptian scholarship, and this particular book is a major work of reflection by Egyptian scholars on the subject of modern Egyptian history. The remaining chapters take up the problem of blind spots that arise from the retention of the Oriental despotism paradigm and consider whether the abandonment of the paradigm would resolve these problems.[40]

1

The History of Anglo-American Scholarly Writing on Modern Egypt from the Late Nineteenth Century until Today

This chapter takes up the history of the Anglo-American scholarly interpretation of modern Egypt from the late nineteenth century until today through a consideration of representative texts of the three periods under discussion: the formative period (1890s–1920s), the period of the Development Revolution (1930s–70s), and the period of globalization (1970s–present).

What one finds is that the Oriental despotism model was the hallmark of the field through these three periods. There have been several minor challenges to the paradigm, but none have succeeded, at least until now. The first of these challenges dated from the time of the Development Revolution, when some writers began to portray Egypt as a despotism, but a modernizing one. Other writers introduced class analysis, but this was never fully developed. In still more recent times, a number of writers have questioned the binary thinking on which the Oriental despotism paradigm is based. So far, however, no alternative model has appeared.

The Formative Period: British Imperialism from Heyday to Decline

"The formative period" refers to the years during which the study of Egypt underwent some degree of professionalization, not just as a part of university culture, but due to the pressures exerted by the government. This section starts with the work of Lord Cromer, the putative

35

founder of the field, then turns to that of his immediate successors and a consideration of the works of civil servants and academics whose writings were significant at that time. The missionary tradition produced a few writers, but historically their focus was more on Islam or language than on Egypt per se.[1]

There seems to be little doubt about the influence of Cromer's *Modern Egypt* (1908) both inside and outside of the academy.[2] This was because of the author's prominence and perceived mastery of his subject, as well as a matter of timing. In part, its influence might also be explained by the fact that it was an articulate restatement of the familiar. Newspapers of the day had been presenting similar ideas, so the book's publication served as a kind of confirmation of what readers already thought to be the case. As the book straddled traditions, it could be read in the United States for its allusions to Exodus; in the UK it could be read—as Cromer himself perhaps intended—in terms of Greco-Roman models of imperialism.

For those who worked in the colonial service, Cromer's references to the classical world were particularly salient, perhaps because his education and his experiences mirrored their own. Typically, a colonial official like Cromer had a university education that prepared him for a career in public service. We know this because many colonial civil servants wrote memoirs; some were even scholars. In their university days, the future colonial civil servant would have received a literary education, developing his skills as a writer and as a classicist. Minimally, his education in classics would have given him the example of the Greek and Roman Empires as a perspective for understanding the British Empire. Doubtless he would have read Herodotus, the first writer to introduce the idea of the West versus the Orient.

More important, however, was the matter of status. Typically, such an individual would have come from a well-connected family, who would open the door for their son to enter public service upon his graduation. In short order, the young man would become not just an official but an authority on some subject such as the Orient. If he was posted in India, for example, he would have found himself part of a group of like-minded individuals, as Cromer himself did, most of whom saw the country (and indeed Asia at large) as consisting of examples of Oriental despotisms.[3] Assuming someone was transferred to Egypt, the idea of the Oriental despot would be further reinforced by the prevailing colonial views about the Ottoman Empire, as well as by those of the missionaries about the state of Egyptian civilization. For the typical British colonial official in Egypt, whether arriving directly from England or transferring from India, the common view was that Egypt was an appendage of the Ottoman Empire, which was known at that time as the "sick man of Europe." This sick man was an Oriental despot in need of major reform. The West was, of course, the only hope for countries such as Ottoman Turkey.

While Cromer, like most other imperialists, was more interested in empire building than in religion and missionaries, he realized that the two went hand in hand. And, concerning the missionary movement, it must be remembered that, for all one reads about Victorian doubt and skepticism, for many in England (and for even more in the United States) the Victorian age was one of spiritual renewal and the spreading of the Word. While this was satirized and ridiculed by some at home, it was much appreciated by colonial officials abroad who came to realize the contribution these religionists made in justifying the British presence in countries like Egypt. Biblical stories such as Exodus seemed to make saviors of the British. Moreover, the presence of these religionists stimulated the development of Egyptology, a field of knowledge that was useful to British officials, as it widened the acceptance of the colonial project internationally and in Egypt, at least in the circles of the royal family.

By the time of the British occupation of Egypt in the 1880s, Lord Cromer was a rising star in the colonial service. He was, after all, a Baring, a member of the family connected to the bank bearing that name. Upon his arrival in Egypt, Lord Cromer professed to be concerned with the efficiency of the irrigation system and with the condition of the peasantry. Reforms were needed. His task, he said, was to reform Egypt.

Cromer believed that the only way to reform the country was to make it fiscally sound, and that the only way to do that was to help it reach its true agricultural potential. This, he believed, would in turn depend on the expansion and centralization of irrigation. Later commentators such as Wittfogel would call this a "hydraulic state"—that is, a state where all of the irrigation management was in the hands of the central government.[4] Wittfogel famously maintained that this centralization of the irrigation system was a more or less permanent feature of such regimes. But, as indicated in the previous chapter, this seems unlikely. While we may not know when exactly the hydraulic state arose in Egyptian history, recent work suggests that when the French savants came to Egypt in 1798 they uncovered little evidence of a centralized agrarian system or irrigation system.[5] Rather, there were different kinds of water regimes in Upper, Middle, and Lower Egypt. Apparently, however, these savants—and then, later, some engineers, also mainly French—must have thought that a centralized hydraulic state was or ought to have been the norm for the country. As no such system existed, there developed the myth in these circles that this lack of centralization was the cause of decline, that such a system had once existed under the Pharaohs, and that the French could help Egypt restore what once must have existed. Subsequently, the British took over and set out to complete the task of centralizing irrigation.

"Myth" is a laden term, but its use is justified here, I believe, because, as was noted earlier, the technology needed for a centralized irrigation system only became available in the nineteenth century. This would have been known by the engineers of the period, who would have been aware that the hydraulic society did not exist in antiquity. Nonetheless, many educated people of the nineteenth century and beyond—Egyptians, among others—chose to propagate this myth.

While Cromer may have been a reformer in the eyes of his contemporaries, today some would see him as the closest thing Egypt ever had to an Oriental despot. During his reign, Egypt was run for the first time in a basically centralized fashion, give or take the government's haphazard connection to Upper Egypt. As one would expect from an Oriental despot, Cromer showed little concern for qualifications, professionalism, or legal or political rights. He depended on his cronies and, to the extent that he could, on his charisma. He was articulate, he had strong opinions, and he expressed them in a memorable fashion. It was he who so unflatteringly compared the Egyptian character to that of the English; it was he who used this character comparison to justify lengthening the period of British rule that Egypt would need to become modern, or, as he put it, if Egypt was to develop a sense of itself as a nation rather than simply a bunch of fragments. It is from Cromer that we learn that there were no Egyptians per se, simply dwellers of the Nile Valley, and that, under modern conditions, Egypt was experiencing something of an identity crisis. Copts, he believed, were more Eastern than Christian, and Muslims by and large lacked rationality, at least compared to Syrian Christians and Armenians. The Anglo-American reader of that day absorbed ideas like these, traces of which one can find even now.

Cromer's emphasis on Egyptian character led him to believe that Egypt needed structural and moral reforms. It had to abolish slavery, and it had to abolish the practice of whipping its workers, whence came the term "Kurbash." What he found, however, was that while slavery could be abolished, whipping the workforce could not, nor could reliance on unpaid forced labor. It would be impossible for Egypt to pay its debts without retaining this system. To get the work done, the worker had to be whipped.

Cromer also believed that Egypt needed to eliminate corruption, especially judicial corruption. His solution was to modify the Napoleonic Code, which he thought was inappropriate for Egypt, simplify administrative procedure, give courts more power, and diminish the right of appeal in cases involving minor offenses. He also believed, in an equally literal-minded way, that eliminating corruption would require that Egypt eliminate vice. Egypt had too much vice, too much smuggling of hashish, and too much prostitution. The Greek moneylenders were responsible for a good deal of it, but they were hard to get rid of, given the capitulation agreements and, as a result, the support these individuals could count on from the Greek embassy in Egypt. The problem of vice, Cromer decided, basically stemmed from the Egyptian character; therefore, the real corrective was moral reform. It would be a long-term process, involving the education of Egyptian women. Cromer believed that educated women were essential for the education of their sons, an idea often associated with the reformer Qasim Amin, the author of *The Liberation of Women* (1899).

But, for all his interest in character formation, Cromer set quite modest goals when it came to the development of the Egyptian educational system, be it for women or for men. He had several concerns: not just the cost, at a time when debt repayment was doubtless a more pressing concern, but the risks inherent in producing a class of "over-educated" and "unemployable" people who would not be grateful for their education but would likely cause trouble. Gratitude was not an attribute he found among Egyptians. Basic elementary technical education seemed to him to be appropriate in order to produce more skilled workers.

As Jennifer Kernaghan, the author of a recent study on Cromer, has noted, Cromer's ideas on education and uplift of moral character were intertwined with his ideas about Islam.[6] Islam in itself was dangerous to tamper with, he thought, as its beliefs and practices were fixed. Attempts to challenge these beliefs might lead to insurrection, so reform of al-Azhar or even of the Kuttab system was not advisable. What was therefore feasible was for Egyptians to be exposed to a government that followed the Christian moral code. Over time, this would lead them to aspire to more than a fatalistic acceptance of bad conditions.

What is noteworthy in all this, and perhaps not widely understood, is that Cromer's writings shaped the intellectual horizons of the field of modern Egyptian studies in the English-speaking world, having an impact on both academic scholarship and government policy toward Egypt until the present. It is this man, who was not regarded as especially intelligent by his peers, nor even by his own family, who may be considered the founder of the field.[7]

Let us now turn to subsequent works of colonial scholar officials and others who developed the modern field of Egyptian studies, in the process uncovering some of the contradictory features of a British colonial Egypt.[8]

Lord Lloyd

Lord Lloyd (1879–1941) was high commissioner of Egypt from 1925 to 1929 and the author of *Egypt since Cromer* (1933).[9] His career as high commissioner ended in 1929 when it was sacrificed by Parliament to avoid confronting problems that long predated him. Lloyd wrote that when Cromer came to power in Egypt, the empire was at its height, Egyptian nationalism had suffered a big defeat, and Cromer was able to insert himself as the administrator who would restore the country's prosperity and look after the Fallahin. Despite this set of fortuitous circumstances, even Cromer faced his share of problems. Problematic from the start was the fact that Britain had occupied a country, all the while acknowledging that it rightfully belonged to the Sultan. Elsewhere, Britain typically annexed countries and declared them colonies. This was not the case in Egypt. A few years later the Ottoman Empire was dissolved, and there was no longer a Sultan. At that point, Egyptian nationalists began to argue that there was no longer a legal basis for Britain's presence in Egypt. What complicated this even further was the rise of welfare colonialism. As a result, the high commissioner was obliged to argue that while Britain stood for progress and democracy, countries like Egypt and India were not yet ready to really appreciate either. This was not a position that either the Egyptian nationalists or the British expat community in Egypt found acceptable, albeit for different reasons.

Lloyd's work, seen by its detractors as an effort at self-justification, was nonetheless praised in a number of reviews both in the UK and the United States, not only for the work itself, but also for the author's career as a loyal and intelligent statesman. His book exhibited an unusual awareness of the forces arrayed against Britain's traditional imperial presence in Egypt. Beginning in 1904 against the backdrop of the Anglo-French Entente Cordiale, the author notes how much change had occurred since the British had occupied Egypt. In the early 1930s, the strength of Germany called into question many aspects of traditional British policy. At this point, Egyptian nationalism was an established force, the Ottoman Empire was a relic of the past, and Pan-Islamism was on the rise. This was no longer the world of Lord Cromer, and it was not yet the world of the more contemporary coalescence of elite interests.

In his discussion of one of his predecessors, Sir Eldon Gorst (1907–11), Lloyd suggested that changes in Britain were continuously influencing British policy, a view that Lloyd no doubt also applied to his own experience. It was not easy to satisfy Egyptian nationalists and British expatriates at the same time, given that each had their supporters in Parliament. This made even the most necessary reforms difficult. Consider, for example, reform of the capitulation agreements: at one point those agreements in their original form were necessary, but by the 1920s they were subject to abuse and needed to be revised. But how? Britain lacked the authority to undertake such measures, even in its own colonial sphere. Its claim to support reform had been undercut during World War I—in Egyptian eyes, at least—by its need to rely on forced labor, which the UK had originally condemned and outlawed but then allowed to be reintroduced. Such were the dilemmas of the period.

Henry Dodwell

In 1931, Cambridge University Press published Henry Dodwell's *The Founder of Modern Egypt: A Study of Muhammad ʿAli*.[10] Dodwell was a civil servant but also a historian. While his career was mainly based in India, and he was primarily known for his books on South India, this work has remained a fixture in Egyptian studies until today. While it has doubtless been read over the years largely for the information it provides, a closer look reveals that it was not written for that purpose, or at least for that purpose alone. Rather, as the text makes clear, it was written to counter the view emerging among Egyptian nationalists after World War I that Great Britain had always been hostile to Egypt, a case in point its hostility to Muhammad ʿAli in the 1830s and 1840s. To show that this was not the case, Dodwell reconstructs that bygone era, noting that Lord Palmerston was merely protecting the

British access to India, and that if one took an impartial view of the interactions of Egypt and the UK throughout the nineteenth century, one would conclude that the relationship between the two countries was generally a positive one. Dodwell goes even further, defending Muhammad 'Ali's administrative policies in Crete and Syria against the charges made by Palmerston, noting as well the stand Muhammad 'Ali took for religious tolerance in Syria. As Dodwell puts it, in a backward Oriental country a great ruler has no choice but to use violence against the corrupt Zamindars, or Multazims, as the case may be.

Dodwell's experience in India, it appears, may well have influenced his decision to write this book. In India, in order to confront the challenge posed by Indian nationalism, the British tried to portray themselves as authentic continuators of the best of Indian history. To this end, they identified themselves with the figure of the Mughal emperor Akbar while ignoring more recent rulers. Applying this approach to Egypt, Dodwell set out to build up and identify with Muhammad 'Ali, the analogous figure in the Egyptian context.

Sir Valentine Chirol

Sir Valentine Chirol (1852–1929) was an ardent but pragmatic defender of the British Empire. A widely traveled diplomat and an author of works on concerns of the day, he was among the earliest to use the term "Middle East." His book *The Egyptian Problem* (1920) defends the imperial identity of Egypt.[11] Eldon Gorst and Lord Lloyd cover some of the same ground in their work, but indirectly. Not Chirol: he is quite forthright.

One of Chirol's claims—one found in scholarship to the present day—is that England was not in Egypt by choice, but by necessity. Who else could have saved the peasantry and the economy and protected the country from the Mahdi? Chirol's analysis is of a pragmatic sort. To hold Egypt, one had to hold the loyalty of the peasantry. In Chirol's view, this had worked in the time of Cromer, but, given the abuse of labor during World War I, the peasantry now sided with Sa'd Zaghlul and the Wafd Party. In other words, poor management was to blame. The bureaucracy had become increasingly aloof from the people that it was supposed to serve and increasingly preoccupied with infighting. How was the opportunity missed to honor the Egyptian army that defended the Suez Canal against Turkey on behalf of Britain? Why was Egypt not formally invited to participate in the Paris Peace Conference when lesser countries were? The Milner Mission was another lost opportunity; it was so delayed that it sparked anger and led to a boycott, which defeated its purpose. Taking the needs of the empire as a whole, any senior official should have realized that some kind of stable political solution would be needed. Egypt was only one part of the wider world of problems facing Britain.

The Suez Crisis: The End of the Colonial Era and of the Paradigm's Heyday

The Suez crisis crystallized trends that had been progressing for several decades but then exploded into the British political arena. Among them was the movement of Egypt toward independence and the increasing disinclination of the United States to continue following the UK's lead in matters concerning Egypt. The result for the UK was feelings of anger and frustration, perhaps even incomprehension. This was all the worse because no one of stature was on the scene to write the kind of analytical book Lord Lloyd wrote in the 1930s, analyzing the situation of the empire as it actually was. The writers attempting to maintain the imperial narrative at this point wrote more narrowly about Nasir in terms of World War II or Nasir as psychobiography.

Walter Laqueur may serve as an example of a defender of the empire through the lens of World War II. Born in Europe in 1921, Laqueur fled the Nazis and lived for some years in Mandate Palestine. He subsequently became a journalist and political analyst of eminence, first in the UK and then in the United States, with his work cited in academic writing as well. Laqueur's framework of reference was Europe and World War II. In a pamphlet written and published in London in 1956 entitled *Nasser's Egypt*, he set out to locate Jamal Abd al-Nasir in this framework, concluding, however, that he did not fit in certain respects.[12] He was not like Kemal Ataturk, who made peace with the Greeks and respected borders; instead, Nasir made enemies and showed imperialistic tendencies. Some of the Nasirite rhetoric was fascist, and some of it was pro-Soviet, but, according to Laqueur, Nasir was neither a fascist nor a communist—probably because (and here I paraphrase) Egypt was too primitive to allow for this to be the case.

The politics of Nasir's rise to power seemed to Laqueur simply a matter of circumstance. The cotton market had collapsed, leaving the economy in bad shape. The army did not intervene to stop looting during the Cairo Fire of 1952. This meant that some new government had to come to power and take charge, because King Farouk was hated and the Wafd hopelessly corrupt; this gave the young officers the opportunity to seize control. As this approach did not explain the 1952 land reform, the creation of free education, the housing of workers, the medical and social welfare programs, and the promotion of industrialization, Laqueur claims that the officers enacted such programs because they all came from the same lower-middle-class background. Ultimately, he concludes that the regime was mysterious. In a conclusory and covertly pro-war section entitled "Egypt and Britain," Laqueur argues that Nasir was a continuing threat to British interests in East Africa, the Middle East, and the Persian Gulf. Sooner or later even his well-wishers would understand he was no Ataturk, but more like the evil Enver Pasha. The Oriental despotism implied in the reference to Enver Pasha comes out as well in his idea of Nasir as an imposter, trying to imagine developing the country without British investment.

P. J. Vatikiotis (1928–97), a Palestinian educated in Egypt and the United States who made his career as an academic in the UK, is known for a number of books on contemporary Egypt written between the 1960s and the 1980s. He may be taken as the culmination of the Suez era of British Orientalists who worked on Egypt. His work *Nasser and His Generation* attempts to explain what transpired in Egypt through a psychobiography of Nasir.[13] Nasir, he believes, had an unhappy relationship with his father and an unhappy childhood generally and had grown up suspicious of those around him. Where other writers have emphasized his struggles with the Muslim Brotherhood, the communists, Naguib, and the older generation of politicians such as 'Ali Mahir, here the emphasis is on a Freudian analysis of personality development. Vatikiotis's overall contention is that Nasir wanted undivided power, which was what the Egyptian people wanted their ruler to have as well. Nasir was ambitious, and the adulation he received made him more so. By 1967, Egypt was a totalitarian police state. While this view is not unique, Vatikiotis prioritizes this over other dimensions of his analysis. For example, he does not cover Kamshish, the symbol of the recovery of the power of the traditional landowning class. As various reviewers have noted, in titling the book *Nasser and His Generation* Vatikiotis understood the term "generation" to mean his generation in Egypt. Other writers would have approached the issue in terms of the leaders of the Non-aligned Movement and of the decolonization movements more generally, but the Suez generation of Anglo-American scholarship did not. To think in such terms for those scholars would have been too pro-Soviet.

Signs of Change

In the generation of Lord Cromer, the prevailing Anglo-American view about Islam was that it was unchanging and best left alone. Cromer himself held that view. He had, in fact, once characterized Egyptian culture—in effect meaning Islam—as needing centuries more of British tutelage. A generation later, British officials in Egypt needed to demonstrate to both Egyptian public opinion and the Labour Party in the UK that this was overstated: the colonial presence had in fact produced progress, but for it to continue, the colonial presence would indeed need to be extended.[14]

The British claim about the progress of Islam in Egypt under its aegis was closely tied to the rise of a liberal reformist trend in Islam prefigured by Muhammad 'Abduh but then increasingly developed in the writings of such figures as 'Abd al-Raziq, al-Maraghi, and, still later, al-Shaltut, as well as various modernist authors who were Muslim and wrote about religion, such as Taha Hussein. What the officials naturally hoped was the Anglo-American reader of these later works might conclude that Cromer was wrong to a degree, and that, under sustained British tutelage, Islam had in fact begun to evolve. It was in this context that the Muslim Brotherhood made a limited debut as well.

British Orientalists played a leading role in substantiating claims about Islam and modernism. Here one thinks of two well-known works by H. A. R. Gibb, *Modern Trends in Islam* (1947) and its companion, *Mohammedanism* (1949).[15] In these books, what is striking is how at home Gibb was in Islamic society—more so, one suspects, than most other British scholars before or since. In fact, he dedicates *Modern Trends* to one of his Egyptian teachers, a scholar with whom he used to stay when he went back to Cairo in later years: Muhammad Hasanayn 'Abd al-Raziq, an individual who did not live in a Europeanized neighborhood and was neither wealthy nor famous.

In both of these two works, today's reader will find something of a collision between the author's own experience and his formal education. And one could, if one chose, read into it some of the contradictions of British Egypt. In *Modern Trends*, for example, Gibb casts doubt on the golden-age-and-decline model he had learned as a university student; Islam must have kept on developing, he states. Further, he disputes the view that Arabs had no art, arguing that this construed the idea of art too narrowly. Similarly, he argues against the view that Arabs lacked rational thought. Such a perspective, he claims, failed to acknowledge that their concern with the concrete allowed for enormous progress in empirical sciences. Of course, Gibb was drawn to liberal Islam, and it's here that one finds the imperial linkage. Liberal Islam was, he claims, better established in India than in Egypt because it began there earlier and more deeply institutionalized than it was elsewhere; here he alludes indirectly to British influence. When it comes to his discussion of neo-Hanbali trends, Gibb's focus is on the Wahhabis of Saudi Arabia, thereby bypassing the subject of the Egyptian Muslim Brotherhood, which Britain had been financing since at least 1942 as a counterweight against the Left and the nationalist movement.

Another Orientalist of the period was Jamal Ad-Din Heyworth-Dunne. Heyworth-Dunne was a onetime British official in Cairo and later a professor at Georgetown University's School of Foreign Service. What is noteworthy about his *Religious and Political Trends in Modern Egypt* (1950) is that it contextualizes the Muslim Brotherhood in modern Egyptian history the way they themselves sometimes did.[16] This, too, fit with the idea of a British Egypt. Muhammad 'Ali began modernization, his successors failed to carry it on, and the British invaded the country, which gave rise to the nationalist resistance led by Sa'd Zaghlul. In time, nationalism became stymied, and the country fell back on its true Salafi nature. This was not surprising, given that nationalism was a European idea and not understood by many Egyptians.

Modern political life, Heyworth-Dunne finds, only began in the twentieth century. The early twentieth century was a period of social chaos, and, as a result, Christians and Jews formed societies to protect their way of life. This was soon followed by the formation of the Young Men's Muslim Association, which in turn gave rise to the Muslim Brotherhood. In 1936, when Egypt was in a state of near revolution, the government appreciated Hasan al-Banna's support. The book links al-Banna with the Mufti, arguing that it was the Palestine question that gave the Brotherhood its opportunity and that it was the Mufti who connected the Brotherhood to Hitler through intermediaries, connections that allowed the Brotherhood to carry out anti-British activities. Heyworth-Dunne notes these last points as if they were of no great concern. In a similar manner, his text brushes aside the cult-like quality of the Brotherhood as being a touch of the Mahdi, and the militarization of the movement associated simply with Palestine. Written in 1950 after the assassination of Hasan al-Banna, the book concludes that Hasan al-Banna was ahead of his time, too visible too early; he allowed the ruling class to see that he was following his own interests and not theirs, thus making his removal foreseeable. The Brotherhood's history, according to Heyworth-Dunne, was over after the assassination of its leader. At the time of its writing, the author was teaching at Georgetown's School of Foreign Service; arguably, this may therefore have been the American introduction to the Muslim Brotherhood. The reason for writing the book and doing so at that time was not made clear.

Another feature of these later years was the reliance on Egyptian scholars by the British; their work showed the general British reader that not only could Egyptians write in English, but what they wrote clearly fit into the world of British imperial thought and indeed reflected it to a considerable extent. In the 1940s, this was still something of a novelty; Egyptian authors no doubt thought that their works therefore had to be vouched for by established British academics. For example, we find A. C. Cawley, an eminent British medievalist, introducing a work written by M. Rifaat Bey, an Egyptian history professor, on modern Egyptian political history. In *Cultural Survey of Modern Egypt* (1947–48), a two-volume work by literature professor Moustafa M. Mosharrafa, we find that the introduction for volume 1 was not written by the same scholar whose name appears in volume 2.[17] Volume 1 was introduced by the chemist John Murray, who for many years was the principal of University College Exeter, where the author taught. Volume 2 was introduced by J. B. S. Haldane (1892–1964), a British scientist who wound up taking citizenship in India. In these introductory sections, one notes some differences in emphasis, perhaps reflecting changes in the author's worldview or in the public acceptance of the work. In any case, where John Murray in volume 1 emphasizes the author's arthritis, Haldane in volume 2 emphasizes that it had been a misfortune for both Britain and Egypt that Britain had occupied Egypt, and that it behooved the British reader to read what Egyptians were writing, to understand not only Egypt, but themselves. Haldane then notes the contributions of the Pharaonic period to modern civilization, expressing appreciation of the author's delineation of the cultural differences between classes in Egypt and of the broad outline of history presented in the book, one in which the country went from being more feudal to more capitalist.

Mohamed Rifaat begins his book noting that it arose out of lectures given to the Anglo-Egyptian Union in Cairo, and although the idea of writing it had been on his mind since his days as a student in Liverpool many years earlier, now seemed the time to do so, given the wartime exigencies that brought the two countries close together. Rifaat approaches the subject of intercountry understanding through an interwoven account of elite personalities from 1798 to World War I, with brief comments about some who came later, his Egyptian centrism expanding the imperial gaze but not disrupting it. As the author makes clear, he does not support the "radical nationalism" of the 'Urabi era, but he points to the problem of officers' pay and other such issues that doubtless played a role in why it occurred. As for 1919, he notes that one could have foreseen the outcome, given the tension between the local Egyptian *mudirs* (village headmen) and the British inspectors sent from Cairo. Thus, both these upheavals emerge as conflicts from within the elite ranks into which society was drawn, which the author doubtless hopes would not be repeated.

Writing in the early post–World War II years, with the empire on its last legs, some criticism of imperial practices was to be expected. British administration, Rifaat claims, generally succeeded in principle, but sometimes it failed in point of detail, which again references the issue of the mudirs and inspectors. Still, the work comes to an end by praising Cromer and those who followed for allowing freedom of the press as a way to avoid secret underground trends, as well as for improvements in sanitation, prisons, education, medicine, and law.

In the *Cultural Survey of Modern Egypt*, Moustafa Mosharrafa adopts a slightly different approach. He appears less concerned with the intertwining of the two countries and more with correcting various false impressions. He begins by stating that his goal is to give the English-language reader an idea of modern Egypt seen against its "ancient and rather chequered history," doing so to overcome the rather more common approach found in the UK of simply fixating on the Pharaonic past without making any effort to connect it to more recent Egyptian history. Here Mosharrafa appears to be aligning himself with the Pharaonic school of Egyptian historiography, which was prominent in the liberal age in Egypt and even to a degree in Great Britain.[18] Volume 1 proceeds to itemize the various fields of culture and industry of the Pharaohs, noting as well their influence on Judaism and Christianity, and it concludes with some references to the revival of Pharaonic art forms in the twentieth century. This, Mosharrafa suggests, is a reasonable way to connect the Pharaonic past with more recent history. Volume 2 takes a more chronological approach to Egyptian cultural history, noting the contribution of the half-dozen odd civilizations that imposed themselves on Egypt over the past millennia while allocating most of its attention to European contribution in modern times. At that point, the tone becomes anti-imperialist, perhaps explaining Haldane's appreciation of this volume. Cromer's Five Feddan Law, the author claims, was a plot to create a pro-British petit bourgeoisie, no matter how faulty the economic rationale for this may have been. But, despite Cromer's policy, Egypt had become a modern country; in recent years, it had developed the arts, radio, film, and crafts found in modern countries. The book concludes on a somber note, asserting that the narcotics habit lived on in the circles of the mystical organizations of the lower middle class, as a way of dealing with a life of frustration for those caught between a destitute peasantry and a comfortable middle-class lifestyle.

Missionaries in this period also contributed to the development of the idea of Oriental despotism. American missionaries went to Egypt to convert Muslims, and, while most of them were not scholars, some were, and their ideas about Islam and Egyptian culture seemed to have found their way into the works of the colonial officials. Lord Cromer devotes many pages to issues about which the missionaries also wrote. One famous American missionary author was Duncan Black Macdonald, the scholar who founded the Muslim Lands Department of the Hartford Seminary. Macdonald knew Arabic, studied medieval Arab-Islamic culture, and was an early proponent of the "golden age of Islam" approach, which evolved as a part of the move toward dialogue and away from evangelism. Samuel Zwemer, a leading American evangelist, appears to have been more concerned with matters of conversion than anything else; in his writings, one finds endless unflattering sociological observations about Egypt that the author associates with Islam. Given his eminence, it would not be surprising if some of his views were those echoed in the writings of Lord Cromer.[19] In any case, it is a reasonable hypothesis that in the writings of Zwemer and of the other missionaries, one finds as well the origins of an Anglo-American idea of modern Islam.

Taking the period as a whole, what one observes is that not only did the British officials retreat from the extremism of Lord Cromer, but so did the missionaries shifting from evangelism to dialogue.[20] As the field continued to evolve, such was the extent of the retreat that Cromer and the colonial period were treated as a part of the prehistory of the field. The reasons for this are not hard to determine: not many wanted to defend colonialism anymore. Moreover, Cromer was clearly a racist and a very cruel administrator, functioning like a surgeon who was practicing his trade but not in the patient's best interest. In his 1908 essay "The Government of Subject Races," one sees more clearly than in some of his other writings his detachment from the misery caused by his policies in Egypt.[21] Yet Cromer is not a part of the prehistory of the field. His idea of Oriental despotism and many of his other ideas remain with us today, give or take small changes.

Among these long-lasting ideas is that of the UK as the active agent of history and of Egypt as a panorama of social problems and a culture ruled by a despot reacting to Britain. This despot was found to be isolated from his own society, making him ineffectual in numerous ways.[22] But, as Cromer's successors noted, in just a few short years, under direct British tutelage, the governmental system grew modern, as did Islam, which had similarly been fossilized for centuries. For modernization to succeed, however, many more years of British tutelage would be needed.

The Development Revolution: 1940s–1970s

This section takes up Anglo-American scholarship on Egypt between the 1940s and the 1970s. While there were some important changes during this time, there was also continuity, one reason being that the rise of the United States as a new center of gravity during the Development Revolution did not immediately bring an end to the ongoing tradition of British Egypt. This only occurred gradually after 1952.

What is striking about this period, however, is the decline of the missionary. Also striking is the entrance into the field of an increasing number of scholars from a middle-class background, individuals with no significant connection to the Anglo-American power structure or to oil or missionary interests. This trend began following the passage of legislation in the 1950s, leading to the creation of Title VI grants, monies given to students to support the study of critical languages, among them Arabic. Finally, it's striking to see the appearance of specialized scholarly institutions, including some for the study of Egypt.

In many academic fields, the confluence of such developments would mark a watershed, but the evidence suggests that this was not the case in regard to the study of modern Egypt. Rather, the new institutions became mere sites of bureaucratic struggles between funding bodies, which wanted policy studies, and scholars who wanted funding but had no affinity to such studies. As the interests of the one diverged from those of the other, the funding bodies realized they did not need scholars in the universities; they needed native informants or employees in think tanks, as the British once did. Still, as historian Zachary Lockman shows in *Field Notes*, his study of the development of US Middle East studies, and as historian Osamah Khalil demonstrates in *America's Dream Palace*, this was a long, slow process. The era witnessed the federal government investing in Middle East Centers, hoping to orient scholarship at least in some general sense to issues of modernization.[23]

But it appears that many of the students who developed competence in language and area studies were only peripherally interested in matters of development and the Cold War, much less modernization. Even when encouraged to write about the contemporary period, many still produced works that were expressions of nostalgia for the colonial past more than anything else and shed little light on the present. Quite a number of doctoral dissertations and books from that period focused on the liberal age or the Nahda. For many, the model was Albert Hourani's *Arabic Thought in the Liberal Age* (1962). While that book did not devote much attention to Egypt, many others like it did.

In this section, we begin with two well-known examples: Nadav Safran's *Egypt in Search of Political Community* (1961) and Morroe Berger's *Islam in Egypt Today* (1970).[24] Berger was a product of the social science data revolution of the period and did not come out of Arabic studies, while Safran was closer to political theory and Arabic cultural history. Still, their works had much in common. They were both optimistic about the future to an extent not seen since

Lord Cromer. Safran was nostalgic for the liberal age past, but he managed to channel his nostalgia in a way that served policy, while most others did not. Berger simply had no nostalgia; he assumed that despotism could be useful, that a despotic government could, if it so chose, impose modernization on traditional institutions, by force if necessary.

The Development Revolution rested on a kind of collaborative approach between the United States and Egypt. In this period, Egyptian intellectuals began to help shape Egyptian studies in the United States, doing so on a scale that would have been unthinkable in the UK.[25]

In her well-received book *Egypt and Cromer* (1969), Afaf Marsot stays close to the British documents and to the papers of the Egyptian elite.[26] It is in some ways a scholarly version of a kind of book the British had become used to since the 1940s, and it was received well. However, in her next book, *Egypt in the Age of Muhammad 'Ali* (1984), she raised considerable controversy, particularly in the UK, by arguing that the British undermined Egyptian development as far back as Muhammad 'Ali—in effect a refutation of Henry Dodwell's book.

Nadav Safran

Safran begins his book on Egypt in search of a political community with a model of the Islamic state, which he compiles from various classical authors. This he takes to be the traditional political order that would be displaced by modernity, given enough development. For Safran, the modern began with Muhammad 'Ali, a figure who developed Egypt under the aegis of Europe. After Muhammad 'Ali there was a hiatus, but once again development continued in the liberal age between the two world wars. The developments of the intervening period did not seem so important.

What an older generation had called the influence of Islam became for Safran the influence of ideology, or, simply, culture. As if echoing Émile Durkheim, Safran argues that states need some overarching ideology to bind their citizens together and allow a ruler to rule; in other words, citizens need a culture to cling to in order to avoid anomie. Egypt tried to adopt liberalism as its ideology or culture, but this failed, so the country was still in search of a political community. As liberalism began to fail in the late 1930s, many turned to the Muslim Brotherhood. For whatever reason—perhaps the influence of the Cold War—Safran does not take up the fact that in this period many turned to socialism as well.

Safran looks at the liberal age as an experiment in development, one in which the Oriental despot was induced to experiment with decentralization by giving some space to the liberal intelligentsia. This experiment was for Safran the forerunner to the Development Revolution, which came a few years later. Safran's account follows the careers of various prominent figures through the heyday of the Liberal Age and beyond.

The liberal age, of course, ended with the 1952 Revolution. Even after the revolution, however, Safran remained optimistic about the eventual triumph of liberalism, although he was fearful of the rising influence of the Muslim Brotherhood, which he took to be an extremist organization, somewhat similar to that of the Mahdi. The book was reviewed skeptically by the older generation. Some reviewers thought that Nasir's great popularity proved that the predisposition to autocracy was still alive, if not still inherent, in Egypt, and that liberalism had quite a ways to go before it would become rooted. They saw Egypt as a static society that would be difficult to develop. In this sense, Safran's work was a part of the newer literature of the Development Revolution.

Morroe Berger

Morroe Berger was an empirical social scientist whose *Islam in Egypt Today* (1970) typified the propensity toward data gathering and quantification that was typical of post–World War II scholarship. Berger states that, because of the secularization of the Western academy, few chose to study religion, and that this was a mistake for those hoping to understand Egypt. His work redresses the matter by examining the existing religious institutions of Cairo in the 1960s. To this end, he distinguishes between the more traditional ones, such as the Sufi orders, and the more modern ones, such as the secular voluntary associations. He notes that the government supervised both types: the voluntary organizations were supervised by the Ministry of Social Affairs, and the Sufi orders by the Ministry of the Interior.

Berger also attempts to categorize the different types of mosques—an undertaking yet to be satisfactorily accomplished. His approach is to correlate size with degree of government backing, resources, and number of personnel. He finds a few larger mosques and a myriad of smaller private mosques. While smaller private mosques were often tax abatement projects, and thus not only smaller but rather different in nature, Berger's approach to categorization is simply one rooted in quantification. He attempts to determine who chose to go to which mosque, how old the mosques were on average, and whether age was a factor in their cleanliness. He also inquires into salary structures of the various functionaries. Clearly, his book resonated with the students of that era. What interests us here is his assumption that information in the hands of modernizing officials could bring about the hoped-for developmental revolution.

While in some obvious ways Safran and Berger differed from one another, one might also note that each in his own way was carrying on an experiment started in the later colonial period: using the Oriental despot as an agent of change. Both Safran and Berger assumed that development could be carried out by some elite entity under the aegis of the United States, but managed locally.

Afaf Marsot

The work of the Egyptian American historian Afaf Marsot shows the limits to which this experiment with development would be allowed to go. In *Egypt in the Realm of Muhammad 'Ali* (1984), the author takes up the subject of Egypt's experience with development, noting how development was thwarted as soon as it conflicted with Anglo-American interests. Marsot pictures Muhammad 'Ali as a reformer, making alliances and building institutions. The logic of his policies led to more and more advanced industrialization, which in turn required more markets. However, these developments brought Egypt into conflict with the UK in the person of Lord Palmerston, the most influential statesman of the most powerful country of that time. In due course, Great Britain backed the Ottomans, thwarting Egypt's drive to develop autochthonously. Permissible development would be dependent development.

During the Cold War, the desired emphasis was on development of the sort that was harmonious with Anglo-American objectives, meaning anti-Soviet. Some have termed this periphery "capitalism." At the end of the Cold War, and with the dawn of globalization, the Oriental despotism paradigm kept on developing to fulfill new needs.

The Period of Globalization: 1970–Present

In the 1970s and in the years thereafter, a majority of scholars rejected the orientation of the preceding period—not only the usefulness of the idea of a development revolution, but in some cases even that of the nation-state as a unit of analysis. In place of the nation-state often came a renewed interest in empire, notably the American empire. In the more policy-oriented work in that context, the debate involved whether authoritarianism was a positive or a negative trait, with advocates of democracy on one side and imperial pragmatists on the other.

Much of the work in this period was somewhat theoretical, somewhat feminist, and somewhat critical of various aspects of the Oriental despotism model while at the same time still coexisting with it. To introduce these developments, the following section is divided into two parts, the first part taking up a discussion of the dominant theory of the period, commonly known as New Social Theory (NST), and the second considering scholarly works of the period, many of which were influenced by the NST.

New Social Theory

This section takes up pieces of NST, a body of work sometimes also called New Liberalism, neoliberalism, or postcolonial discourse: a group of theoretical positions underlying some of the most influential Anglo-American scholarship on modern Egypt of this period. In so doing, it attempts to show some degree of continuity and some degree of change in the framework of assumptions we have encountered up to this point. While NST appears to represent some degree of change in its attraction to Nietzsche, overall in Egyptian studies it appears to adopt much of the liberal Hegelian tradition, allowing it to assume the general validity of the Oriental despotism approach while being critical of pieces of it.

One of the assumptions of NST scholarship is that from the 1980s onward there was a radical break with the historical past. This break, it is assumed, came about as a result of new computer technology, the breakdown of the Soviet Union, the worldwide acceptance of democracy and free trade promoted by the United States, and the rise of new ecological challenges. This led to the conclusion that the history of countries understood as nation-states was no longer meaningful; the world had entered a period of globalization. Further research of course showed the limitation of these formulations. Scholars soon realized that the nation-state and nationalism had not ended at all. However, in circles committed to the idea of a historical rupture, one started to see such terms as "neonationalism." In applying NST to the study of "Oriental" countries, scholars naturally confronted the problem of how to characterize the state. In the case of Egypt, the idea of despotism was retained.

Here as an aside, it is necessary to note that NST, for all its popularity, has had to confront a good deal of criticism. Following its rise, historians, especially those who were oriented toward materialist explanations, saw it as the most recent wave of ahistorical idealism and wondered why NST theorists were prepared to give up so much of the historical terrain that liberalism once controlled. Is the abandonment of historicism the price one has to pay to survive in the academy?

One of the major targets for NST was the narrative of national history; others included social history, peasant history, labor history, comparative history, Third World history, and Marxist political economy. In the view of NST, the narrative of national history serves to perpetuate elitism and patriarchalism. Accordingly, one objective has been to encourage historians and others to go beyond the nation-state as a framework, replacing it with a civilizational approach to analysis, an imperial approach, or some variant of global and local. While this suggests some kind of rupture, perhaps it should not. One could claim that NST draws its sustenance from nineteenth-century liberal thought in its preference for empire and civilization over the nation-state, but not really at the expense of Hegel. As was the case in the nineteenth century and remains so today, historical agency was taken away from Egypt as a country and returned to the imperial metropole. In both the colonial (or classical liberal) period and our own neocolonial (or globalization) period, scholars denigrate the study of Egyptian national history, often using the term "nationalist" in a derogatory sense. In both periods, scholars appear to assume that there are limits to how far Egypt could develop, given its propensity for nationalism. Thus, where Cromer understood Egypt to be a long way from modernity, today scholars repackage this idea as hybrid modernity, thereby suggesting the limits to which Egyptians can advance in the short term and still retain their authenticity. Authenticity here means true identity.

But are we not on the other side of the Saidian revolution? Are we not post-Orientalist? Obviously, in some sense, this is also the case. Theorists today, taking their cue from Said, set out to overcome the binaries of Middle East studies: the Easts and the Wests, the Orients and the Occidents, and Orientalism and history. To that end, they have introduced a new set of concepts such as transnationalism, urban network analysis, cosmopolitanism, identity politics, migration studies, and secularism studies. This critique of the traditional binaries of which the field was constructed is new. Insofar as there are any antecedents, they appear to be no more than a few passing remarks made by Anglo-American women who visited Egypt and expressed a feeling of kindredness with Egyptian women.

NST might also be understood—at least in part—as a product of a new moment in the history of gender relations in the United States and in the UK. For specialists in Middle East gender studies, a field emergent in this new theoretical context, it was obvious that there was not much room for development of their form of analysis, given the version of the Oriental despotism paradigm that had come down from the Cold War. If one assumes that power is unitary, highly centralized, masculinized, and coercive in nature, where does that leave women? For a number of scholars, the best approach appeared to be one of engendering the dominant paradigm as opposed to rejecting it out-right—that is, entering into it at a strategic location and challenging the interpretation of power relations commonly assumed at that point, an interpretation that was of course a male-centered one. One scholar, the historian Leslie Peirce, did just that. As she shows in *The Imperial Harem: Women and Sovereignty in the Ottoman Empire* (1993), when one looks at the Ottoman Empire in the seventeenth century, a period in which the ruler's weakness is assumed to be an issue, what stands out is how this detail has been used by historians to promote the idea of a male-centered view of Ottoman history. Given that the ruler was weak, the period has been characterized as one of decline, due to the influence of the women who raised the future rulers and who in the process softened their characters, making them less manly and despotic.

Following the publication of Peirce's work, the narrative of the seventeenth century began to change. Historians began to realize that it would be more persuasive to hypothesize that women were compet-ing for political power. The queen mother, responsible for raising the heir apparent, had to be included in the story. Peirce is an Ottomanist, but her influence was felt across Middle East studies. Had she sought to challenge the rise and decline paradigm more directly, the book of Rifaʿat Abou el-Haj on the changing nature of the Ottoman state would have been useful to her.[27]

To conclude this section, one might turn to the work of the histo-rian Zachary Lockman, who termed the years between the late 1960s and the early 1980s "a period of turmoil."[28] Many would agree with him and would agree as well that this turmoil subsided in the years that followed, because of the consolidation of NST's hold on the academy. What had caused the turmoil was the brief appearance of Third Worldism and Marxism. It was brief, one suspects, because the

government continued to be the principal funder of Middle East studies programs and had no interest in promoting such trends.[29]

The Era of Globalization and NST

In shifting from a general account of theory to a consideration of the
works of particular individuals, one finds that the main preoccupation in recent years among Anglo-American scholars studying Egypt
has been with the study of women and gender. Not all this work is
theoretical, but many of the institutional histories, biographies, gender identity studies, and socioeconomic studies of women written in
this period were influenced by NST. Moreover, women's studies often
came to serve as the basis from which to attack the traditional reliance
on binary categories that were so noticeable in this field. To represent
what has transpired in recent years, this section surveys a number of
different scholarly trajectories directly or indirectly influenced by NST.

Women as a Part of History. It is scarcely an exaggeration to claim
that until a few years ago, scholars had felt obliged to show there were
sources to prove that women played some role in economy, society,
politics, and culture, much less history, as none of this was conceded
by the variant of the Oriental despotism paradigm then in use.

Gradually, scholars did overcome these challenges. In 2001, the
historian Margot Badran published a monograph on the history of
the leading Egyptian feminist institution, giving due importance to
its founder Huda al-Sha'rawi as a historical personality.[30] As time went
on, however, it became apparent that supporters of the older version
of the paradigm would try to absorb women like Huda al-Sha'rawi as
individuals who played traditional philanthropic roles without having
to acknowledge that there were women in the public sphere or in history in a strict sense. In reaction to this renewed attempt to dehistori-
cize women, Beth Baron's *Egypt as a Woman* (2005) attempts to move
the discussion to where power indisputably was, the Wafd Party.[31] She
argues that Safiyya Zaghlul, the wife of the party's leading personality, was a historical figure in the lifetime of her husband Sa'd Zaghlul

and thereafter as well. After his death, there were struggles over his succession and over tactics the party adopted; finally, the Wafd Party split. Even after her late husband's papers were stolen from her by her party colleagues, Zaghlul was still involved in the politics of the day. Baron uses her example to raise a fundamental question: How and when did elite women become involved in the politics of nationalism? Baron's inquiry leads her to reopen the subject of the Women's Demonstration in 1919, an event in which Safiyya Zaghlul, among others, was involved. In traditional scholarship, Baron finds, the importance of this event is often understated; historians sometimes look at it as an isolated act of a few women, sometimes treating it simply as further evidence of the unity of the nation against the British, but never viewing it as an expression of the historical evolution of gender power, which would seemingly be a logical way to approach it as well. Historicizing the event as a part of gender history, Baron set out to study the developments leading up to this demonstration, eventually writing an entire chapter on the question of the preconditions for women to turn toward Egyptian nationalism and to support the 1919 Revolution, finding that what was perhaps most decisive was the breakdown of the large multiethnic, multiracial, Ottoman-style households that were prevalent through the end of the nineteenth century. This involved, among other things, an end to the slave trade, a beginning of the education of women, and the rise of the ideology of monogamy and companionate marriage.

Two other students of women's history arrive at similar conclusions about the presence of women in modern history, doing so using somewhat different materials. In her first major work, *Women in Nineteenth-Century Egypt* (2002), the historian Judith Tucker introduces the idea that by the mid-nineteenth century, the majority of Egyptian women had to work. A decision to regard all of these women as outside of history even though they were workers is more revealing of the Oriental despotism paradigm than of the reality at hand.[32] More recently, historian Cathlyn Mariscotti has argued in *Gender and Class in the Egyptian Women's Movement, 1929–1935* (2008) that a

close examination of Egyptian feminism shows class to be an important factor as well, with the more affluent advocating for women's role
in philanthropy pitted against a growing middle strata calling for the
broadening of feminist struggles to include the issues of women with
professional careers. Here the top-down Oriental despotism paradigm
is replaced by women's history as a dialectic.[33] Here NST makes something of an exception to allow for national history.

Cosmopolitanism. For many scholars, cosmopolitanism has long been
one of the main signifiers of modernity. This continues to be the case,
although in recent scholarship some concern is expressed that the
term "cosmopolitanism" rather easily lends itself to binary reasoning
and to a Eurocentric view of how Egypt became modern. As some
have observed, cosmopolitanism has functioned as a kind of binary
opposite to the unmodern and parochial. Additionally encoded in the
term is a certain degree of masculinism, as, for example, in references
to specific groups.

In the study of Egypt, historians and literary critics have long
applied the term "cosmopolitanism" to the study of Alexandria and
Cairo, and more particularly to certain groups that were assumed
to be exogenous but lived in those cities in certain periods and were
assumed to have played a role in modernization. More recently, critics have become dissatisfied with this application of the term, because
it still does not transcend the East-West binary. In an article on this
subject, historian Will Hanley, a specialist on the history of Alexandria, expresses frustration at the limited development and application
of the term. He finds that it is currently being used in three ways,
none of which breaks with the received paradigm: as a prop in the
discussion of elites, as a prop that allows for nostalgia about the colonial past, or as a prop associated with Europeans but having no fixed
content of its own.[34] Thus, not only is there nothing new in the concept; it actually lacks a common-sense grounding in the local history
it purports to explain. For example, "cosmopolitanism" is frequently

used with respect to Alexandria as a way to explain what is important about the second largest Egyptian city without discussing the Egyptians who live there. But why? Why is something so seemingly illogical so important to so many people? Why would historians assume that Europeans in the nineteenth and early twentieth centuries would be cosmopolitan when it is well known that for Europeans this period was an era of hypernationalism that led up to World War I? Why not emphasize—and this would be a contemporary Ottoman studies perspective—the Europeans living in Alexandria in the eighteenth century, when cosmopolitanism was possibly more common?[35] Upon closer examination, there appears to be a connection between the idea of an Alexandrian cosmopolitanism and the Oriental despotism paradigm, and it might seem that a critique of the one would imply a critique of the other; this was what NST would have to confront. If the coming of the West explained how modernization began and what allowed it to progress, one must then explain how Egypt kept modernizing, as it did even in periods when there was a dearth of Europeans in control.

In the Muhammad 'Ali period, while there may not have been that many Europeans, the modernization that was achieved could be interpreted as having been done under the aegis of the French. But what about the period that followed? Egypt continued to modernize with few Europeans in positions of influence. The solution arrived at was that one could interpret the continuing modernization in terms of the presence of a cosmopolitan elite in Alexandria, a handful of ultra-sophisticated European residents creating a modern way of life and giving Egyptians something to emulate. Local minority groups and Syro-Lebanese immigrants, who were more receptive to this way of life, were clustered in Alexandria, and they provided a way for modernity to trickle down to the "native" population.

But, as Hanley argues, what this shows is that much of the writing on cosmopolitanism today is the same as it always was. It simply equates cosmopolitanism with the presence of Europeans or with members of minority groups, which Hanley finds unsatisfactory. The role one might ascribe to certain individuals is one thing, but homogenizing entire groups is something else altogether; there were class differences and political differences within and among them. Is that irrelevant to one's understanding of cosmopolitanism?

Literary critic Deborah Starr takes a different approach while critiquing old ways of understanding cosmopolitanism. According to Starr, cosmopolitanism came to Alexandria, then left, but will perhaps return sometime in the future. Starr finds it hopeful that Alexandria's present mayor is emphasizing the city's cosmopolitan roots, doing so by changing the city's physical appearance. She finds reason for optimism as well in the openness of the work of the Alexandrian novelist Ibrahim Abdel Meguid.[36] But, for Hanley, this would be primarily an example of the tag meaning of "cosmopolitanism," as something simply being appended to Europeans or to minorities without designating anything in particular. For Starr, on the other hand, the idea that cosmopolitan Alexandria could return implies a critique of history understood in the Hegelian way, as stages.

New Urbanism. Another part of the discussion of Egyptian modernity where one finds the New Liberal critique of the binaries of the older scholarship appears in a body of recent work loosely called "New Urbanism." New Urbanism ties the idea of cosmopolitan modernity to the existence of global networks as opposed to ethnic or national origins or emulations of the West, thereby transforming our conception of all the cities in the world, including "Islamic cities," from closed-off patriarchal entities to transnational networks. Egyptians in these transnational networks, whatever their religion or gender, are clearly modern. A recent article by Bruce Stanley introducing the assumptions of the New Urbanism argues that we lack an approach that explains how the Middle East holds together—in other words, what gives it identity.[37] We are presented with two unsatisfactory forms of explanation: the bounded city and nation-state, or the "mosaic of essentialist religious solidarities."[38]

Stanley and others suggest shifting to a different conceptual vocabulary that goes beyond the underlying binary of Western democracy–

Eastern despotism, with all its related details coming down from older thought. Why not look at a city as a node, and the modern citizen as a part of some set of networks that makes use of it? By doing so, one could evaluate a city in terms of connectivity, centrality, black holes, and brokers, which would tell us more than do facts about urban quarters, new cities, old cities, downtowns, exurbs, suburbs, and the like. Why, Stanley asks, must one keep on debating questions of whether or not there is an Islamic city?

Applying theory, any theory, is not always that easy. In bringing the New Urbanist methodology to bear on specific Middle Eastern cities, Stanley finds that the sources at his disposal are limited and, even more important, that the connectivity of urban-based networks is often very low. Nonetheless, he argues, there are analytical advantages in dropping the framework of capitalism and the nation-state and looking instead at the city as an urban node caught up in the *longue durée*. Without some such change in categories, how can one explain that power in Iraq is really in Amman and Washington and not in Iraq itself? How would one know that a city like Baghdad is not living up to its potentiality of being a global city but remains disconnected, like a "black hole"?

While this line of thinking seems promising as a way to get beyond "East" and "West," one would need to guard against the possibility of simply generating some new set of binaries around connectivity and lack of connectivity in the process. That said, what is important here is, first, the scholarly recognition of the problems associated with the Oriental despotism paradigm, and, second, the attempt to surmount some of them. Still, one might wonder why actors cannot simultaneously be local and national, a part of wider networks, à la the rise of the rich. Why one or the other? Perhaps it is simply a matter of paradigm development.

In addition to the discussion of going beyond binaries through the study of women's history, cosmopolitanism, and New Urban Studies, yet another strand of NST is found in the discussion of modernity studies, sometimes called "new modernity" or "hybrid modernity studies," and sometimes applied to the study of the Nahda or to the study of the religious reaction to it that followed.

NST and the Critical Rethinking of the Nahda. The Nahda, or modern cultural movement, is an essential subject for a student of modernity, especially given how male-centered it has been made to appear.

In fields such as literature, scholars have long maintained that cultural modernity is symbolized by the appearance of the novel, which in Arabic studies is taken to be the defining feature of what is called "the Nahda." The traditional idea was that if men wrote novels, then men were the bearers of modernity. This idea continues to inform scholarship even now: the woman writer or literary critic is someone who has entered a male domain. Today, however, there is at least an initial questioning of the underpinnings of this line of thought and some awareness of its loose ends. First, the Nahda involved more than the development of the novel, but also the development of the symphony, as well as modernist trends in the fine arts and other fields. The more this is recognized, the more easily one could show that modern culture is not gender specific, even if men have written most of the novels. Here NST has had to deal, to repeat, with the strong preference among scholars to study the history of the novel as opposed to the history of music, theater, or film, the inclusion of which would make the subject of the Nahda more gender neutral.

Given how important the idea of the Nahda is to the subject of modernity in the Arab world, it is not surprising that all the divisions that exist in the Arab world and in Western countries are found in the scholarship on the subject, and yet researchers have yet to embrace the idea of a gender-neutral approach. That point noted, efforts to understand the background of the Nahda, or the circumstances of its arising in Egypt, or to what extent it was indigenous, or to what extent it was influenced from abroad, nonetheless make for interesting reading.

As the next chapter will show, the timing of the early Nahda has long been found to have coincided with the arrival of Europeans in

Egypt after the 1798 invasion. Its progress depended on the student missions to Europe, which brought new knowledge to the Middle East. A translation movement arose, producing such important early translators as Rifaʿah al-Tahtawi and ʿUthman Jalal, which solidified the connection between Egypt and the early Nahda. So far, at least, NST has not chosen to contest this set of formulations.

As regards the later Nahda, traditional scholarship has said that it began in Lebanon and was brought to Egypt by the community of Syrians and Lebanese who immigrated to Egypt in the second half of the nineteenth century. What is then further assumed is that the missionary educators in Lebanon brought Western culture where there had been none before. Doubtless some of them did, but what is also clear is that by the later nineteenth century, the Arab world had gone beyond a reliance on missionaries to a reliance on schools, universities, and newspapers. Egypt too had its share of such schools, but, following the traditional historiography, it was the Syro-Lebanese community in Egypt in the 1870s and 1880s that introduced nineteenth-century European thought after the stalling of Muhammad ʿAli's cultural reforms of the 1830s. As noted before, one also typically finds the idea of the importance of Syro-Lebanese community tied to the idea of the importance of Alexandrian cosmopolitanism.

But here NST critical thought begins to appear. Some Syrian and Lebanese Christian immigrants received a missionary education, but did that make them modern? Some Muslims did as well; did that make them modern, too? Perhaps. But then what about the immigrants who played a role in the Nahda but had only indirect or minimal relations with missionaries? For example, Rashid Rida, the Lebanese journalist, had had some casual contact with missionaries in Lebanon. Later in life he immigrated to Egypt; there, he published with Shaykh Muhammad ʿAbduh the journal *al-Manar*, which covered a wide range of topics from the threat of missionary activity to developments in the natural sciences.[39] For the old Nahdawi school, with its binary method of narrative construction, Rida was a difficult figure to deal with; he did not fit their modernity and tradition paradigm very well. Nonetheless, he was the single most influential representative of the

Syro-Lebanese community in Egypt and thus had to be a part of the Nahda, even though later in his life he developed Salafi tendencies. In the older scholarship, the question lingered: How could he be a part of one but also a part of the other? More recent writing from NST suggests that this may not be that difficult a matter to resolve. Rather than assuming a binary between modernism and Salafism, one could assume Salafism is a form of modernism, with Rida serving as an example of hybrid modernism.[40] One could assume the same for other journalists as well, such as the feminist writer Zaynab Fawwaz.[41] Fawwaz was a Shi'ite from South Lebanon who immigrated to Egypt. Like Rida, she did not come from a missionary school background. Nonetheless, she was an important figure in the early feminist journalistic and literary circles of the period. The case of Fawwaz underscores once again the problems of the traditional interpretation of the Nahda.

At this point, the subject of the Syro-Lebanese in Egypt is up in the air. What we know is simply that there was a diverse group of individuals who all happened to come to Egypt from Lebanon or Syria at a time when most Lebanese and Syrians immigrated elsewhere. Whether they formed a community in Egypt is uncertain; that Egypt or any other country was stagnating and needed them in order to wake up seems unlikely. Why, in any case, a stagnant country would attract new migrants is uncertain. For these reasons, there must be some additional explanation for the prominence of a few of these individuals who did in fact participate in the Nahda. What were the dynamics driving these developments, and why did certain émigrés fit so well? A series of questions about the Syro-Lebanese school inspired by NST has all but taken apart this venerable buttress of the Oriental despotism paradigm in Egypt.

Let us now turn to NST analysis of the later Nahda. Following the 1952 Revolution, colonialism was over, and the reputation of Naguib Mahfouz, the novelist, was on the rise. Decades later, in 1988, Mahfouz won the Nobel Prize, suggesting for some scholars that the Nahda, whatever its background, was an authentic path for modern culture, one that went beyond colonial binaries. Others, however, were not persuaded by this interpretation; in fact, it seemed to propel the proponents of the older, more colonial binary thinking, such as the Orientalist Bernard Lewis, to make one last stand. In 2001, Lewis republished his book *Land of Enchanters: Egyptian Short Stories from the Earliest Times to the Present Day* (1948), which conveys the idea that Egyptians have always had a knack for telling stories, one that goes back to Pharaonic times, making Mahfouz in effect a part of eternal Egypt, as opposed to a part of the evolution of the Nahda.

More interesting was the NST reformulation of the Nahda paradigm that emerged after Mahfouz received the prize. Its premise was that Egyptian literary figures were creative in their own right and not simply as individuals who were skilled at emulating Western writers, and that logically it could not be otherwise. If one made Egyptian modernity dependent on translations from Western culture, these translations would have to be literal replications of the original to perform their function. But how could a translation function like that? Translation is not simply a literal rendition of a text from one language to another following some mechanical process that can be replicated; rather, it is an interpretation, and as such it is influenced by many factors, among them the size and nature of the market. If the market for Sherlock Holmes was anticipated to have been much larger than that for some famous novelist, would that not be a factor influencing a translator or a publishing house? The older Nahdawi school had other views on these matters. Popular culture—including Sherlock Holmes—was not a part of the Nahda. The Nahda was not just what was foreign inspired, but in addition what was elite oriented and scientifically accurate. The Nahda thus involved a radical separation from the popular and from "the imprecise." New Social Theory would disagree. For its protagonists, a translation is an interpretation, and popularity, if anything, suggests authenticity.[42]

Here the writings of Naguib Mahfouz would serve as an interesting example. Mahfouz was on the one hand the ultimate triumph of the Nahda, and on the other hand someone whose inspiration supposedly came from listening to ordinary people in coffee houses in Old Cairo, not from reading European books. Is it not surprising that

New Social Theorists have been focusing on the case of Mahfouz? Here is proof of the necessity of getting beyond the binaries of East and West, elite and mass, which are holding back our understanding of the Nahda. If Mahfouz got his material listening to the stories of ordinary men and women, would this not suggest that the Nahda had popular roots after all?

Authentic Identity, Religion, Law. Yet another dimension of Egyptian modernity for NST is bound up in the issue of authentic identity. In older scholarship, modern identity was assumed to be authentic as well as secular, and modernity was understood to be a universal and interchangeable set of ideas and practices. Islamic modernism, as the Nahdawis and as the Anglo-American scholars of the age of colonialism more generally understood it, was religion encapsulated in a secular framework. For the NST, on the other hand, modernity was not universal and need not be secular.

In effect, if Salafis were what society produced, as per one of the variants of that line of thought, Salafis might well represent modern authenticity. Still, if authenticity is tied to religion, how does the researcher escape from the binary of religious East versus secular West, or of the discourse of authentic religious tradition versus inauthentic secular history?

Consider the work of Indira Falk Gesink as an effort to resolve these conundrums. A student of Islamic law as well as a historian, Gesink argues that, contrary to what has been commonly assumed at least since Cromer's day, the Salafi attempt to impose Shari'ah law on Egypt was a recent innovation. It does not even date from the eighteenth century, much less from medieval times, nor is it a restoration of anything that had ever existed before. Rather, it is one in a series of modern constructions, which, in the case of Egypt, began in the mid-nineteenth century and is still ongoing. In a recent article, Gesink draws our attention to the figure of Muhammad 'Ilish, a mid-nineteenth-century Maliki Mufti.[43] 'Ilish argued in matters of law for the importance of Taqlid—that is, the obligation to follow tradition.

However, in contrast to the practice of earlier figures, 'Ilish's use of Taqlid appears to have been of a modernist sort; he was attempting to cope with the too-rapid and detrimental change of society that was occurring with the coming of the market. This, Gesink argues, was an important moment in the development of Salafism; it shows that Salafis could use Ijtihad, but sometimes it was more strategic for them not to.

Most scholars pass over 'Ilish as simply another traditional writer preferring Muhammad 'Abduh, who is of interest because he was an ideologue in favor of the use of Ijtihad (i.e., of man-made change). Gesink's argument is that, in practice, in opting for Ijtihad over Taqlid, more might be lost than gained. Historically, those who tended to use Ijtihad on an extensive basis were the reformers, who instrumentalized it to legitimize state policy. Sometimes state policy was good for the society, but sometimes it was not.

My own work reaches similar conclusions, although of course I am not involved in legal studies.[44] When Muhammad 'Ali chose Hasan al-'Attar to be the Shaykh al-Azhar, he knew al-'Attar was the unusual Shaykh who supported his reform program as well as the use of Ijtihad. In the same period, however, the most influential figure, Shaykh Ibrahim al-Bajuri, remained a critic of Muhammad 'Ali's policies and a defender of Taqlid, and he and al-'Attar did not get along. The life of al-Bajuri sheds light on the struggle to hold Egyptian society together as it was being impacted by reform. While al-'Attar was a modernist in one sense, al-Bajuri was a modernist in another sense, the two together seemingly antecedents of 'Abduh and 'Ilish.

Irfan Ahmad, a political scientist who is also a student of modern Islamic legal history, makes a similar argument, but one about the modernity of Salafism. The traditional upholders of the Oriental despotism paradigm, he notes, found it convenient to take at face value what the Salafis said about true Islam because it was always wrapped up in the idea of the eternal and the unchanging, which was also the argument of the Oriental despotism paradigm. He gives as an example the idea of Islam as in some sense a combination of church and state, arguing that in modern times Islam only became a combination of church and state—the so-called fusion thesis—as a reaction to modern conditions. What preceded the era of the fusion thesis involved not only a great variety of forms and relationships, but a very considerable degree of separation of church and state. This was the case at least in part because the Waqf system assured the virtual independence of the one from the other. In the nineteenth century, however, this independence broke down when the state encroached on the religious system, depriving it of its Waqf revenue and disrupting its method of teaching in the madrasa by imposing curricular reforms and by offering incentives to students to attend schools, which would qualify them for government service.

This fusion of church and state that Cromer took to be eternal actually came as a surprise to religious modernists. To them, it was not only something new but something undesirable, an obstacle to individual development and, by extension, to all progressive reform. If Allah had wanted some particular eternal system he would have said as much, and this he never did. Even most traditionists would agree with this point. Only the Salafis deeply embraced the fusion of church and state, some examples being Mawdudi and Sayyid Qutb.[45] What they called for was an Islamic state.

In the work of historian Amira Sonbol al-Azhary, another specialist in the field of contemporary Islamic legal studies, one finds modernity, be it Salafi or colonial, to be quite ambiguous, especially as it relates to gender matters. As concerns marriage, for instance, it turns out that modern women are actually in a weaker position than were women of the premodern period. Before the impact of the Europeans and the Salafis, women enjoyed relative equality with men, evidence for which can be extrapolated from the conditions written into their marriage contracts. This changed with the rise of the modern state, which, in the case of Egypt, coincided with the imposition of French law and Salafism; at that point, women became increasingly powerless. Thereafter, the modern state promoted the idea of male power over women, and marriage contracts became empty formalities as marriage was transformed into a sacrament. According to Sonbol, the Salafi trend not only accepted these changes but declared them to be the eternal word of God.[46] What is needed is a way to discuss reactionary religious modernism as a part of hegemony and to separate it from the issue of authenticity on the one hand and progressive trends in Islamic history on the other.

Subalternity. As we have discussed, writers on Egyptian modernity have tended to focus on the male elite, contrasting its culture to those of the peasants, the tribes, and the urban poor. While this continues to be the case, some recent work on modernity influenced by NST blurs the distinction between the elite and the subaltern, once again calling into question the adequacy of research based on such polarities.[47]

Lila Abu-Lughod, an influential commentator on the Awlad 'Ali women and a cultural anthropologist influenced by Clifford Geertz, initially took the Oriental despotism paradigm as a given. But, in analyzing feminine protest embodied in tribal poetry, she ended up challenging the received ideas of gender hierarchy that are commonly associated with that paradigm. Abu-Lughod observes that while numerous studies of tribes have noted the importance of the oral tradition and of seers and bards, few have considered the poetry of the ordinary person, which would require a different approach. Rather than going to the one Bedouin who was the poet and welcoming him or her into the pantheon of Egyptian culture, Abu-Lughod focuses on the ongoing role of the ordinary Bedouin women's poetry as an exercise of ordinary women's power, which is difficult to do. The Awlad 'Ali are a challenging community to study, as their economic situation depended on the ups and downs of the black market, and this would not be something to be disclosed to an outsider.

Perhaps Egypt's neoliberal economy had made the black market after 1970 more lucrative than before. This is, of course, a matter of speculation. What is more certain, and more observable, is that some of the women Abu-Lughod was studying were in the process of becoming housewives and consumers for the first time and starting to make use of piety strategies in their struggles. What she found was that even those women still chose to retain and make use of the older tradition of female love protest poetry, thus still exerting their power in marriage, politics, and alliances.

Resistance, Abu-Lughod concludes, in any form, should serve as a diagnostic of power, and the women whose emotions or drive for power induced them to recite this poetry clearly were exhibiting some power. Here Abu-Lughod reveals herself to be a critic of a part of the older paradigm, the part that took power to be centralized in the hands of the official elite and to trickle down in a predictable way though the hands of male functionaries. Resistance of the sort she discusses does not have a place in this formulation. In a manner reminiscent of the well-known book *Weapons of the Weak* (1985) by the political scientist James Scott, she argues that the weak, too, have their weapons and their powers of subversion, in this case the subversive power of subjectivity. Consider what the free discussion of feelings of love in this poetry does to the attempts to impose modesty: apparently, even today, love poetry can be a weapon in Awlad 'Ali society for any woman.[48] Perhaps the larger sense of this is that the struggles of the women of Awlad 'Ali are in some ways evidence that subalternity does not automatically imply powerlessness.

In a more recent book in the same vein, Abu-Lughod argues that the Egyptian state television serials have been playing an important role in constructing the nation during the period of the 1970s and beyond, in which the neoliberal state was not otherwise investing in national institutions. As her study shows, the outcomes on the level of audience reaction especially among women were not, however, necessarily what the government might have been hoping for. While the TV serials were very popular for their story content, they were often looked at quite critically on other grounds. Upper Egyptians, for example, did not appreciate the way their region was presented in some of the episodes; this was less the case for Lower Egyptians. The Oriental despotism paradigm assumes the efficacy of state coercion, evidence of which is that the society is passive and static. The idea of a critical audience is not compatible with this paradigm. However, as the research shows, entering empirically into the issue of governmental control of mass culture requires us to adjust our conclusions as to how the ruler/ruled relation may actually be functioning. It is not just top-down; it is somewhat interactive.[49]

The Idea of the Dictator. As we have noted, the idea of the dictator has always played an important role in the paradigm. Traditionally, it was contrasted, at least implicitly, with Western democracy. However, for a generation that has grown leery of East/West and dictatorship/democracy binaries, dictatorship in Egypt became an important subject to try to understand more precisely.

A well-known attempt to do just that is Timothy Mitchell's *Colonizing Egypt.*[50] At first glance, Mitchell's book appears to be another study of how nineteenth-century colonialism remade Egypt; reading on, it becomes clear that it follows a quite different trajectory. Inspired by the French philosopher Michel Foucault, Mitchell develops an argument about the coercive nature of the modern state as such and not simply about the state in Egypt. In the case of France but also of Egypt, the use of the census and of statistics proceeded hand in hand with the expansion of the bureaucracy's reach. Soon language was standardized, as was the calendar. The dictatorial nature of the regime can thus be acknowledged, but the older East-West binaries of the dominant paradigm are not what is most important. All states show these tendencies. Is there then no opposition?

For Mitchell there is. In a later book, *Rule of Experts*, the author focuses on the consequences of reducing one's understanding of politics to technocratic change as one finds under centralization. To do this, he explores several actual examples of change in Egyptian history, commonly interpreted as the achievements of architects, irrigation engineers, planners, foundations, businessmen, and others, all of whom possessed some knowledge of abstract science, which only a small handful (of mainly Europeans) possessed. Looking into each of these examples, he finds that the technical factors on which historians have placed such weight were actually overwhelmed by a plethora of other factors, most of which had nothing to do with science at all. The problem with the paradigm at its core, Mitchell argues, stems from the

faith of its supporters in a science that is not scientific. None of the traditional historians have adequately reflected on what these attempts at
abstraction and systematization that we call science amount to, leaving open the question of whether historians in the past were thereby
avoiding the actual subject of politics.[51]

A variant of this line of thought is also found in the work of the
historian Zeinab Abul-Magd, who makes the critique of the Oriental
despot a part of the critique of the use of the Egyptian nation-state as
a unit of analysis. The dictator, she maintains, is the face of the empire
and not simply of the nation.[52] Her book, *Imagined Empires*, high-
lights how the use of empire opens up historiographical possibilities
that nation-based historiography does not; her work is among the first
serious attempts to discuss the generally neglected subject of the modern history of Upper Egypt. What the author shows is that while Upper
Egypt is a very large and obvious subject, it is one that the nation-state
historiography has generally failed to address. Three world empires—
the Ottomans, the British, and the Americans, in alliance with the
Egyptian state—have all tried unsuccessfully to subdue Upper Egypt.
This, Abul-Magd claims, is explained in terms of the long-term tradition of resistance among Upper Egyptians to aggression from outside.
Nation-state historiography does not make any of this clear.

Think Tanks and Policy Studies. In this, the era of NST, only a
fairly small number of scholars self-consciously uphold the imperial-
maintenance version of the Oriental despotism paradigm without trying to overcome its binaries. These tend to be in policy circles, where
Egypt is still thought to have a patrimonial-cum-military-style regime.
Countries such as the United States would like to help Egypt become
a democracy, and in fact US policy toward countries such as Egypt
is constructed on that basis. This writing puts less emphasis on the
fact that, over the years, the US government has actually given a very
large amount of aid to the Egyptian police and army. Policy writing
about the Egyptian political system separates these two facts; it does
not speculate about how this aid might influence the way the system

might function. What gets emphasized instead is simply the dictatorial nature of the regime and what to do about it. For some, dictatorships are a challenge for the West. They produce terrorists, raising the question of how the West can penetrate such a society and help it reform so it will not produce them. Some shrug their shoulders. For them, it is the wrong question to ask. As one recent work by the political scientist Jason Brownlee argues, somewhat in the NST tradition, the vast majority of countries supposedly making transitions to democracy actually got stuck somewhere along the way. Failure to achieve democracy, he argues, is not specifically a problem of the Middle East or of Egypt. What policy makers need to acknowledge is that the persistence of authoritarian regimes in the world is, if anything, a phenomenon that needs to be better understood before jumping to policy conclusions. Given the number of examples of authoritarian regimes, singling out Egypt does not make sense at this point. Political scientist Vickie Langohr agrees: all we know, she writes, is that past efforts to generalize about the Middle East as a region fostering one-party (i.e., Oriental) systems have not brought us the expected results. Some Middle Eastern countries actually have fairly strong opposition parties functioning in parliament.[53]

Not all scholars, especially policy scholars, would agree with the advisability of such a laissez-faire approach. In one of his articles, the political scientist Robert Springborg takes up the subject of patrimonialism and policy making in Egypt to distinguish Nasir from Sadat.[54] He defends US support for Sadat and his system, claiming the genus was patrimonial and the species was exclusionist, whereas, in the case of Nasir's system, the genus was patrimonial and the species was inclusionist. By "inclusionist" he means more centralized power, more large-scale decisions, and more presidential activism, while the exclusionist approach was the opposite. In the latter variation, the president remained a bit aloof, letting the infighting work itself out, thereafter seeking only small-scale change. Of course, both regimes shared quite a bit in common as well; as patrimonial setups, both were run by patriarchs who ruled through an administrative structure that was an extension of their households, as opposed to through corporate

structures. This formulation allows Springborg to justify his preference for Sadat while at the same time arguing for the need for continuing long-term US intervention.

Policy writers following the dominant paradigm further buttress
their arguments for some kind of US intervention in Egypt by pointing to the economy. Their observation has long been that the Egyptian economic system was characterized by crony capitalism and not
by true market capitalism, so of course one should assume that there
would be stagnation and a lack of democracy. In recent years, however, even this line of thought has been open to question. As concerns
about stability have mounted in policy circles as a result of terrorism,
some have been taking a fresh look at crony capitalism. One policy
specialist writes that, to an extent, merging the political and economic
structures was not so much a matter of confusing the two but of sta-
bilizing the system.[55]

Still others reinforce the theme that Egypt is closed off from
the world and not receptive to ideas about history and methodology
found in the West. As one writer sees it, history is a science; one needs
to keep up with the latest techniques.[56] For others, no doubt, turning
history into scientific techniques dissociates it from its context. As the
UNESCO attempts at world history have shown, historians around
the world actually do not seem to have that much in common.

What we can take away from this characterization of the Anglo-
American field of modern Egyptian studies is that it is still a part of
the tradition of colonial knowledge; that it arose during the heyday
of the old Hegelian paradigm, which made of Egypt an Oriental despotism; but that today scholars aspire to break with that past. While
no new paradigm has arisen as yet to replace the Oriental despotism
model, the groundswell of critique augurs well for anyone who might
be inclined to undertake such a task.

At the same time, based on previous attempts, one could predict
that paradigm change will not be that easy. The Hegelian structure of
knowledge with its Orients and Oriental despotisms has been essential

for disciplines such as history all through the age of the nation-state. In reflecting on why this continues to be the case and why there are not more challenges to it, some weight, as I indicated in previous chapters, must be given to the desire of important segments of both the power structure and of the scholarly community as well as of society at large to preserve the nation-state and its structures of knowledge even when signs of its obsolescence appear. Thus it is that, until now, critics are more inclined to tinker with the Hegelian paradigm than to replace it. Nonetheless, the Hegelian tradition with its fixed ideas of East and West continues to erode before our eyes. In recent years, to give one example, what Egyptian historians write is increasingly cited in Anglo-American scholarship on Egypt not simply for detail but also for interpretation.[57] For the upholders of the Hegelian paradigm, this may come as a surprise. Egypt is not even supposed to have an academic tradition that produces original scholarship; rather, it is presumed to be intellectually stagnant or derivative.

To sum up, this chapter showed that, despite signs of discontent in the field, what one still observes are variants of a very oppressive paradigm maintained in place by various dominant interests. The next chapter takes up the question of how the narrative of Egyptian history has been made to fit this paradigm down to the level of the minutiae.

2

The Orthodox Narrative

The previous chapter showed that Anglo-American scholarship on modern Egypt has long conformed to one or another permutation of the Oriental despotism paradigm. This chapter carries the argument further, hypothesizing that one finds the influence of paradigm logic not just on the level of individual studies, but on the level of the commonly accepted—what I am terming here the "orthodox"—narrative of modern Egyptian history as a whole and even, seemingly, on the level of the choice of facts that go into that narrative.

In making this claim, the chapter further proposes that, in the case at hand, the conventional view of how historical narratives get formed and what role paradigm logic plays in the process needs to be rethought. The conventional view is that the narrative emerges as the result of the facts unearthed by scholars in archives, meaning that while philosophical frameworks such as the Oriental despotism may exist, they do not play the role that facts do. My finding, to the contrary, is that in this field, paradigm logic is much more determinative. Some facts get selected by scholars, and some lines of inquiry get pursued, but others do not, and those facts that get selected tend to get organized in a particular way that is defined by the paradigm logic. There are few loose ends. And yet, I would insist, the scholarship in the field is as technically competent, and the results are as objective, as are those in any other part of the discipline. In few other fields do scholars have comparable technical skills. And, last but not least, this should not be taken to mean that the history of this field is simply art—that is, constructed by a historian who chooses certain facts and rejects others. Based on the findings of the previous chapters, history in this field is art and science in a cage, albeit not recognized as such. The Oriental despotism paradigm is the cage. To pursue the hypothesis of the determinative nature of paradigm logic, this chapter takes up the question of how the narrative is put together, what gets included, and what gets left out or sidelined. Subsequent chapters pursue the matter further, taking up the issue of blind spots.

As with the previous chapter, so with this one: one significant problem is the representation of the subject. The repertoire of possible materials from which one might choose is enormous, and the commentary literature on this material that might serve as a guide is limited or altogether nonexistent. Given this situation, I chose to base the discussion of the orthodox narrative on two multiauthor works of interpretation of modern Egyptian history—one Anglo-American, one Egyptian—choosing in each context to cast the net as widely as possible but in an organized way. The works I chose were *The Cambridge History of Egypt, Vol. 2: Modern Egypt, from 1517 to the End of the Twentieth Century*, edited by W. W. Daly,[1] and *Deux cent après Expedition d'Égypte: Vision Égyptienne*, an Arabic-language collection edited by Nasir A. Ibrahim and Ra'uf 'Abbas Hamid as *Mi'atay 'am 'ala al-hamlah al-firansiya (Ru'ya Misriyah)*.[2] In the former, Anglo-American case, the dominance of the one paradigm stands out, while in the latter, Egyptian case, it does not. Paradigms appear to compete with each other, as one might expect to find in most areas of historical study.

The Cambridge History of Egypt is part of a tradition of carefully edited reference books that Cambridge University Press has been producing for many years about the history of different countries. The Egyptian *Deux cent après Expedition d'Égypte* came out of a conference held by the Egyptian Society for Historical Studies in conjunction with the French Civilization faculty of Cairo University and other Egyptian institutions. The conference had been held in reaction to the French government's decision to celebrate in 1998 the bicentennial of the Napoleonic invasion of Egypt by holding a conference in France. Most Egyptian historians boycotted that conference and held their own in Cairo. This series of events caused a strain in diplomatic relations between the two countries, and diplomatic efforts were made thereafter to patch matters up, with this book serving as a part of the process. For this reason, the controversy is mostly downplayed in the book itself; its main rationale, the editors claimed, was to address the problem that the writing on Egypt in 1798 available today to students lagged behind the times, based as it is on scholarship produced many years ago. Given the existence of more recent scholarship, it should now be possible to construct from the older and newer bodies of writing, taken together, a more balanced and up-to-date picture.

Why not, one might wonder, select more contemporary works of the sort referenced in the preceding chapter? Why choose books that are twenty years old? Clearly something could have been gained from relying on newer work. The short answer is that the choice was in some sense faute de mieux: NST has been more successful in deconstructing than in building systematic studies of its own, so when one seeks to understand how historians approach modern Egypt in a systematic way, the Cambridge University Press series seems like the obvious choice. As for the Egyptian book, one has to go back a few years to an occasion when the field had enough funding to support the publication of a work on this scale.

The Cambridge History of Egypt

In the *Cambridge History*, the study of modern Egypt covers a total of five hundred years. It does so, however, in a very particular way, as part "Whig History," part Oriental despotism. History slowly unfolds over centuries, but change takes place only with the coming of the West. Chapters begin and end in such a way as to draw attention to the politics of the elite in Cairo and to the empire of the day. The sources used primarily concern Cairo and not the provinces. On the level of factual information, the facts selected lead to the conclusion that the country by its nature is static, and that, as a result, foreigners play a conspicuous role in whatever development takes place.

In chapter 1, the historian Michael Winter covers the period between 1517 and 1609.[3] He takes up some of the well-known events of the era—for example, how, in the last part of the sixteenth century, when the empire failed to pay the salaries of the Sipahi troops, the Sipahis then defied the central authority and imposed their own tax on the Delta. Winter characterizes this period as one of weakness compared to the period of the Conquest: the Sipahis' tax aroused the ire of the Sultan, who sent a high-ranking official, Muhammad Pasha, to put an end to this practice in 1609. Winter's chapter thus begins and ends with the strong ruler in Cairo. The facts emphasized and the periodization chosen are those that fit the narrative. Nonetheless, what also catches one's attention are the side references about tribal shaykhs and others, individuals who apparently did not cooperate with the central authority, which raises a question: Does a Cairo-based political narrative of this sort, beginning and ending in the way this one does, actually makes clear who had power in Egypt or what they were doing with it? Even as regards Cairo, the narrative seems to have its limitations. How do we understand the quick rebound of the Mamluks, who were defeated but returned to power with their land system intact? Obviously, they were not doing this on their own. Why is this not a major subject for those specialized in this period? Again, one is led to assume it is not a major subject because of the paradigm logic. Those particular Ottomans who forged an alliance with the Mamluks whom they had just defeated were doing something that was not a part of previous patterns; something new was occurring, and it involved unexpected changes. Both those Ottomans and those Mamluks, I assume—and this would be a possible alternative interpretation—were out to succeed as much as possible in the newly emerging world of mercantilism. They wanted a share of commercial profits, and they wanted to invest in local businesses and to intermarry. They had more interests in common than they had differences. This seems more likely than hypothesizing, as Winter does in following the paradigm, that the Ottomans in Egypt were simply all functionaries following orders from Istanbul. No doubt there were a few functionaries of that sort, but, as regards the majority of the soldiers who stayed on in Egypt, this seems doubtful.

In chapter 2, the historian Jane Hathaway looks at the subject of Egypt in the seventeenth century.[4] Her chapter stresses the importance of Egypt as a bread basket for the Holy Cities and even for Istanbul itself. While this is fair enough, Egypt per se emerges only seren-dipitously—as, for example, in references to the fact that the warring military factions of the seventeenth century were involved in the cof-fee trade.

Very probably, Hathaway is simply giving priority to what was most important. Following paradigm logic, Egypt followed Istanbul, so one would focus on events in Istanbul. Istanbul was a part of a declining Orient witnessing a rising West; therefore, by extension, so was Egypt. Yet, as Hathaway mentions in passing, change was taking place—it was not simply a matter of decline. A struggle among the military-political factions had resulted in the consolidation of power by one of them: the Qazdogli Mamluks.

Of course, what stands out as well is the preference for the idea of decline as opposed to that of change. Egypt and Turkey were different than Europe. They fell behind the UK in economic terms in the years leading to the Industrial Revolution. Of course, so did nearly every other country in the world. And, such being the case, one does not learn much about the specificities of Ottoman or Egyptian history by characterizing this situation as one of decline.

In chapter 3, the historian Daniel Crecilius deals with the eigh-teenth century, ending in 1798.[5] This chapter logically had to charac-terize the period as one of decline, and to that end the author looks at what he terms "Mamluk misrule," a shorthand for the way the failure to maintain centralization of authority in Egypt led to a breakdown of law and order, which destroyed what could have been a period of prosperity as the country gained more autonomy from the Ottoman Empire. Given this set of assumptions, it is not surprising that a his-torian seeking to demonstrate decline might turn, as Crecilius does here, to the more outspoken critics of the Mamluk policies of the period, among them the French merchants and the Egyptian historian al-Jabarti, yet this seems rather arbitrary. No doubt the merchants were bitter about their affairs in Egypt, and they had reason to be: they were caught in a situation in which France needed more and more foodstuff from Egypt at a time when it had less and less to offer that the Egyptians were willing to buy in return. The merchants thus fell into arrears in their payments, and the Egyptians tried to collect what was owed them in any way they could. The French merchant memoirs record all this, and in so doing they convey the idea of increasing Mamluk misrule. This in turn got picked up, as it fit the Oriental despotism paradigm then in formation by scholars, in which it has played a role ever since.

Crecilius also makes use of the work of the Egyptian historian al-Jabarti, who also alludes to Mamluk misrule and Egyptian decline, in ways leaving open, however, the question whether in reality the French merchants and al-Jabarti were actually talking about the same thing. It would seem reasonable to suppose al-Jabarti missed the Egypt of his youth.

There cannot be any other interpretation of the late eighteenth century but that of decline: so goes the dominant paradigm. The Mamluks must therefore have stood in the way of progress. But, as detailed studies would subsequently show, this was not in fact entirely the case. Modern military technology had begun to arrive, and the Mamluks made what use of it they could, raising the question of how scholars could doubt Egypt's receptivity to modern technology. Here, as the reader might note, was a potential threat to the paradigm. Ultimately, paradigm logic was salvaged by scholars' hypothesizing that it must have been the Christians in Egypt who would have introduced progress as opposed to the Muslims, since progress depended upon contact with the West, and Egyptian Christians were the ones who had such contacts. From this, scholars further hypothesized that Egyptian receptivity might be explained in terms of the country being run by Mamluks who had converted from Christianity to Islam (e.g., 'Ali Bey al-Kabir). But where does this hypothesis take us? If 'Ali Bey and some of the other Mamluks were originally Christians, this was not the case for the majority of the other Mamluks in this period. And there is certainly no evidence to show that some Mamluks used new weaponry and others refused to do so for religious reasons. Again, it would seem that what gave such assumptions their plausibility was the paradigm logic more than anything else.

Problems associated with the defense of the paradigm persist. As we shall see in the following pages, when Napoleon invaded Egypt there was the issue of how to characterize the enemies that he encountered, especially in Upper Egypt. The narrative required that historians identify them and briefly fit them into history, but then, as they have no true place in history, drop them out again, returning them to the "eternal peasantry." As this was not persuasive, historians characterized Napoleon's enemies as Bedouins, thereby granting them a tentative historicity as enemies while denying historicity to the Fallahin altogether. This would explain how certain Egyptians could be said to have military capabilities while others did not. But, as we will now see, this approach to defining the Bedouins, while solving one problem, created others. Overall, they have played a role in Egyptian history—actually, many different roles. The Hawwara, for example, often did not cooperate with the governors appointed to the Sa'id, but pursued their own interests in the grain trade. This threatened French interests because it was in the Sa'id that the grain that the French wanted was grown, so Napoleon captured that region and defeated the Hawwara. The Hawwara then appeared to disappear from history. But, of course, they did not disappear; they have continued to play a role in Egyptian history right up until the present. One other such example must suffice here: in the Delta, the confederation of the Haba'iba were found to be troublesome, but they maintained their ties to Cairo, for which reason historians include them at least on the margins of history.

So, are Bedouins a part of Egyptian history or not? This would depend on how one defines the term. If one were to historicize the Haba'iba, doing so by making their willingness to deal with Cairo and to be sedentarized the main prerequisites to be a part of history, one would exclude a great many other Bedouins who neither maintained such contacts nor chose to sedentarize.

Putting the paradigm aside, one might ask, as if beginning from scratch, why individuals chose a Bedouin lifestyle in this period. We can of course speculate. For some individuals who remained Bedouins, it might have been out of a desire for a freedom of lifestyle, or at least a freedom from being a day laborer on a cotton plantation; those seeking that freedom might group themselves together as Bedouins. Sometimes they would sedentarize, sometimes they would not. The Hawwara, for example, who opposed the French in Upper Egypt and the government in Cairo and were briefly included in history, were one of the more sedentarized of the "tribes" of Upper Egypt. They were centered at the time of Napoleon in the city of Farshut.

As a result of the influence of the Oriental despotism paradigm, one can find very few Bedouins acknowledged to be a part of modern Egyptian history. In the chapter from the *Cambridge History* under discussion, Shaykh Hummam, the famous leader of the Hawwara, is described dismissively in terms of the number of Nubian slave girls he possessed. However, other accounts of this individual by Egyptians coming from Upper Egypt (e.g., by Rifa'ah al-Tahtawi and Lu'wis 'Awadh) describe the Shaykh's long rule as marked by an early form of republican government in which the security of conditions allowed merchants to traverse the routes to the Red Sea and the Sudan. In other words, under Shaykh Hummam, the Hawwara state was, like Cairo, a mercantilist regime, until 'Ali Bey conquered it in 1769. In Crecilius's chapter, however, the 1769 campaign of 'Ali Bey to conquer Shaykh Hummam is simply a passing episode emanating from Cairo.

In chapter 5, historian Darrell Dykstra examines the period of the French Occupation of Egypt (1798–1801).[6] The chapter begins with a depiction of events in Egypt seen as an extension of the European theater of war, which at a certain moment happened to include Egypt. The rationale for proceeding in this way was no doubt based on the assumption that Egyptian history did not have a dynamic of its own, so that if one could no longer write Egyptian history as an extension of Ottoman Turkey, the Ottoman presence being quite limited, it would then make sense to turn to France. In a later period, following the same logic, the book turns from an emphasis on France to an emphasis on the UK.

The chapter then proceeds to highlight particular aspects of French policy in Egypt such as the registration and appropriation of the lands of "enemies," leading to the author's claim that these actions presaged the end of the Mamluks and hence represented progress. However, this formulation is as much paradigm driven as fact driven. In point of detail, neither tax farming nor sharecropping nor mercantilism—the hallmarks of the Mamluk system—actually came to an end for many years thereafter. Paradigm logic, however, would dictate otherwise: Napoleon brought reforms. Historical continuity extending from the eighteenth century into the nineteenth century would therefore seem unlikely. The larger metanarrative of the "Rise of the West" and of the waking up of the "sleeping Orient" depends on the Napoleonic invasion of 1798 being a rupture.

In an assessment of the era of Muhammad 'Ali in chapter 6, the historian Khaled Fahmy considers three themes: the growth of ties to Europe, the colonial adventures, and the exploitation of the peasantry.[7] Fahmy's emphasis is the coercive treatment of the peasantry, which while fitting the paradigm does not distinguish Egypt from many other countries of that period.[8]

As the chapter also makes clear, 1798 is a watershed. The modern period beginning in 1798 and extending through the reign of Muhammad 'Ali is understood as one of sustained and systematic development followed by a long hiatus in which nothing much happened. Another possibility would be to look at the first half of the nineteenth century as a part of a longer transition dating from earlier times in which the mercantilist system of the past several centuries broke down and the capitalist nation-state of the mid-nineteenth century started to emerge. Muhammad 'Ali struggled, ultimately unsuccessfully, to keep a mercantilist regime in place. Given too much emphasis on a rupture in 1798 and its aftermath, the historian writing on this subject is likely to miss these slower-moving but equally fundamental changes. If too much emphasis is put on the creation of the new army, as is often the case, too easily forgotten is the fact that the army was all but disbanded following the treaties of the 1840s. In light of such details, an alternative interpretation pointing to how the formation of the army and of the bureaucracy coming at the time they did was important not because they symbolized the birth of sustained and systematic development but because they slowed down the development of an indigenous middle class by giving power to a small landowning class and a surrogate bourgeoisie made up of foreigners. In this way, Egyptian history diverges a bit from some others, where the growth of the indigenous middle class, while slow, was not hindered to the same extent. Were it not for the demands of the paradigm to conflate the coming of the West with modernization, perhaps researchers would make the argument that the technicalization of Egypt in the Muhammad 'Ali period in some ways slowed its modernization. Fahmy, to his credit, finds a solution to the problems brought about by the paradigm by invoking the idea of modernity as dystopia. He presents details concerning how Muhammad 'Ali treated his peasantry, how he crushed revolts, and how he dealt with those who were late with their taxes or unable to perform the corvée.

In chapter 7, entitled "Egypt under Muhammad 'Ali's Successors," the historian F. Robert Hunter notes the expanding range of both European involvements in Egyptian affairs from afar and of the Egyptian bureaucracy in the affairs of its own people up close. The author mentions events such as the construction of the railways, the construction of the Suez Canal, and the rise of the Egyptian debt, none of which necessarily relate to Muhammad 'Ali.[9] But, as the chapter's title suggests, what Hunter assumes is that this was a period of time in which rulers were weak, as European tutelage was more limited, the two points being connected. Nonetheless, some development was still taking place. This requires an explanation. One possibility would be to see this period as a part of the heritage of Muhammad 'Ali, in conjunction with the presence of cosmopolitan Europeans in Alexandria and Cairo.

Freed from the Oriental despotism paradigm, it would seem more logical to see the period between 1849 and 1863 on its own terms. For example, there was the rise of the public debt. Debt plays an important role in the formation of Third World nations. Nubar Pasha and the others who incurred the debt for Egypt let loose a chain of events leading to the creation of a huge starving landless peasantry that has not yet found a way out of poverty a century or more later. This is an event of gigantic importance, but one that clearly had little to do with Muhammad 'Ali. However, to fit the paradigm, Hunter suggests that Nubar Pasha was a modernizer, as if he was in some sense a continuator of the reform agenda of Muhammad 'Ali.

In chapter 8, the historian Hasan Ahmed Ibrahim takes on the subject of the Egyptian empire in Arabia and in the Sudan.[10] In the Arabian section, he emphasizes the Pasha's duplicity and ambitiousness in fighting the Wahhabis. The Oriental despot paradigm is sustained at this point by exploring Muhammad 'Ali's Machiavellian side. Others have taken the view that, then as now, jihadist regimes such as the early Wahhabis were a menace to others; the Ottoman Empire as a whole felt threatened. But the approach here does not consider that possibility. It confines itself to speculating about the Pasha's potential motives for his involvement. In the section on the Sudan, Ibrahim emphasizes the supposed foolhardy belief of the Pasha in the likelihood of finding gold and other riches along with slaves for his army, no matter how devastating Egyptian imperialism might have been for the Sudan or how wrongheaded were the Pasha's beliefs, thereby underscoring the irrationality and extravagance of the Pasha. But why frame the issue this way? Why not ask what was going on among investors and others who were promoting this campaign? The building of an empire was scarcely the pipe dream of one man.

In chapter 9, the historian Donald Reid takes up the 'Urabi Revolution and the British Conquest (1879–82). He begins with an argument against what he calls the partisans of Tawfiq, who thought 'Urabi was a revolutionary, while others thought what took place was simply an insurrection or a revolt—a line of argument leading one to expect the chapter would break with what went before and be more Egypt-centered.[11] However, this is not the case. The chapter remains centered on the British, with brief references to members of the Egyptian elite, concluding, as if as an aside, that the defeat of 'Urabi brought a loss of power to the Khedive. And, indeed, paradigm logic does not encourage the historian to go any further than that. Following the paradigm, there is actually no such thing as a revolution. Society does not rise in revolt. How could it? Egyptian society is not even a part of history. Thus, there would be no reason to inquire whether or not the mass population did or did not support 'Urabi. More fruitful would be to inquire why the Coptic elites supported 'Urabi as opposed to why the Muslim ones did, Reid's assumption being—to return to an earlier point—that these two communities had little in common with each other, so their support for 'Urabi would doubtless need to be explained in different ways.

In chapter 10, the historian M. W. Daly surveys the period of the British occupation from 1882 to 1922. In doing so, he adopts a pragmatic imperialist position reminiscent of that of the British diplomat Valentine Chirol discussed in chapter 1 of this book.[12] The British occupied Egypt more or less accidentally, but, once in control of the country, they realized that its finances might take some years of careful management to be brought back into order. The chapter focuses on this supposed mission of financial recovery. As this interpretation develops, the paradigm logic is once again quite apparent; it is not surprising that the modernization of Egypt once again began to progress as a result of the presence of Europeans. In regard to the 1919 Revolution, Daly notes simply that Egyptian frustrations with the Protectorate were made worse by Reginald Wingate's meeting with Sa'd Zaghlul, which gave the false impression that Britain might grant Egypt independence.

In chapter 11, the historian Ehud Toledano takes up the subject of socioeconomic change in the long nineteenth century, beginning with the claim that socioeconomic processes are not like political ones—they do not just start and stop.[13] This is in effect one of the corollaries of the dominant paradigm: that history is a matter of events involving the political elites, and that whatever else may have taken place is not a part of history or causally related to it in a predictable way. Thus, a historian studies subjects such as social history or demography after he or she has covered the more important aspects of the subject, such as political history. While this set of assumptions is not unique to Egyptian studies, it is much less common in the study of the United States, the UK, or other Western countries. The apparent reason, once again, is the paradigm, which allows for only a few actors. Following the paradigm, the dynamic of history that results normally takes place between those actors and their imperial counterparts and not their fellow countrymen. So, by definition, the rest of the population is simply demographic detail. If the population rises up, such an uprising is—for a historian at least—essentially a matter of passing detail, as it would be for a chronicle writer. To explain the rise of the figure of Ahmad 'Urabi, some modification of the paradigm was, however, required. Toledano was forced to come up with the idea of a slowly evolving challenger stratum that rose up over the preceding years.

In chapter 12, the historian Selma Botman deals with the subject of Egypt in the Liberal Age (1923–52). In doing so, she confronts the problem of explaining the rapid political change and development occurring in this period.[14] Egypt, she notes, went from a country with a very small elite in the days of the British Protectorate to a country with a growing middle class as it moved toward independence. There was not only a king and a parliamentary system at this point, but also a mass party, the Wafd. Here, Botman appears to follow the work of a number of eminent liberal-age historians, from George Antonius to Albert Hourani, who were all a part of the dominant paradigm as well.

As the chapter shows, the 1923 Constitution marked the beginning of independence, even though—as Botman notes by way of qualification—it reserved considerable power not just for the British but for the King as well, and, as regards the latter, neither King Fouad nor King Faruq believed in parliaments or democracies. As Botman also points out, neither the parliament nor the political parties of the Liberal Age were fully developed institutions. Participation in them amounted more to a status symbol than to a defined set of responsibilities. In these ways, one might infer, the subject would conform to the interpretation of Egypt as an Oriental despotism. There was still a tiny circle who actually had the power, whereas others simply had titles.

Botman's conclusion is that one should think of the breakdown of the liberal age in the late 1940s as an unnecessary tragedy for Egypt, perhaps even something of an accident: it followed from Britain's inability or reluctance to negotiate its withdrawal on suitable terms, a matter that has never been satisfactorily explained. Some have blamed the ineptitude of the Labour Party in foreign affairs, others Sidqi and the Egyptians. Either way, logic would lead to the conclusion that the 1952 Revolution had come too soon; the country still needed more years of British tutelage.

In chapter 13, the historian Joel Beinin considers Egyptian society and economy (1923–52). His treatment thus differs from that found in chapter 12, which took up politics.[15] Beinin argues that, during this period, the middle classes—or Afandiyya—emerged as the progressive element in society, pointing the way to a better future. And, as Beinin then notes, while segments of the Afandiyya were found in the countryside, his emphasis would be on the more Europeanized, more urbanized Afandiyya, especially those from the minority communities. They were a vanguard, and this was their heyday. Perhaps! Yet, at the end of this period, they virtually disappeared. How and why this was the case is unresolved. Was it the breakdown of the British Empire, the rise of nationalism or the Muslim Brotherhood, the deepening crisis of capitalism, or simply the spread of education? Whatever the case may be, one might wonder at the role the author assigns to these communities; "progressive elements in society" may not be the most precise term for them if they simply disappeared in thirty years, but it is a way of making the subject fit the paradigm. As a somewhat Europeanized community, they brought change, and 1952 marked the end of that change.

In chapter 14, the political analyst Alain Roussillon considers the post-1952 period, in the process confronting yet another challenge, that of explaining how a country with supposedly no internal dynamic—a country supposedly dependent on foreign influence for its history—could become independent without falling back into the chaos, misrule, and stagnation one associates with the eighteenth century.[16] What kind of history could such a country then have? Roussillon's answer is that the history of Egypt after 1952 was cyclical: there would no longer be linear development as such, but simply a replaying of what went before. Nasir, in this view, was a replaying of

Muhammad 'Ali, and Sadat and Mubarak were a replaying of Khedive Isma'il. While one cannot dispute the consistency of this line of thinking with regard to the logic of the paradigm, one might well have questions about whether or not a useful insight is being pushed too far. After 1952, there was land reform and Egypt's role in the Non-aligned Movement, and there were trade unions. Trade unions did not exist in the Muhammad 'Ali period, and there were reasons for this. Add to this the obvious fact that the neoliberalism of today is not the same as the classical liberalism of the nineteenth century, and that neocolonialism was not the same as the colonialism of the Victorian era. In sum, a cyclical approach to analyzing Egypt today limits one's capacity to deal with what all historians have to deal with, and that is change.

In chapter 15, the literary critic Paul Starkey deals with the subject of modern Egyptian culture though the 1980s, leading with the traditional claim that modern culture in Egypt began in 1798. In putting this forward, Starkey appears to be relying on the scholarship of the liberal age, a time when the dominant paradigm was less open to debate than it was later. Since the fall of the Muhammad 'Ali dynasty in the 1952 Revolution, a generation of scholars has been raising questions about the adequacy of the 1798 watershed for the study of modern cultural history. A number of studies of al-Zabidi, al-Jabarti, al-Damanhuri, al-'Attar, and other figures of the eighteenth century suggest that modern culture existed before 1798. In 2012, with the publication of the doctoral dissertation of the literary historian Ahmad Hamid Hijazi, *Izdihar al-adab al-'Arabi fi al-'asr al-'uthmani*, one comes to realize the importance of the pre-romantic landscape poetry for Egypt as well as for many other countries in the eighteenth century. While some of the poetry in Hijazi's collection is virtually unknown to modern readers, some of it was known to scholars as early as the 1960s. But, coming as it did before Napoleon, for Starkey and others following the "Coming of the West" approach, such poetry would be deemed irrelevant to a discussion of modernity.[17]

In his coverage of more recent times, Starkey naturally makes reference to Naguib Mahfouz winning the Nobel Prize, and to other notable achievements in literature, concluding that, nonetheless, Egyptian literature is marked by several unresolved tensions, among them the divide between serious and popular literature. And, while this might be said about the literature of any country, here this was doubtless yet another reference to the radical division between elite and mass (*al-khass wa al-ʿamm*) thought to exist by those following the Oriental despotism paradigm. Another unresolved tension arose from the fact that Egyptian literature was tied up with Third World literature and development and thus not as pure as literature in the West, where one finds true art that is art for art's sake. Egypt's literature is thus not true art.

Granting Starkey's point, that Egyptian writers are involved in society, the reader comes away with a tableau of two hundred years of their struggle defined as outside of history because literature itself is outside of history; thus, in a work of history such as this one, logically what one says about literature is relegated to the end. One wonders whether Starkey believes that Naguib Mahfouz should have won the Nobel Prize for literature if he was not in a position to produce art for art's sake. Yet another unresolved tension, according to Starkey, arises out of the question of how art can be produced given the censorship writers face from religionists. Here Starkey appears to disallow the possibility that censorship might stimulate art. Oriental censorship by its nature is apparently different from censorship in Europe or in Russia.

This chapter, like the others, stands in contrast to chapter 4, the only one not part of the dominant paradigm. As the Egyptian historian Nelly Hanna notes, the study of culture in Egypt in the Ottoman period has been unsatisfactory for reasons associated with the paradigm question.[18] Scholars simply assume a relative absence of cultural change from the time of the early Mamluks through the nineteenth century, despite the paucity of studies for most of this period and the obvious differences in the patronage of the arts in different periods.

In sum, what emerges from the *Cambridge History* is an image of Egypt as a country developing technologically but still Oriental and dependent in nature, its modernity essentially an import, every detail accounted for. We now turn to a work that shares in many of these dilemmas but that, to its credit, problematizes the paradigm of Oriental despotism.

Two Hundred Years since the French Invasion

While overlapping with the *Cambridge History* in various ways, *Two Hundred Years since the French Invasion* naturally focuses on 1798 and on what its authors take to be the mythology surrounding it. As this mythology—or, in our terminology, paradigm logic—is deeply ingrained in existing scholarship, the goal the authors set for themselves is not an easy one to achieve. The approach ultimately adopted involves sticking close to the empirical details found in archival materials and in other primary sources, maintaining balance, and avoiding the kind of narrative approach suggesting finality.[19]

Given the context that gave rise to the book, a number of the chapters allude to the recent reassertion of the old French colonial idea of *mission civilatrice*, originally associated with the Napoleonic invasion. As several authors mention, the French government seemed to have entirely forgotten that Napoleon had invaded Egypt, committed what amounted to war crimes, and then left. What kind of civilizing mission was that? What also becomes clear, however, is the degree of uncertainty among Egyptian historians as regards a potential alternative view of the origins of Egyptian modernity in terms of 1798. For the senior historians at least, the idea of an eighteenth-century background to Egyptian modernity does not seem persuasive; to them, it would be more reasonable to go forward from 1798, not backward. Here one detects something of a generational divide.

The book begins with a chapter by the historian Nabil al-Tukhi on the French invasion of the Sa'id.[20] Here the myth of the "civilizing mission" is met by an account of the actual details of that campaign. Al-Tukhi based his work both on archives and on a careful rereading of the well-known primary source *Voyage dans la basse et la haute Égypte pendant les campagnes du Général Bonaparte* by Vivant Denon (1802). What is clear from al-Tukhi's account is that Denon provided observations about the French campaigns of a disturbing nature that were either never noticed or ignored by readers from then to now. Was this because it was not a book about Cairo and therefore the details were not important, or was it because the unflattering detail about the French troops was not compatible with the Napoleonic myth of waking up a sleeping Orient? The answer is not clear; we do not know enough about Denon.

In the second chapter, the historian Nasir Ibrahim takes up the old canard that the Copts collaborated with the French because they were Christians and hated the Muslims. This chapter shows how the Coptic intendants, with their detailed knowledge of land and taxes, were initially embraced by the French, who were desperately trying to raise revenue, only to then be rejected as the French figured out they were not on their side.[21] In effect, these Mubashshirun resisted the French demands by being habile and by tempering their cooperation. This chapter thereby casts serious doubt on the assumption of some kind of an affinity among Christian elites. Certainly Napoleon did not rescue the Copts, as claimed by some of the earlier books, nor did they rescue him.

The next two chapters, by specialist in French civilization Layla 'Inan and historian 'Ali Kurkhan, respectively, consider the subject of Napoleonic propaganda and myth construction.[22] What they show, following Kurkhan, is that enormous effort and expense went into controlling French public opinion and knowledge about the Egyptian campaign. Napoleon mobilized musicians, artists, playwrights, and literary figures to manufacture the image he sought to promote. Apparently it scarcely mattered what in fact he was doing, be it to his own troops or to the Egyptians. As we learn from 'Inan's account, Napoleon poisoned to death his own soldiers who were wounded or sick on at least one occasion, which certainly never made the headlines.

In the chapter that follows, the historian Sabri al-'Adl challenges the claim that Egypt was isolated from the world of science and medicine as if it had been asleep for the past centuries.[23] He notes various details from accounts by travelers, to which he appends a list of Egyptians in the eighteenth century known from the Arabic-language sources for their scientific or medical prowess. We learn, for example, of a clinical tradition outside the circles of the Azhar that continued uninterrupted throughout the eighteenth century. Even in the nineteenth century, bits of this tradition carried over and could be found in the early Muhammad 'Ali period.

The historian Ra'uf 'Abbas Hamid summarizes an example of the traditional historiographical thought that has stood the test of time: that the invasion should be seen primarily as a part of the history of a long-running rivalry between France and England.[24] Beginning in the eighteenth century, both of these great powers sought to control the route to India and the East. The Napoleonic invasion was one moment in this series of events that presaged the eventual British control of the seas. The rivalry, however, did not end there.

The book then turns to consider problems of communication in Egypt during the invasion, questioning the idea that Napoleon's proclamations would have been understood in Egypt as Napoleon had intended them to be. As linguistics professor Madiha Doss writes, there is evidence to show that translators confronted the problem of how to make proclamations, orders, and questions understandable to the different levels of Egyptian society.[25] These translators were obliged to experiment; there thus began what today is called modern standard Arabic, the invasion accidentally becoming an event in linguistic history. As Doss also notes, while there were different groups of people involved in translation work, the leading French Orientalists, who were in charge, had all been trained to regard colloquial Arabic as "Arabe Vulgaire." They were not aware of the tradition of written colloquial Arabic, a tradition that could have served their needs, so they aimed at creating a new mix of language levels.

In her chapter, Cairo University professor of linguistics Dalia 'Ali Muhammad sets out to identify what sorts of people were involved in translation.[26] She finds that there were prisoners of war (among them Turks, Bedouins, and North Africans) and Orientalists (including Syrian and Lebanese Christians), as well as some of the French savants. This odd mixture of individuals with their own disparate histories raises issues in themselves—of technical skills in Arabic, of knowledge of Egypt, of motivations in translating, and, of course, of Napoleon's motivation in depending on these people in the first place.

Professor of French Maha Jad al-Haqq addresses in her chapter yet another language-related issue, involving the work of the translator Alexander Cardin.[27] Cardin, a prominent French intellectual of the first half of the nineteenth century, is credited with translating and publishing a book in Paris in 1838 entitled *Journal d'Abdurrahman Gabarti pendant l'occupation Français en Égypte suivi d'un précis de la meme campagne*, among his other achievements. What is known to the modern reader, thanks to recent scholarship, is that Cardin's translation took in a rather casual fashion pieces from three different writings of al-Jabarti, to which he appended an essay by Niqula al-Turk. This raises the question of how and why Cardin presented the Paris audience with a mix of al-Jabarti and Niqula al-Turk, and why he did so at the time he did; there would be no reason to expect these two writers to be similar. A quote from Cardin suggests that the timing of the publication may have been connected to the needs of the ongoing French occupation of Algeria of that period. In other words, as with some other studies of the Orient done in the name of science (including, as we shall see, the *Description*), there was a politics, in this case of an ongoing imperialism.

Next, Cairo University French professor Manal Khedr takes a close look at the *Description de l'Égypte*, the major intellectual production coming out of the Napoleonic invasion, most often used to substantiate French claims that they brought civilization and enlightenment to Egypt.[28] Khedr concludes that the main use of the "modern state" would be for a scholar studying French imperial policy in the years of the Bourbon Restoration, the period during which the book was edited and published. Its views of Egypt, Khedr states, were suspect for a number of reasons. It was certainly not, as it was often made out to be, a scientific achievement: the empirical work was carried out under the supervision of the French military as conditions allowed and thus bore no relation to science. Furthermore, the work was conducted by young men who were not yet specialists and in fact whose scholarly reputations evolved only in later years back in France, where the *Description* served them as a career vehicle. The fact that there is so much uniformity in thought throughout the text, which is something that one would not find in a real scientific work, is also something to be looked into. Would it be explained by the education that the savants had received in France, or was it simply the work of the editors? The sociological part of the *Description*, Khedr finds, was organized according to three main categories: peasants, city dwellers, and Bedouins. The justification for the use of these categories, she says, was not a scientific one, but reflected the ease (or the difficulty) with which the French were able to collect taxes from them.

Maha Jad al-Haqq continues the discussion of the modern state, shifting from textual analysis to an analysis of the artwork. From a study of the various plates, she shows that the 'ulama' appeared in closed rooms, suggesting their closed universe, and that the peasants appeared in a desolate countryside, suggesting their poor agricultural techniques. As for the French, their pictorial self-representations were often elided with those of the Pharaohs themselves.[29]

French-language specialist 'Aidah Husni extends the discussion of the plates, noting the juxtaposition of modern-day peasants and Pharaonic priests, which conveys the impression of an unchanging Egypt.[30] Meanwhile, Husni shows French soldiers to be guardians of the Pharaonic temples, as if they were a link back to that civilization: the French painters even painted themselves in the corner of various paintings. The author concludes that this was related to the artwork's intended audience, which wanted to believe that linkages existed between the French and Pharaonic civilizations. Such an audience might well have appreciated seeing these juxtapositions—that is, figures wearing a mixture of the clothing of these two civilizations. Mixture, the author suggests in her conclusion (perhaps as a critique of contemporary terms such as "hybridity"), was a step in the direction of possession and absorption.

The book's next section begins with a chapter by Hina' Farid, a professor of languages, on the writings of Joseph-Marie Moiret, an officer who participated in the invasion. While obviously a French patriot, Moiret departed in his *Memoirs* from the official line of

Napoleonic invincibility, discussing the challenge posed to it by the Egyptian resistance.[31]

This section concludes with a biographical sketch of Vivant Denon by the French-language specialist Raghda Abu'l-Futuh.[32] Denon, we learn, was from a well-off provincial family, was drawn to artwork at an early age, dabbled in many occupations (including being a diplomat), and even promoted the Louvre, but, all the while, he was also something of an antiquities thief. His success began when Napoleon recognized the propaganda value of some of his drawings. His lasting fame, however, no doubt came later, back in France, with the publication of his travel book on Lower and Upper Egypt that went through more than thirty editions, which was unheard of at the time. As a close reading shows, it was not simply a work of Napoleonic achievements, as it was introduced, but a work filled with critical asides about the activities of the French in Egypt. Apparently, despite this, Denon's book continues to have a market; Abu'l-Futuh's bibliography cites a 1990 edition of the work.

At this point, *Deux Cent* takes up the way the Napoleonic invasion appears in school textbooks and in scholarship, leaving the reader with little doubt of the importance of that subject in the pedagogy of both France and Egypt until the present day, especially in upper-level classes. In covering French elementary school pedagogy in history as it evolved from 1945 to 1969, the French-language specialist Farida Jad al-Haqq finds that the subject rated very little attention.[33] It was referred to simply as an event connected to French/British rivalries over access to India. As the student progressed, however, through and then beyond the years of elementary education, the role of Napoleonic art grew in importance, art appreciation substituting for the narrative and its justifications. On a still more advanced level, one begins to find both a glorification of Napoleon as well as some references to French defeats. As the author notes, these defeats are not attributed to the struggle between France and Egypt, leaving some ambiguity about to what they should be attributed. In an indirect way, this chapter answers the question that the book as a whole implicitly set out to address: How was it possible for the French Ministry of Foreign Affairs in 1998 to imagine that Egypt would want to celebrate its invasion? The answer lay in the French education system and in its tendency to glorify Napoleon.

In a survey of Egyptian education covering the years 1960–2006, the French-language specialist Hina' Farid continues the discussion by examining the role played by 1798 in Egyptian pedagogy.[34] Pedagogy, she notes, is of course a domain that provides its own challenges. If a teacher's objective is to create a young person with positive feelings about themselves and others and about being Egyptian, what room, she asks, is there for a discussion of French deceptiveness? The idea of deceptiveness would not be suitable for young people. As the Ministry of Education saw it, what 1798 finally amounts to are two overlapping subjects: one, the heroic struggle of the Egyptian people against the foreigner occupier, and, two, the more positive legacy of contact with the French, found in the policies of Muhammad 'Ali, the builder of modern Egypt. In this optic, the quicker the Mamluks lost to the French, the quicker that part of history could simply be forgotten.

The next section looks at the level of the academy, its first chapter beginning with a consideration of academic writings on Napoleon through the reign of King Fouad (d. 1936). As French-language specialist Jihan al-Qadi explains, this was the heyday of French cultural influence in Egypt, the reason being in part that it was a period of Egyptian nationalism, and the Egyptian nationalist movement was in need of France to help put pressure on the British.[35] Not surprisingly, of the four most widely read historians of the period, it turns out that two were French, and a third was an Egyptian Francophile. From al-Qadi's reading of Henri Dehérain and Charles Roux, it is clear that their writing is imbued with the mythic side of Napoleon: Napoleon was not an imperialist from an imperialist country but a bringer of civilization. These historians regard General Jean-Baptiste Kléber, and especially his report to the Directory in 1799 and the Treaty of al-'Arish, as a betrayal of the Napoleonic legacy and the explanation for the collapse of the French position. The Egyptian historian Muhammad Fu'ad Shukri shares most of these views, emphasizing in his work the military prowess of Napoleon, picturing him as an eternally unfulfilled "Ulysses." The fourth of the four historians is 'Abd al-Rahman al-Rafi'i, who emerges as the one closest to contemporary thought, taking Egypt as his center of gravity, emphasizing French imperialism and Egypt's popular resistance to it. Al-Rafi'i criticizes the French historians for justifying the criminality of the French army and for their uncritical treatment of the role of the French savants, as well for their claim that Napoleon protected the rights of Copts, for whom he was said to have been a savior. In closing, al-Qadi expresses appreciation for the contemporary French historian Henri Laurens, whom she finds to be a great improvement over this earlier generation.

The discussion shifts to contemporary, French, American, and Egyptian historical thought on the subject of Napoleon in Egypt.[36] In a lengthy and complex account, the historian Muhammad Sabri al-Dali shows that the vast majority of historical writings from these three countries has for a long time accepted the dominant liberal-Marxist view of the coming of the West or change in the mode of production as represented by 1798. In his treatment of the French, al-Dali begins with André Raymond, who skirts the subject of 1798, and then turns to the more recent works of Henri Laurens, who acknowledges French colonial intentions. Raymond shows wealth and commerce in eighteenth-century Cairo, but he did not set out to undercut the Egypt-in-decline narrative as applied to the century's last couple of decades. Laurens does not engage the narrative either, beyond acknowledging French colonial intent.

In his treatment of American books, al-Dali starts with J. Christopher Herold, a popular writer who concentrates on French history. A Czechoslovakian-American refugee from the era of World War II, Herold gradually became acknowledged as a leading critic of the European dictators past and present. His most famous book was on Mme De Staël and the liberal opposition to Napoleon. His work on Napoleon in Egypt does not dispute the narrative but decries Napoleon's dictatorial methods. Al-Dali considers the generation of Stanford Shaw and Helen Rivlin, both of whom worked in Egypt, funded by the early area studies programs that were starting up in the 1960s, and who were archival historians trying to learn details about particular subjects: Shaw was interested in the Ottoman structure of Egypt, Rivlin in Muhammad

'Ali's reforms. The chapter then turns to my generation, which was formed in the 1960s and early 1970s. Here al-Dali tries to make sense of various books in terms of an American tradition of which the writers were presumably a part; in a sense, his work is an antecedent of the present work. Al-Dali characterizes my first book, *Islamic Roots of Capitalism* (1979), as one from the Left as opposed to from liberalism, and this despite the fact that leftist historiography has generally assumed that 1798 was the Egyptian 1789—that is, the quintessential moment of rupture from precapitalism to capitalism. The idea of an eighteenth-century background to modern Egypt, therefore, at least from a Marxist point of view, was simply incorrect.[37]

Al-Dali goes on to discuss Kenneth Cuno's study of relative continuity and slow change in family structure from the eighteenth into the nineteenth century. As al-Dali indicates, Cuno did not try to become involved in paradigm issues. As a result, his work has been interpreted in different ways: some read it as a variant of the eighteenth-century-roots-of-modernity argument, while others read it as a study of "the private" in a context in which history dwells on the public, not on the private.

Al-Dali then takes up Egyptian historians, beginning with the founders of professional history in Egypt, and carries his account down to his own generation. After some brief comments about al-Rafi'i and Muhammad al-Surbunni, al-Dali focuses on the historians of the 1960s and the years thereafter.

In the following chapter, 'Abd al-Raziq 'Isa and Ramadan al-Khuli pursue the subject of contemporary views of 1798 by interviewing their colleagues.[38] They began their work by interviewing a group of their senior colleagues to ascertain their views on the idea of 1798 as a watershed ushering in modern times. Not surprisingly, the answers they received from the more senior historians tended to support the 1798 watershed view while those of some of the younger professors did not.[39] Arguments put forward supporting the watershed idea often had to do with the fact that late eighteenth-century Cairo lacked a coherent enough state to allow a leader to create a viable modern government. Given the absence of what one could call a viable state, how could there be a viable economy or a viable way to bring in market capitalism and keep it regulated? It is clear, one interviewee is quoted as saying, that neither the Ottomans nor the Beys were even contemplating pursuing modernizing or reformist programs. In addition, the state of natural science in general and military science in particular was so low that it would be difficult for a government, had one existed, to create a modern army.

The collection then turns to a contribution by Muhammad Isma'il Zahir, a historian with a Pan-Arabist formation, whose question is how one can one put so much emphasis on 1798 when other similar events were happening around the region at about the same time. As Zahir wrote, first the French invaded Egypt, then they invaded Algeria.[40] Why should 1798 be given such status?

The book then introduces the views of the professors who remain uncertain about the utility of the idea of 1798 as a watershed, among them the historians Ra'uf 'Abbas Hamid and 'Asim al-Disuqi and the philosophy professor Magdi 'Abd al-Hafiz, all three of whose chapters take the position that 1798 might best be characterized as a jolt. Ra'uf 'Abbas Hamid hypothesizes that after a severe military defeat (which was what 1798 amounted to) one would logically expect to find its influence, if there was one, in the approach to the rebuilding of the army by the next ruler (i.e., Muhammad 'Ali).[41] He concludes that this was the case, with the caveat that the actual influences on Muhammad 'Ali and his reform program over these years may also have come from the ongoing threats posed by Europe: these, too, were real, which makes for a bit of a dilemma in terms of how much weight to assign to 1798 per se. Moreover, one needs to be critical about the common view that the French defeated the Mamluks because of their technical superiority. Napoleon was a military genius, a fact that also makes the importance of technology in explaining the Egyptian defeat a difficult one to assess. There was a technological dimension, but certainly it was not the only one. Napoleon overcame a number of foes who used the same technology as he did; he would fool them as he fooled the Mamluks. So, while one might agree with the idea of a jolt in terms of what it implies in term of technological modernization, there remain these unresolved matters.

'Asim al-Disuqi notes that, while 1798 was a jolt, there is no need to romanticize matters by drawing a false comparison to the Ottoman conquest, or by distinguishing between good conquests and bad ones.[42] Warfare is not ethical, and both of these foreign armies did many of the same things even if the circumstances were different. Thus, we should not exaggerate the fact that the French rode into al-Azhar on their horses; the Ottomans did much the same. This is the nature of combat, and something we tend to forget. While doubtless there was some intellectual influence resulting from the occupation, the record also shows the reactions of several of the 'ulama' and others who regarded the savants as magicians brought along to further the military enterprise. Therefore, the matter could be construed as a jolt, providing one also assumes that actual change was a long-term phenomenon, not a short-term one, where one would say the French brought X or Y and that in and of itself amounted to change. Perhaps the question of the intellectual impact is easier to clarify a few years later, when the Egyptians began to compare the French to the British. But, in making that claim, we leave 1798 behind.

For Magdi 'Abd al-Hafiz, the reaction to the jolt of 1798 should be looked at on the psychological level, as elements of the Cairo population started to identify with the French as a result of their own perceived weakness, a problem we find persisting even to the present day.[43]

The last section of the book, "Critical Readings," begins with an essay by the aforementioned Layla 'Inan entitled "Napoleon and the French in Egypt and the Holy Lands, a Critical Reading."[44] In it, she mentions that at the time the Egyptians were rejecting the idea of celebrating the occupation's two hundredth anniversary, the Israeli Napoleonic Society held a commemorative conference naturally focused on the Holy Lands. 'Inan reports that the organizer of the conference dwelt on what some assume to be a forged document, "discovered" by the writer Franz Kobler in 1940, in which Napoleon made a statement in 1799 promising that, if African and Asian Jews rallied around the French, he would reestablish the ancient Jerusalem. The article by 'Inan thus makes another connection: it links Egyptian modernism to the Palestine Question.

The next chapter tells us that, while the Egyptians were rejecting holding a celebration, the French themselves held a large-scale conference of a celebratory sort in June 1998, the proceedings of which were edited by Patrice Bret and published a year later. Shortly thereafter, a review of this work by Philippe Bourdon, a professor from Blaise Pascal University, Clermont Ferrand, appeared.[45] Bourdon's review was subsequently translated into Arabic for the purpose of being included in the book. Basically, it gives a brief account of the papers, many of which, he finds, shed light on the savants and on their interpersonal relations. The review is mildly critical, however, of the celebratory nature of the conference. It notes the cautionary statement of André Raymond, one of the few actual specialists of Egypt as regards French influence in attendance. Raymond suggests that the influence of the savants might well have been limited to Shaykh Hasan al-'Attar and to Mu'allim Ya'qub. Bourdon concludes his essay by remarking how it could have been otherwise in the context of a military occupation, that a bunch of scholars could do other than lend credibility to what turned out to be a failed imperial adventure.

For Layla 'Inan, there is more to the book than one finds in Bourdon's review.[46] The savants went to Egypt expecting to find the residue of Pharaonic wisdom and civilization; not finding it, they came up, rather curiously, with the term "modern Egypt." As 'Inan points out, it seems rather curious that Bourdon does not mention the contribution of Ghislaine Alleaume. According to Ghislaine Alleaume, a specialist in modern Egypt, the only achievement of the Savants of any lasting importance was their mapmaking; even 'Ali Mubarak used their maps. 'Inan's overall view is that, despite certain misleading remarks about the reason for the absence of the Egyptians from the conference, the papers do present, as Bourdon himself makes clear, some useful material and do not conform to the chauvinistic idea of the occupation bringing enlightenment. As Raymond states, this bringing of enlightenment never happened.

Juxtaposed to this paper, and coming last in the volume, is once again the article by 'Abd al-Raziq 'Isa and Ramadan al-Khuli from *Égypte/Monde Arabe*, this time used to underscore the point that the

Oriental despotism paradigm has less influence in Egyptian scholarship at this point than it does in Anglo-American scholarship.[47]

This chapter attempted to pick up where the preceding one left off by demonstrating how scholars have made the subject of modern Egyptian history fit the logic of the Oriental despotism paradigm, and it raised a number of questions along the way as to how feasible this would be from a purely scientific point of view. Would not one expect there to be some gap between the theory and the facts, as not all the available information on a subject can be made to fit any theory? Here, however, this does not apply.

As we noted before, the problem that Anglo-American specialists on Egypt face is that the Oriental despotism paradigm differs from other paradigms in knowledge. Not only does it have more prestige than do most others, but it is embedded in the identity of the researchers themselves: they too are a part of the West. Were we living in earlier times, we might compare this situation to that of astronomers in the heyday of the Ptolemaic worldview. In its time the Ptolemaic worldview was, according to the church and the state, the only acceptable way to understand the importance of God and his creations. Under those conditions, the field of astronomy allowed for research but smothered common-sense queries, and sidelined empirical results that did not fit. Over time, this led to blind spots, as fairly obvious questions were never squarely addressed.[48]

This book's next chapter attempts to show that this is the case here as well. Basing itself on a consideration of the careers of two individuals of the period, it finds that the reliance on 1798 as one's historiographical divide raises a number of fairly obvious questions that the logic of the paradigm obscures, and that these questions have never been squarely addressed, much to the detriment of the subjects concerned.

3

The Orthodox Narrative's Blind Spots

1798, Shaykh Hasan al-'Attar, and Muhammad 'Ali Pasha

Previous chapters examined the dominant paradigm in the field, by looking into its history and internal logic. This chapter takes up another aspect: its blind spots, falling back on the well-known "1798 watershed" as a case in point. The argument of the chapter is that the idea of a watershed has wrought havoc on the study of the period, as much of what went on at that time cannot be subsumed in the watershed framework and, as a result, has fallen by the wayside. The chapter illustrates this point through a consideration of the lives of two individuals that cut across the year 1798: Shaykh Hasan al-'Attar and Muhammad 'Ali. Brief references are made to a third figure, Rifa'ah al-Tahtawi, whose life figures intimately with the two mentioned above.

The term "blind spot" is used here in a sociological sense: to denote the result of a worldview that somehow induces scholars in general to look but not to see, to see but to do so in a distorted way, or to choose not to look and consequently not to see. The term is chosen here in preference to that of "lacuna," which conveys the idea of something that was overlooked in the past but is likely to sooner or later be dealt with and, if found to be important, given its due. Blind spots, on the other hand, may never be dealt with—given the prestige of the dominant paradigm, which created them.

In using the term "blind spot," what is not in question is objectivity or rigor. Blind spots do not result from a lack of objectivity or some technical weakness; rather, they result from the weakness—or nonscientific quality—of the paradigm on which the scholarship is based. A blind spot is not, therefore, to be associated with error in the ordinary sense, as something in need of correction. A blind spot may well allow for the production of knowledge that is technically sound. As I have also tried to make clear, in the case in hand this is not the fault of the field—or, at least, of this field alone. Functioning in an Anglo-American context, it is hard to imagine professors of modern Egyptian history assuming anything other than what they have been assuming.

Some fields are in a different situation in this regard. Scholars control the paradigms they use and not the reverse. In certain fields, the coming of the West once played or still plays some role but, looking closely, one finds that the initial scholarly interpretation was then replaced after further study with a much more nuanced, interactive one. Here one might include the research done on the discovery of the New World by Columbus now termed the "Columbian Exchange"[1] and the history of Admiral Perry's opening of Japan.[2] In each of those cases, one finds specialists now viewing the original paradigm of the coming of the West as something that has been outgrown, whereas in Egyptian studies this has not yet been possible.

To dramatize the significance of the 1798 blind spot, this chapter begins with an account of a figure who plays a major role defending Muhammad 'Ali's program but who came out of eighteenth-century Egypt and not out of the missions that returned from France. It then turns to Muhammad 'Ali himself and asks who this man was in a cultural sense: What inspired him, given the particularities of his background? These questions would never arise if one is oriented to studying the ties between France and Egypt. The chapter argues that the failure to address such questions should be seen as blind spots.

Shaykh Hasan al-'Attar

We begin with the study of Shaykh Hasan al-'Attar, noting gaps in the received scholarship that, from a purely scientific point of view, are hard to explain. Two in particular are briefly discussed in this section: First, why, given the general interest in reform and reformers, has no one inquired as to how al-'Attar, a noted reformer, became a reformer? The most reasonable hypothesis is that the question of how he became a reformer cannot be addressed in the framework of the dominant paradigm, so it has never been pursued. At most one finds fleeting references to the brief and traumatic meeting that al-'Attar had with the French during the Occupation. Second, why, given the general scholarly interest in reform and reformers, has al-'Attar been so marginalized in all of the standard accounts of the nineteenth- and twentieth-century Nahda (modern cultural awakening)? The explanation, once again, is tied up with blind spots.

Shaykh Hasan al-'Attar (d. 1835) was a Shaykh al-Azhar and an influential teacher in the last years of his life. Earlier on, however, he was a fairly unknown private individual. During that time, he lived abroad for fourteen years and on his return was appointed to various leadership positions. The period of his life preceding this series of appointments has scarcely been studied because it has been assumed—following the paradigm—that, since he did not go to Western Europe, his travels did not matter. From a scientific point of view, this seems illogical. Were it not for the blind spots caused by the 1798 "Coming of the West" paradigm, this period would have been studied. The question would also have arisen of how al-'Attar could jump from relative obscurity into positions of leadership in the years after 1815, following his return to Cairo.

Modern scholarship recognizes al-'Attar as a reformer because he supported Muhammad 'Ali's project of acquiring modern technology and know-how from France. As an Arabic language teacher, he worked with several students who gained prominence as translators and as journalists, professions that were useful to the government. There is thus no question that he was a reformer. How, then, did he come to be a reformer? While this has not been pursued in depth, one could begin to form some sort of hypothesis by considering his background, then his travels in Turkey, Syria, Palestine, and Albania over the course of fourteen years. In considering this, let us keep in mind that we lack some crucial details. Al-'Attar, it will be recalled, returned home and, a few years thereafter, was offered a high position, with some involvement on the part of Abd al-Rahman Sami Bey.[3] We do not know how Sami Bey, the chief of Muhammad 'Ali's cabinet, came to know al-'Attar and then recommend him for high positions.

What we do know is that al-'Attar did not go abroad unformed intellectually. He was not a student. This fact makes the subject of his travels and their influence on him a complicated one to interpret, in that it obliges a consideration of the experiences of his youth in eighteenth-century Egypt as a part of an interpretation of his life thereafter. What we know about his youth is that al-'Attar studied with various well-known scholars and participated in the literary salons of Cairo. Along with others of the period, he was concerned with language issues. Written Arabic was not adjusted to the needs of the period, nor was spoken Arabic, and, from what information we have, it appears that his concerns about adjusting and teaching the Arabic language remained with him throughout his life. For this reason, if no other, it would seem logical to assume that, rather than his travels being a hiatus in some wasteland (as per the Nahda scholarship), they were a stage in his development, a period of time during which he was apparently drawn to reformism more deeply than he had been before and, for that reason, became someone who could contribute to Muhammad 'Ali's reforms.[4]

Paradigm considerations, however, preclude taking such a common-sense approach. During the nineteenth and twentieth centuries, modernist scholars closed the door to the possibility that there might be a background to Egyptian modernism before 1798 and to the possible significance of someone traveling around the Ottoman Empire as al-'Attar did. Beginning with 'Ali Mubarak, scholars interpreted al-'Attar as a reformer but also as a traditional man, his only lasting claim to fame being that he was Rifa'ah al-Tahtawi's mentor. In this view, it was Rifa'ah al-Tahtawi, the founder of the translation school, who was the first true modern reformer.

Even here, however, the paradigm runs into problems. A close look at al-Tahtawi's life shows that he was well educated before he left Upper Egypt for Cairo, where he met al-'Attar and became involved in the world of translation. This being the case, it would seem logical to hypothesize that, for al-Tahtawi as for al-'Attar, eighteenth- and early nineteenth-century culture must have played some role in his turn to reformism; in this period, after all, there were some important intellectuals. For this reason, it would make more sense to assume that the early Nahda began in the late eighteenth century and that the translation movement of the 1830s ought to be looked at as a second phase of the Nahda and not as the first. Were one to adopt that approach, al-'Attar's career as a reformer would also make more sense, and there would be no need to rush to study al-Tahtawi. Very likely, al-'Attar would be seen as a continuator of the cultural revival of the eighteenth century, which in turn would be seen as the birth of modern culture. Most historians today, however, following the paradigm, prefer to look at the early Nahda as translation and not as revival of heritage. This is one of the reasons why Shaykh Hasan al-'Attar, who was a major figure in Muhammad 'Ali's reform movement because of his work in heritage revival and Arabic-language modernization, is little remembered today, even by the specialists of the early Nahda.

To understand why scholarship has proceeded this way, it is necessary to look more closely into how the early Nahda has generally been studied. On doing so, what one finds is that, whether the early Nahda is taken to be a time period (i.e., the culture from 1798 through the first half of the nineteenth century) or an orientation toward French culture (as was reflected in the student missions and the translation movement), what is assumed is that the revival of heritage that was taking place in the same period should be put aside in order to focus on the cultural development resulting from the interaction with France. As a consequence of these blind spots, which resulted from what appears to be an exaggerated idea of the importance of the coming of the West, the actual history of modern Arabic culture in Egypt remains quite undeveloped as a field.

Fidelity to the paradigm also explains why scholars attempting to distinguish between the earlier and the later Nahda have run into other blind spots as well. Recall the assumption that the early Nahda was associated with translation, and the later Nahda with literary creation (e.g., Haykal's *Zaynab* [1913 or 1914]): this makes the culmination of the Nahda to be the first Arabic novel, a work widely understood as a successful imitation of the French novel of the period. This, too, however, seems like a part of the blind spot. The very idea of the Nahda was supposed to be one of escaping from imitation and tradition, but somehow no one sees *Zaynab* as a matter of imitation and tradition.

In fact, the early Nahda might more logically be seen as a phase of the revival of heritage than as one of translation. The evidence for this is well known to scholars. In the nineteenth century, private printing presses and periodicals grew rapidly in number, and by World War I a range of older works had been revived. While this point has been recognized as a matter of detail, it has not attracted much attention on the assumption that heritage is a subordinate feature of the Nahda at most.

Another assumption embedded in the orthodox view of the Nahda—and one of equally limited utility, in my view—is that the Nahda was dynamic and that heritage was static. Although this set of assumptions may serve the Nahdawi paradigm logic with its demand for a static Orient, it amounts to a blind spot for someone studying modernity in Egypt from another point of view. It would be more defensible to postulate that as the nineteenth century progressed, not only was heritage being revived but, as one can see from al-'Attar, the way Egyptian intellectuals understood it kept evolving as well—meaning that the study of heritage itself needs to be pursued as one part of modern cultural history.[5] This would overcome the problem of binaries in Nahda studies of a supposedly stagnant past and dynamic present.

Let us now attempt to explain why al-'Attar has been all but forgotten in scholarship on Egyptian modernity, whereas most other figures who were reformers have fared much better. We noted that he did not speak French, nor had he visited France. One other reason stands out as well, one related to al-'Attar's association with Muhammad 'Ali's reform program. During his lifetime, Muhammad 'Ali was not a beloved figure in Egypt. As he grew weaker, and the reform period came to an end, the cultural aspect of the period—which al-'Attar had helped to develop and preserve—was quickly put aside, and a kind of romantic, religious reaction to the liberal positivism of the reformers became more dominant. What this meant was that not only did the later Nahdawi scholars abandon al-ʿAttar as a figure lost in an era of religious revivalism, but so did his contemporaries, who were, like the Azharites, part of the romantic revival; indeed, some of the latter actually actively disliked him for his having served Muhammad ʿAli. In sum, since neither one of these two main cultural traditions claimed him, this is very likely an important part of why he was forgotten.

However, in making al-Tahtawi the leading figure of the early Nahda and in marginalizing al-ʿAttar, still other problems arose as well those already mentioned. Nahdawi scholars found that they were not able to make use of more than three of the twenty-odd books he had written: the account of his trip to Paris, his essay on the education of boys and girls, and his later book on politics, *Manahij*. The rest of his writings were put aside, the reason being that most of them dealt with religion and heritage. This point is known, at least to specialists, since copies of most of his works have been located, and an initial effort to collect and publish them was made in the 1970s. In addition, his library still exists more or less intact: the part containing the Arab-Islamic materials is in Tahta, and the part containing European materials is supposedly locked up in ʿAyn Shams University Library.

Since the 1970s, al-Tahtawi has been referred to in hundreds of publications around the world, but there has been little effort to connect the one part with the other. Following the Nahdawi paradigm, al-Tahtawi continues today, as in the past, to serve as a model of secular reform. As a result, what we remember is that when the Muhammad ʿAli reform period came to an end, ʿAbbas Hilmi Pasha, who opposed the reforms, not only pushed him out of government service but exiled him to the Sudan, along with one or two others. Most in his circles, however, for whatever reasons, managed to continue working as before, although the language school was closed. Al-Tahtawi was unhappy in the Sudan. For the Nahdawis, this was to be expected because the Sudan was backward, and, naturally, al-Tahtawi would dislike backwardness. What he meant by what he wrote is open to some interpretation, as he was a complex individual; to proceed further, one would need to know a lot about him, his Upper Egyptian background, and Egypt in the Sudan in this period.

In any case, it is known that Sa'id Pasha brought al-Tahtawi back from the Sudan in 1854 and that life for him thereafter seemed to improve. His subsequent career, first as a school administrator and then as an editor of the journal *Rawdat al-Madaris* under Khedive Isma'il, was highly successful. This, too, fits with the paradigm. Looking at this narrative more critically, it seems odd that we do not read of some major attack on him by his detractors either at the time of his exile or at the time of his return from exile, as we do on a couple of occasions in the case of al-'Attar. Al-Tahtawi was certainly more of a Francophile than al-'Attar and could easily have run into problems, leading to more than simply exile.[6] Would it not be logical to assume that, as a reformer, he would inevitably have angered various traditionalists, as al-'Attar did in his time? In fact, we know that he did have some problems, and it has been acknowledged in an oblique way that Al-Tahtawi's problems had more to do with Europe than with Egypt, that by the time of 'Abbas Pasha, England was more important to Egypt than France, and that al-Tahtawi was associated with France. While perhaps true, this scarcely seems to be an adequate explanation, given that France and French influence continued to be important in Egypt even when British influence was growing. One might recall that al-Tahtawi's work for Khedive Isma'il included translating the French Civil Code. There must have been more to his life, which was successful but not without troubles.

We now come to another point about the dominant paradigm that affects how al-Tahtawi is remembered, a point introduced earlier in a very general way concerning the propensity of historians to defer to authority—in this case, to the authority of philologists. Philologists assume that the authors of texts know what they were writing about and that their work could be understood by anyone who could read Arabic. Yet in al-Tahtawi's *Manahij*, one encounters a work that is written in a slightly abstract way, but that hints at a context containing a conflict, suggesting that the book is probably some sort of intervention in that conflict. However, since we lack a precise knowledge of that context, it still even now is difficult to go beyond a literal, philological reading of that book or for that matter those of al-'Attar. In sum, had it not been for the various blind spots created by the paradigm, some of the issues might have been resolved as far back as the nineteenth century.

It is thus only recently that there has been anything new to report on the subject of al-'Attar and the origins of his reformism. Egyptian, Turkish, Syrian, and Albanian scholars did not engage the subject. As a result, many basic details are still missing. In 2012, the situation changed somewhat. In that year, an article about Shaykh Hasan al-'Attar in Albania appeared in the *Hayat* newspaper under the byline of the Jordanian professor Muhammad al-Arna'ut and was then reprinted in the Egyptian *Wafd* newspaper almost immediately thereafter.[7] This article catches one's attention not only for its subject matter, but for its reference to Albanian-language sources and, more specifically, for its claims about Hasan al-'Attar, Muhammad 'Ali, and Albania.

According to Muhammad al-Arna'ut, the author of this article, al-'Attar spent a decade in Albania, mainly in the city of Scutari. The author's source for this claim is *Scutari and Its Traditions* (*Shkodra wa sunun*), a study of the history of the city of Scutari by the Albanian historian Hamdi Bushatli. All I can attest to from general knowledge is that Hamdi Bushatli, who died in the 1980s, was not an unfamiliar name to scholars; he was the author of many books on Albanian subjects, some of which are cited in Anglo-American scholarship. The article states that, according to Bushatli, al-'Attar spent a decade teaching in Scutari upon his departure from Egypt, beginning in 1801 and ending with his departure from Albania around 1810–11 for Syria. How he came to be there is not clarified, but what al-Arna'ut suggests is that al-'Attar's lengthy stay there was important in terms of his later career, given the tradition of reform and modernization in Scutari by the dynasty in power and given the fact that Muhammad 'Ali had a relationship with that dynasty, in later years, modeling his own reforms in Egypt on those of Kara Mustafa Bushatli (d. 1796), and those of his brother Ibrahim Bushatli (d. 1810), who succeeded him.

What is commonly known about Kara Mustafa is that, during his rule, he modernized the city of Scutari, making it the main city of Albania; that he maintained relations with the European powers; and that he supported Islamic scholarship, but got caught up in the many political intrigues of the period. At one point, he was approached by the Austrians and Russians with the offer that, if he converted to Christianity and fought the Ottomans, he and his descendants would be recognized as the kings of Albania in perpetuity. He agreed, but then learned that the long-term plan of Austria and Russia was to make Albania a vassal state of Montenegro; on learning this, he had the delegation bringing him the offer beheaded and their skulls sent to the Porte. Suffice to say that in 1796, he, too, was beheaded, and his skull is apparently still in a monastery in Montenegro. Al-Arna'ut makes the additional point that, because of the good relations of the Bushatlis and Muhammad 'Ali, a number of Egyptian 'ulama' worked in Scutari, and some of their descendants still live there. The article is vague about what exactly al-'Attar was doing in those years, beyond teaching in the madrasa in the old market and writing.[8] It is also not clear what he wrote in this period.

As an aside, one might note that if al-'Attar actually spent so many years there, as the article claims, one can scarcely account for all the teaching and writing he did in Turkey, Syria, and Palestine. But, small imprecisions aside, al-Arna'ut's article offers an explanation where none other exists as to how al-'Attar could have had connections with Albanians, some of whom later seized power in Egypt, and how he himself may have acquired ideas about social reform, having been exposed to Scutari, a reform-minded model of society. To sum up, al-'Attar's years of travel clearly ought to have been understood as something more than a hiatus in his life.

However, as we also know, back in the mid-nineteenth century, when 'Ali Mubarak's team interviewed Hasan al-'Attar's son Asad about his father, it appears that the latter hinted at his father's visit to Albania, but the team chose not to pursue the matter. From a paradigm perspective, this is quite understandable. Details such as these, which may seem innocuous enough in themselves, would force the narrative to change, were they to be pursued. The upholders of the Nahda paradigm would have to abandon 1798 and go back to the eighteenth century and include aspects of Albania. This was not going to happen then, and one doubts it will happen now or anytime soon. Blind spots arise, I argue, when paradigm logic has the power to stand in the way of scholars pursuing common-sense lines of inquiry, with the result that various subjects such as that of Shaykh Hasan al-ʿAttar and the history of modern reform thought suffer accordingly.

Muhammad ʿAli Pasha

Muhammad ʿAli Pasha is, arguably, the figure of the single greatest interest for many scholars, yet one for whom no credible account of his background, worldview, and cultural preferences has emerged. Once again one would assume that the reason for this is that the dominant paradigm has put obstacles in the way. For Muhammad ʿAli to fit the framework of the Oriental despot, he had to be an outsider who was free from traditions and would therefore be like putty in the hands of the French. From a scientific point of view, this is a highly improbable set of assumptions, but few look at it in these terms.

For a long time, scholars have taken Muhammad ʿAli to be Ottoman, or Ottoman Turkish–Albanian, and yet somehow also Egyptian. The claim that he was Ottoman is the orthodox view. An Albanian-centered view of Muhammad ʿAli of the sort al-Arnaʾut is suggesting, were it to be developed, would challenge the orthodox view, not only because it would bring in Albania, a country that was trying to break free from the Ottomans for some time, but because it would have an eighteenth-century dimension and pose the question of who this man really was—a question that apparently remains a blind spot for the Nahdawi tradition, which needs Muhammad ʿAli to be mysteriously free of tradition.

There are, of course, reasons why scholars have interpreted Muhammad ʿAli as they have. He arrived in Egypt as an Ottoman, not as an Albanian. Muhammad ʿAli was a pragmatist, very keen to have power and not obsessed with traditional loyalties. One recalls his willingness to get rid of the "old Albanians" who had accompanied him to Egypt after his apparent falling out with some of them following his rise to power. The explanation given is, to put it bluntly, that they no longer could help him. If Muhammad 'Ali sought out Hasan al-'Attar in 1815, there must have been more than simply the Albanian connection, but that may have helped.

Still, the implications of any Albanian dimension whatsoever are considerable. If Muhammad 'Ali was pursuing policies in Egypt based on the experiences of Scutari, one's interpretation of the whole reform period in Egypt would change; one would have to rethink the assumption that Muhammad 'Ali was trying to emulate France. What becomes a possibility is that while he may have needed weapons and help developing his army, and while it may have been in France's interest to supply him with what he needed, he also needed help developing a cultural policy that would allow him to actualize it. In this context, Hasan al-'Attar—thanks at least in part to his years in Scutari—became the first cultural official of the modern Egyptian state, the antecedent of today's minister of culture. For reasons already given, this line of interpretation and the questions it raises can scarcely be said to exist, a point that can be easily demonstrated from a consideration of a more representative work of scholarship on Muhammad 'Ali: *Remembering One's Roots: Mehmed Ali Pasha's Links to the Macedonian Town of Kavala* (2011).[9] This book was written by Heath Lowery, the well-known American specialist on Turkish history, and by the Turkish historian Ismail Erunsel and dedicated to Enver Yucel, who "shared Mehmed Ali's passion for education." Enver Yucel, we learn, was the founder of Bahja Shahir, the college that, along with the Mohamed Ali Institute of Kavala, subsidized the book's publication. Unfamiliar with this institute, I looked it up; according to Wikipedia, it was built around the Pasha's old house, now a museum, and is the fourth greatest tourist attraction in Kavala out of the twelve attractions there.

The book is an informative one, but of a conventional sort. One learns that the Pasha lavished money on the town of Kavala in the form of buildings that he commissioned, and that he gave jobs in Egypt to a substantial number of people from that town as well. Seven in Muhammad 'Ali's immediate family and seven of his close childhood friends wound up being appointed to high positions in the Egyptian bureaucracy. Among the latter was Abd al-Rahman Sami Bey, who served as chief of the cabinet (*bash muawin*), someone whom we are certain knew Hasan al-'Attar. Less certain at this point is how Sami Bey, who was born in Peloponnesus, became a childhood friend of someone in faraway Kavala, or how he knew al-'Attar.

What the authors seem to be trying to do is downplay the role of Albania in Muhammad (Mehmed) Ali's life and to upgrade the role of Ottoman Turkey. Contradicting Afaf Lutfi al-Sayyid Marsot's book on Muhammad 'Ali, the authors claim that the Pasha was not an Albanian, nor were his parents, and that if he, Mehmed Ali, commanded Albanians when he came to Egypt, this was more or less an accident.[10] The book does not take up the point that Muhammad 'Ali's first language was Albanian, nor does it reflect on whether just anyone could command a regiment of Albanians. Another impression: despite its academic footnotes, the book as a whole, with its many pictures, seems as if it could have been designed for tourists visiting a museum gift shop in Kavala as well.

So, who owns the rights to Muhammad 'Ali—Turkey or Albania? On this point, what is clear is that Egypt has chosen sides, and that it has done so in the way one would predict. There have been a number of binational conferences between Turkey and Egypt in which "Mehmed" Ali figured prominently. Meanwhile, there has not been a single conference between Egypt and Albania, and scholars studying Muhammad 'Ali have generally taken their cues accordingly. Thus, the Albanian roots of the Egyptian royal family are rarely discussed. The dynasty is commonly referred to as Ottoman in culture, meaning Turkish. The odd moment a century ago when King Fu'ad nearly became the King of Albania is scarcely ever mentioned. On the other hand, breaking with the Nahda paradigm, one might well want to inquire about the role of Albania in the making of modern Egypt; this is a relatively unexplored subject that very clearly takes us back into eighteenth-century Egypt.

To conclude, let us return to one last example of the dominant paradigm's treatment of Muhammad 'Ali, one that concerns the period of reformism of the 1820s and 1830s. In those years, Muhammad 'Ali was involved in bringing about technical changes in Egypt, under a French aegis. In doing this, he was aware that he was putting himself in a vulnerable situation, ruling Egypt with the help of Europeans. For some in Egypt he appeared to have abandoned his religion. Perhaps he had; he was a Kafir. For him to survive in this context, he needed to have someone of intellectual stature to make clear the Arab-Islamic cultural foundations of his policies. Al-'Attar performed that function for him. This made his contribution important quite apart from the reasons alluded to in the Nahda scholarship. For the Nahda, one may recall, he was a reformer, but one who did not know European languages and was thus ultimately of limited importance. He may have given speeches to the students in the medical school, praising French medicine, and he may have carried on his own study and teaching of classical texts of the sort validating what Muhammad 'Ali was doing in terms of the Arab-Islamic tradition, but the significance of all this has largely been missed. What al-'Attar was able to do was to blunt the criticism of Muhammad 'Ali that he was destroying Islam through his reforms. And, from what is known, he succeeded. No Egyptian doctor, engineer, or officer defected to support the Wahhabis or the Sanusis during the various conflicts.

We also know that among the classical texts that al-'Attar taught, some were in the field of medicine, including a commentary (*sharh*) written by al-'Attar himself on Da'ud al-Antaki's work on anatomy, *Nuzhat adhhan fi islah al-abdan* (2009). Al-Antaki was an influential author in the tradition of Ibn Sina, and al-'Attar's commentary on his book was not, surprisingly, a critique of the deductive approach Avicenna proposed to understanding the body and disease that al-Antaki followed. What becomes clear is al-'Attar's affinity to the empirical study of anatomy, a tradition he had witnessed firsthand in Istanbul and that he read about in the works of Ibn al-Nafis and al-Razi.[11] If students were to move beyond Ibn Sina and accept the empirical approach to the study of anatomy taught by the French doctor Clot Bey, they would have to prepare themselves in a cultural sense. This was what al-'Attar was aiming at.

In sum, this chapter set out to explain the persistence of certain ways of understanding eighteenth- and nineteenth-century Egypt that have remained unchanged despite the growth of knowledge as the result of a blind spot. To do so, it took up as an illustration the treatment of two particular figures with roots in the eighteenth century and careers in the nineteenth century, showing how scholarship essentially ignored the eighteenth-century roots of these individuals and attempted to make sense of their careers simply from events in which they were involved in the nineteenth century. Ordinary empirical research carried out without blind spots would not proceed in this fashion.

The next chapter raises the question of what would happen if one made use of what we know but dropped the idea of 1798 as a watershed and tried to avoid the blind spots; would there be enough relevant knowledge available at this point to allow for an alternative interpretation of Egyptian history in this period?

4

Hypothesizing the Ottoman-Egyptian Roots of Modern Egypt

The hypothesis that early modern Ottoman-Egyptian history (1517–1798) has played a role in shaping modern Egyptian history has not been pursued in any detail. Both the study of Ottoman Egypt and that of modern Egypt are pursued, but as separate fields. This chapter takes up the matter and argues that, based on familiar materials, it seems likely that such a hypothesis might be sustained. And if it were, if it held up to whatever the challenges might be, it would no longer be the case that the 1798 watershed was the only possible interpretation of the origins of modern Egypt.

To this end, the chapter lays out and applies a generic model of early modern history to Egypt. The Ottoman Conquest of 1517 is taken to represent the birth of mercantilism and absolutism in Egypt. This form of political economy lasted to the middle of the nineteenth century, at which point mercantilism was replaced by the open market and absolutism was forced to accept elements of democracy, the one era growing out of the other.[1] The mercantilist phase in Egypt, as elsewhere, was one of empire, but also one within which the dominant trend was state formation, the rulers of empires and states evolving strategies of playing people off against each other to stay in power.[2] The chapter concludes by identifying some of the strategies that rulers devised in the Ottoman period and that continue to be used by rulers in modern times. Therein lie the Ottoman-Egyptian roots of modern Egypt.

There are, of course, other possibilities for contending with the idea of a 1798 watershed. As of now, they remain even more undeveloped.

For example, some would push the idea of modern Egypt still further back in history, even before 1517; still others would push it significantly forward, beyond 1798. Thus, for instance, it is not impossible that early modernity may have begun in the Mamluk period or even earlier, in some era that also had the attributes we associate with modernity (e.g., complex financial, commercial, industrial structures; wage labor; money) and, that being the case, the Ottoman period might well be characterized as less important.

While this line of thought may ultimately prove fruitful, one cannot negate the importance of the sixteenth century as a period of change in world history, or the importance of world history as a guide to formulating national history. After all, there have been capitalist sectors since antiquity as subordinate features of tributary economies. What makes modern capitalism modern, however, is that in the sixteenth century, capitalism on a world scale began to move from being a subordinate sector to being the dominant mode of production. As one finds from a study of Egyptian history from the sixteenth century forward, the rising power of capitalism was such that it could force changes in society and culture of a sort not seen before, a point to which we will return shortly. Still, the retrogression argument is not without merit. In the sixteenth century, the Ottomans appear to have understood the changing nature of world conditions and hoped to position themselves among the leading powers of the new age. To achieve their objective, potential local rivals had to be eliminated, which explains why the Ottomans set out to demolish Damascus, Cairo, and other cities as rival centers of production. And, in this, they were somewhat successful. Looked at in other terms, the Ottomans' regional supremacy meant that Egypt would enter into modern world capitalism but in a weaker position than one might have predicted, given what had existed before. Where the Mamluk-centered argument is perhaps most persuasive is in the idea that the capitalist sector in Egypt was in decline prior to the arrival of the Ottomans, since the sultans had been ignoring it. For the Ottomans, this meant that perhaps this was a strategic time to try to destroy it.

Here a word of clarification is needed as concerns the idea of "watershed." Up to this point, the term appeared only in discussions of the 1798 Napoleonic invasion of Egypt. Its application to Egypt was criticized as a projection of European identity issues masquerading as a contribution to the study of Egypt and for its denial that the Ottoman past would play a role in modern Egypt. Of course, the idea of a watershed per se is not in question; in other applications, it has recognizable analytical value—for example, where the continuation of older trends would be acknowledged, and where claims about change would be less totalistic. The sixteenth-century watershed might serve as an example where scholars have successfully used the term in attempting to characterize the rise of modern capitalism.

The Economy: The Mercantilist Background to the Modern Capitalist Nation-State

"Mercantilism" is the most widely used term to characterize world economic history prior to modern market capitalism. In recent times, with the weakening of Orientalism, it has begun to be applied to areas such as the Middle East; here, the studies of Ottoman Turkey lead the way.

One might also note that, as the use of the term has gradually spread around the world, its meaning has evolved. In the early twentieth century, scholars associated mercantilism with specific economic practices in Europe, such as hoarding bullion and protecting one's market. Gradually, usage broadened to incorporate aspects of international trade and of monetarization of the domestic economy. More recently, scholars are beginning to connect the mercantilist economy with the politics of the period: the age of absolutism, the early attempts at a bourgeois revolution, and an enlightenment and a romantic revolt against it, among other trends. Despite this, it is fair to say that the subject has not attracted much systematic attention until now, as Euro-American economic historians have tended to regard the era of mercantilism as an unfortunate one because the economy was inefficient and therefore not as interesting to study as the period that followed. In some ways, this, too, is unfortunate, given that mercantilism lasted some four centuries and has recurred from time to time as neomercantilism. For that reason, if no other, one might have expected scholars to look at it otherwise. However, as mentioned above, the concept is nonetheless being picked up by historians in a number of countries outside of Europe.

The beginning of mercantilism in Egypt, I am assuming, was in the sixteenth century and inseparable from the newly arising world market. Mercantilism arrived in Egypt via the Ottomans, who were the first in the Middle East to apply the mercantilist approach to the economy. As the Ottoman Empire expanded, it spread mercantilism around the political and commercial centers of the Middle East; the Ottoman Conquest of 1517 brought mercantilism to Egypt. Thereafter, the dominant elements in Egypt began to find new ways to profit from investing in long-distance trade and transit trade, as well as from the gradual monetarization of the economy. In this context, local ruling classes entered into and enforced capitulation agreements to limit participation in international trade to the smallest number of groups possible, in so doing favoring the minority communities that were weak enough to be plundered when need be.

In the seventeenth century, mercantilism in Egypt continued apace. In investing in trade, rulers in that period—there as elsewhere—increasingly risked the dangers inherent in using diverse currencies and in opening their market to the flood of gold and silver from the New World. And they paid a price for doing so. Egypt, along with other countries, suffered considerably from the "crisis of the seventeenth century." Mercantilism as it developed proved to be an aggressive form of political economy. It involved commercial speculation, which often went hand in hand not only with empire and state formation, but with plunder, slavery, colonialism, and, as noted before, absolutist political rule. Indeed, between 1517 and 1867, the dominant classes in Egypt were all autocrats; they made no pretenses of being anything else. When the prospect of great wealth loomed, it attracted them as it did their counterparts around the world. The risks were worth it. Before 1517, there was trade, but the form of the political economy was different. The Mamluk rulers made use of a commercial sector in what for them was mainly a rent-collecting or tributary-based relationship. After 1517, the dominant classes took international trade to be a kind of investment. Unlike investment in land, however, investment in trade always had its speculative side. This speculation propelled mercantilism forward.

Among the trade connections of importance for Egypt, and one that entailed its share of speculation and risk, was Venice, the great commercial connection to Europe for the entire Eastern Mediterranean. Throughout most of early modern history, the main Egyptian link to Venice was the Ladino merchants who were refugees from the Reconquista in Spain given shelter by the Egyptian Jewish community. Coming as they did from Spain, they could bypass the capitulation agreements and acquire luxury goods, weapons, and other items sought in Egypt. Another connection of importance for Egypt was with North Africa. The Maghariba in Cairo included some of the most important merchants of that city. Another important connection came from the Sudan trade.

The period of mercantilism was also one of violent economic struggle for control between and within countries as formal and informal empires rose and fell. In the case of Venice in the seventeenth century, the local Venetian merchants lost control to the Dutch merchants, with the market thereafter controlled from northwest Europe. Among other consequences, the merchants of the Eastern Mediterranean, including the Egyptians, were placed at something of a disadvantage. Mercantilism had socioeconomic dimensions as well: it integrated society in new ways. By the seventeenth century, segments of the ruling military groups invested in Egyptian businesses and intermarried into Egyptian merchant families, and, as the historian Nelly Hanna has shown, wealthy Egyptian merchants bought their retainers positions in the ranks of the local Ottoman military.[3]

By the eighteenth century, the ongoing international economic revolution led to the creation of an aristocracy in cities such as Cairo, some of whose members by this point controlled not just commercial wealth but a great deal of land as well (i.e., as tax farmers). In theory the land was still owned by the Sultan; in practice, however, private property in land was emerging, and tax farms were moving from control by landlords on a de facto basis to private landownership on a de jure basis.

The coming of Muhammad 'Ali supposedly ended the tax-farming system in Egypt—this is an element of the 1798 rupture thesis—but, as records from the period show, villages that could not pay their taxes were taken away from the landlords and given to the Pasha's relatives and most favored employees as tax farms, so, in effect, the old Iltizam system carried on in new hands. Furthermore, the new Iltizams, like the old ones, tended more and more toward private property; land became more alienable and inheritable as the nineteenth century progressed. As in the early modern period but also in the period of Khedive Isma'il, state attempts to regulate trade continued, as if the age of mercantilism had never truly ended.[4] Taking these details into consideration, one could conclude that Egypt experienced the transition from mercantilism to capitalism common to this period. The transition was not a complete one, but it was not in most other countries either.

Politics

Looking at the politics of early modern history, what is important for our purposes is to determine whether certain choices regarding statecraft introduced in the Ottoman period lived on to become embodied in the practices of the modern nation-state of the mid-nineteenth century and beyond. To see whether that was the case, let us take a brief look at how rulers managed class, gender, region, caste, law, and culture in the years of early modern history up to 1867 and then beyond.[5]

Class Stratification Policy

The imposition of mercantilist capitalism in Egypt led to the beginning of class divisions, and the existence of these divisions served as a potential tool of stratification from that point on. However, as capitalism progressed, its utility decreased as rulers came to fear the

masses. In the sixteenth century, class conflict existed, but it was easily deflected, given the other divisions in society; the chroniclers failed
to pay much attention to it. Nonetheless—in retrospect, at least—it is
clear that the growth of poor neighborhoods alongside the aristocratic
suburbs in cities such as Cairo symbolized a new phenomenon, one
in which the central government, the tax farmers, the merchants, and
their various allies tried to deepen market relations throughout society
in the face of a growing resistance. And, indeed, there was resistance.
There was protest; some people fled their land, becoming destitute.

By the eighteenth century, class conflict was becoming recognized
as an issue with menacing potentialities. The historian al-Jabarti, for
example, noted with disdain and some alarm the growth of street
crowds in late eighteenth-century Cairo. From his descriptions, it
seems like a fair inference that these crowds were made up of people
who had been uprooted by the changing economy and perhaps recognized that their strength lay in their numbers and in their concen-
tration in Cairo. In the nineteenth century, Muhammad 'Ali drafted
many of these uprooted people and sent them to fight on foreign bat-
tlefields. Class divisions, however, did not go away. From a series of
well-recorded events from the 1830s and thereafter, one learns that
it was difficult for even the Pasha to force peasants to do the work
needed to expand the canal system. Class issues were also much in
evidence in 1864, when Isma'il, soon to become Khedive Isma'il, had
to go to Upper Egypt to suppress a major uprising. Some twenty years
later, the British ruled Egypt. By then, "the crowd" (to use a term
the British used) was much larger than it had been earlier, and the
British, preoccupied as they were with matters of security, fixated on
it, their police reports filled with what they took to be the menace
posed by city crowds. In more recent times, fear of the urban mass has
been inducing the government to move the capital from Cairo to New
Cairo. This suggests that, from the eighteenth century onward, market pressures led to increasing destitution, which in turn led increasingly large numbers to migrate to the slums of the major cities and
then to loiter on the streets in search of any kind of work. This trend

so often discussed in the British period as something unprecedented actually had a long prehistory, going back into early modern times, and continues in the present day.

Gender Stratification Policy

The watershed of the sixteenth century in world history also witnessed the birth of a new gender policy, euphemistically referred to in scholarship as the "birth of the housewife," which served to enhance the power of men over women. There were housewives throughout history, of course, but at this point the housewife as an institution was imposed by rulers as a universal norm, especially on women from property-owning classes. A significant body of scholarship has examined this matter. Friedrich Engels, for instance, wrote about the housewife in terms of private property and inheritance under capitalism; more recently, Silvia Federici's book *Caliban and the Witch* (2004) has become a modern classic on the subject.[6] Her work describes in very considerable detail the brutality of the state and religious authorities toward the women who resisted housewifeization, but nonetheless some women fought back. The outcome of this very uneven struggle was predictable—for several centuries, women ceased to be a part of public life, a phenomenon the author finds to be the case not only in Europe but worldwide.

As for Egypt, what we know about the subject seems to run along similar lines. Before 1517, bourgeois women were out and about; after 1517, with the coming of mercantilism, they disappeared. We know the Ottomans actually tried to drive women out of the public sphere and that later rulers continued such practices. Not only was the position of women confined by their situation as housewives, but other practices were imposed on them as well, among them the hijab. Of course, the hijab had existed in the Middle East since antiquity, but, at this point, social pressure was put on middle- and upper-class women to wear it whether they wanted to or not and to thereby accept—if hijab meant niqab—having their mobility impeded and their visibility limited.

The coming of mercantilism had other consequences for women as well, the most important being that changes in legal practices served to undermine the assurances given to women in the security of the marriage bond. This change was a long, slow process that of course some women resisted, in the long run to little avail. By the late nineteenth century, it would seem that women had less power than they had had in the sixteenth or seventeenth centuries; by that point, conditions demanded by women and written into their marriage contracts might no longer stand up in court as marriage went from being a contract to a sacrament. Gender as a result became, and today remains, a highly conflictual terrain. As the state was involved, one can legitimately infer that gender policy was a tool of stratification.

The dominant paradigm would, of course, have it otherwise. Modern history is the story of progress. In the second half of the nineteenth century, the "New Woman" arose, thanks to European influence. In a sense this is accurate. The New Woman arrived following a wave of machine-made goods; capitalism required that women of means be made into consumers and buy these goods, abandoning the artisans whom they had previously patronized. Hence there was a need for a new woman. To make women into consumers, they had to be educated to be consumers. Educating women to accept consumerism and its burdens required a new version of education. This new version had to affiliate the history of gender and marriage and consumption with the story of the progress of the nation, making women's trips to the department store a service to the nation. The outcome of these late nineteenth- and early twentieth-century experiments in social engineering are still with us today. Not only did poor women have to work but, from this point on, so did middle- and upper-class women, as consumers.

Regional Stratification Policy

In addition to class and gender, certain states, among them Egypt, adopted policies favoring one region over another as a way to stratify society. Thus it is that in the case of Egypt one can speak of there being in modern times a "Southern Question," and one can find its historical antecedents in early modern history.

Regional differentiation as a strategy of divide and rule began in the Ottoman period, when Jirgah provided Istanbul with grain and was given a certain degree of autonomy from Cairo in return. The modern form of what was to become the Southern Question began when 'Ali Bey al-Kabir captured Upper Egypt in the 1760s. From that point on, the South became an oppressed region, a source of cheap labor for the North, a region known for starvation, revolts, migration, and, more recently, religious radicalism.[7] Khedive Isma'il's campaign in 1864 to annihilate Ahmad al-Tib and his extended family, referred to earlier, was a particular moment in that longer sequence of events. In the years that followed, a new body of administrative law arose, dividing North and South. Finally, there was the construction of the modern city of Asyut as a garrison-city-type southern capital. The struggle to control the South as an oppressed region carries on in more recent times, with the rising influence of the Muslim Brotherhood in Asyut and with the presidency of Muhammad Mursi.

Caste Stratification Policy

Caste, implying the creation of a caste hierarchy, is yet another commonly used stratification device in state formation. In Egypt, the Ottomans changed the meaning of "dhimmi" from that of a defeated nation in the case of the Copts to that of a suppressed caste group or *Milla*, one that would be ruled by a religious figure, specifically a pope. This move marked not only a certain kind of integration of society, one associated with capitalism, but also a certain kind of stratification. By making the Copts a Milla—in other words, a religious community—and by designating the pope as its head, the class nature of the war in Egypt was covered over. With the backing of the state, the pope, the Coptic notables, and the scholars, a Milla-type system has carried on with various mutations until the present day. Socioeconomic conflicts are framed as religious conflicts either between Copts and Muslims or between elite individuals (e.g., the pope and some particular notable). Framing socioeconomic conflicts in this way fits the needs of the state because it acknowledges that they exist, but they do not implicate capitalism. In the nineteenth century, when Egypt turned to the idea of universal citizenship by abolishing the Djizya tax on the Copts in 1855, caste as a technique of stratification faced challenges but still survived.[8]

Law and Stratification Policy

Mercantilism also had an impact on the modern legal system. In Mamluk Egypt, before the era of mercantilism, there had been a degree of decentralization of legal decision making. After 1517, the Ottomans, as part of their statecraft, gave precedence to the Hanafi Code, the one most oriented toward state administrative power, and Hanafism has remained the choice of regimes from then to now, administrative law gradually coming to dominate other forms of jurisprudence. The Ottomans also hierarchized Sunni institutions, building up al-Azhar and the position of Shaykh al-Azhar over others. This, too, was a new set of developments for Egypt, and it, too, has lasted. Thus, when Khedive Isma'il poured money into building up the Azhar and attempted to have the Shaykh al-Azhar present a religious foundation for his policies, he was actually following long-term patterns.

The Organization of Culture as Stratification Policy

All modern states rule through policies of coercion and persuasion. Ordinarily, therefore, one needs to pay attention to state policy toward culture. On their arrival in Egypt, the Ottomans set out to undermine the secular culture of the country in order to make Egypt more docile. To accomplish their goals, the Ottomans poured resources into the local Sufi institutions.[9] This was the core of their cultural policy, which was implemented rapidly, virtually in the aftermath of the conquest; it does not seem to be an exaggeration to claim that it must have been planned. What would seem likely to anyone of my generation who lived through the Sadat period was that the objective was to orient the culture away from a concern with politics, society, and economy toward a more individualistic conception of human progress. Of course, some of the Sufi shaykhs welcomed the Ottoman policy;

there is also some indication of resistance. Evidence suggests that some work in science and medicine nonetheless carried on even without elite patronage and that, by the seventeenth century, Sufism was becoming associated with critical thought. In the eighteenth century, as the Ottoman presence grew weaker, secular culture started to reappear, even among Sufis such as the Khalwatiyya, some of whose members participated in the majlis (salon) culture.[10] By the age of Khedive Isma'il, secular culture was even more dominant but still kept in check by the religious structures.

This chapter concludes the discussion of Oriental despotism, having established that Anglo-American historians specializing in Egypt's modern history have made and can make but little use of the history of the early modern period because of the logic of this paradigm. This situation is an anomalous one. Logically, the paradigm should be abandoned for that reason; a glance at what is known on the level of factual details would encourage such a move. This chapter introduced various details about the development of capitalism and modern statecraft to demonstrate that some of what transpired in the nineteenth and twentieth centuries was shaped by the struggles of that earlier period. This is a major subject area to be developed.

Conclusion

For several decades, the student in modern Egyptian studies has been working in a field with no clear history—that is, with no way to judge where he or she was. Moreover, the field had only one paradigm, and this paradigm failed to account for very much.

Given this situation, this book initially set out to outline the history of American historical studies of modern Egypt, to provide a clearer understanding of the field. This chapter reviews some of the main findings of the book, beginning with the issue of periodization, then moving on to the issue of the Oriental despotism paradigm and identity issues, and, finally, taking up the issue of the role played by the UK in the creation of the field.

Periodization

The history of the field appears to be comprised of three different, if somewhat overlapping, periods. The first coincided with the heyday of colonialism. In the case of the UK, this extended from the last years of the nineteenth century to the Suez War; in the case of the United States, it only extended to the late 1930s and early 1940s. The second of these periods (the late 1930s to the late 1970s) was bound up with the adjustment to the Cold War, the Development Revolution, the coming of decolonization, and Egyptian independence in 1954. The third period, which began in the 1970s and continues today, has witnessed the field's adjustment to globalization and postcolonial discourse.

The First Period

The colonial heyday was marked by the British occupation of Egypt. During this time, British officials produced a number of works whose influence came to be felt in American studies of modern Egypt. Cleavages appeared in the field.

In this first period, one could see the beginning of one of the main internal cleavages in the field, one that still exists today. On the one hand, the government wanted policy-oriented knowledge, finding it more useful than the language and area-based expertise possessed by missionaries and then later by professors. On the other hand, many professors were more interested in questions of science than in those of policy. This cleavage was demonstrated quite dramatically by the decision on the part of dominant elements in the United States to align with Great Britain and to rely on its expertise in Middle Eastern affairs in preference to that of American missionaries. More recently, in the year 2001, the government created—or at least gave its blessing to—a policy association for Middle East studies set up to address policy concerns still not adequately addressed by the academy.

Following the lead of British scholars, American scholars took the subject of Egypt to be a part of Middle East studies, a framework that included Turkey and Iran. The decision to organize the field within these parameters appears to have been a way of avoiding the need to confront the Arab world of which Egypt would have been a part; in other words, it was much more a matter of divide and rule than of science. As the policy priorities of the early twentieth century were the oil fields and the Palestine Question, Egypt became a subfield in what became Middle East studies.

The Second Period

The second period in the history of the field coincided with the Cold War and with Egyptian independence. The US government's response to the challenges of these years was to create a large number of personnel who could serve in development programs, with the intention of forestalling the spread of communism by encouraging capitalist development. To that end, the government sponsored the creation of Middle East centers in various universities, and Egyptian studies benefited from this development. At this point, students from middle-class backgrounds with no particular connection to the government, the oil industry, or policy studies were encouraged to learn Arabic and other languages and to enter public service. On graduation, some of these students did work for the government, while others found employment in the universities. As a result, the field of Middle East studies became larger and more scientific but less policy driven. Policy centers existed, such as the Middle East Institute in Washington, DC, but by this point the actual field was spread out across the universities, and, for the first time, language skills became a prerequisite for one's research to be taken seriously. Last but not least, the field became much more American and much less British, especially after the Suez War. This period came to an end in the later 1970s, when those inclined toward the scientific end of the field began to produce a critique of US imperialism, at just the time when the government was promoting globalization and neocolonialism.

The Third Period

The third period coincides with the age of globalization, spanning from the later 1970s to today. Once again, there were major social changes and intellectual shifts, a number of which were reflected in Middle East and Egyptian studies. It was at this point that one can find sustained attacks on the Hegelian framework of the university from various Nietzsche-inspired trends, which were on the rise for the first time in a century (e.g., Edward Said's *Orientalism*).

As a result of these changes, many in recent years who study Egypt have been doing so through the frames of postcolonial discourse, taking imperialism for granted and thus favoring the study of empires and the global and the local over the study of the nation-states. Nonetheless, the study of nation-states has continued. One reason no doubt is the rising importance of women's history, which has generally remained nation based.

Another result of the revival of Nietzsche has been the abandonment of historicism in favor of presentism. Egypt is now no longer
seen as traditional so much as hybrid modern. It is rated more in terms
of its use of computers and less in terms of its level of industrialization. In the extreme case—and one can find a bit of this in Egyptian
studies—history itself, given its preoccupation with the relevance of
the past, is perceived to be an obstacle to progress. Some following
Nietzsche criticize history by turning to the study of subjectivities,
memory, genealogy, and other subjects associated with antihistory.

In addition, we need to recall the presence of yet two other trends
in this period, the sum of which produced the beginnings of a critique
of the Oriental despotism paradigm. First, in the United States, there
were changes in the alliance structure of the state in the age of globalization, resulting in the inclusion of women in the career world, an
increasing number of whom became professors. With more women in
the academy, a critique of fields such as Middle East studies through
the lens of gender was born. Second, this period saw the arrival of a
number of Egyptian professionals in the US academy. Some of these
individuals became university professors and critics as well.

The Oriental Despotism Paradigm
and American Identity Issues

This book also attempted to explain why Anglo-American scholars specializing in the study of modern Egypt have for a long time
assumed that the country's political system resembled the Pharaonic
political system described in the book of Exodus: autocratic in nature
and highly centralized, presumably more so than other countries.
Most scholars appear to have also accepted the corollary proposition
that not only was the political system little changed since antiquity,
so too was the economic system. It is assumed that Egypt's economy
since antiquity has been largely agricultural and dependent on irrigation, and that, as a result, Egypt has always required a centralized
hydraulic state to manage the water of the Nile. In other words, the
nature of the economy explained the autocratic nature of the political system—hence the term "Oriental despot" and the paradigm of

Oriental despotism. Students of Egyptology and of medieval Egypt share some of these assumptions, but, in their fields, this interpretation of the subject matter is by no means as monolithic as it is in the modern field.

What sustains this paradigm? Here, some would say very little sustains it. Oriental despotism is on the decline. It was a part of the colonial ideology that was ascendant when the field was gaining a foothold in the academy. In that context, Egypt was by definition "Oriental," and Oriental countries were by definition "despotisms."

But then why has the paradigm continued beyond the age of colonialism on up to the present? Here the argument for decline carries on as follows: in the last thirty years, there has been an ongoing critique of Orients and Orientalism, and, as a result, a number of countries that were once studied on the assumption that they were Oriental despotisms are not studied that way today.

However, this argument has its limitations. Compared to the other fields alluded to, the field of Egyptian studies seems like a case of arrested development. While it is true that in this period the field developed more rapidly than ever before—perhaps because it was able to attract different kinds of scholars with very different interests—the choice of paradigm has still remained the same, no matter who was carrying out the research or what they were researching. This has led to the hypothesis of scholarship being written on two different levels: a conscious scientific level, which allows for a colonial/postcolonial contrast; and a less conscious and less scientific level, one associated with identity, which does not allow for such a contrast.

What makes this identity-based hypothesis credible is the sheer power that paradigm logic has been able to exert on the scholarship being produced in what after all is an age of science. Textual analysis reveals that paradigm logic seems not simply to be a factor in the broad outline of the scholarship produced but to be a factor in what scholars find in archives and libraries as well. Perhaps for that reason, in contrast to other fields, archival work in this field does not appear to be changing anyone's fundamental views on anything. Indeed, one encounters few surprises and even fewer loose ends. To illustrate the anomalousness of the situation, the book demonstrated that, with the facts at hand, combined with some sort of common-sense approach, the field might easily have derailed this paradigm a long time ago. Chapter 4 argued that it would have been feasible a long time ago to raise questions about the idea of a Napoleonic watershed in 1798. Specialists have long known that there were Europeans in Cairo and Alexandria before Napoleon, and that the Mamluks of the late eighteenth century tried to buy artillery and other modern weapons from Europe, which should suggest that Egypt was neither isolated nor stagnant, as the paradigm would have it. Moreover, scholars have long known that the later eighteenth century saw the production of a major dictionary and a major work of history, works equal to or surpassing in importance anything produced in the nineteenth century, for which reason the study of the late eighteenth century should not have been neglected. There are still other observations one could make about the influence of the paradigm on historians' choice of sources to reach their conclusions. Certainly science would not encourage us to base our understanding of the eighteenth century on the memoirs of disgruntled French merchants or on parts of al-Jabarti read out of context where the subject of decline appears.

This brings us to the paradigm's assumption of an absolute total rupture separating the world before and after 1798. Assuming that such a rupture occurred, how would one understand the lives of prominent individuals who were born in the eighteenth century but who lived on into the nineteenth century and became quite famous at that point? Is the eighteenth-century background of these individuals to be dismissed? Chapter 3 raises this question apropos to the study of Muhammad 'Ali Pasha. Why, in a field obsessed with this figure, is there so little interest in his background? Why do we only begin to learn a few details about it from Albanian books of the last five years? Eventually, one is left with the hypothesis developed in this book: that, in this case, paradigm logic in the Anglo-American field overpowers everything else, not as the result of failed science but as an outcome produced by the need to maintain one's identity as a Westerner, which trumps one's efforts as a scholar.

In other words, Egypt has to be an Oriental despotism; it has to be Pharaonic. It cannot be a subject that one studies and eventually reaches some conclusions about based on science alone. In this case, one knows from the start what conclusion one will reach. It cannot be other than what it is. The story of Moses and Exodus not only explains but justifies how the West began and how we should understand ourselves as Westerners. The tragedy that ensued first in Egypt and then later in North America upon the arrival of the settlers was not a matter of criminal intent. Following biblical precedent, the settlers were like the Jews in Exodus: for them, the mass death of Egyptians was a matter of collateral damage and not of evil intent. Exodus is thus crucial for Anglo-American identity, as we are Westerners. In short, if Egypt is not an Oriental despotism, one's own self-construction as a Westerner and as a member of a moral society begins to crumble.

And yet the field, even with the constraints imposed by this paradigm, continues to develop. Over the past century, knowledge has grown immensely. The number of researchers has increased, as has the accessibility of source material, thanks to interlibrary loan systems and to the internet. Organizations exist to help with funding and with the publication of results. But, as this book also argued, measuring growth quantitatively is not necessarily the most precise way to evaluate a field's development. Along with this kind of growth of information, one would have to determine whether there was any corresponding growth in self-reflection and criticism, or growth of awareness of who may suffer from the use of a given paradigm. Here, the conclusion reached was that there may be, as evidenced by the rise of groups associating themselves with hybridized identities, with New Social Theory, and with the growing acceptance of Egyptian scholars at home or abroad in Anglo-American academia.

The Anglo-American Nature of the Field

The Anglo-American nature of the field was another discovery for a book of this sort—an unexpected one that was initially not easy to explain. What eventually came to light was that the field was not in any organic sense connected to Anglo-Saxon tradition; it became

Anglo-American as a result of internal issues in the United States, most notably the struggles over sectionalism. These struggles led some of the dominant figures on the East Coast to reach out to the imperialists in the UK because they lacked domestic support for imperialist projects beyond those in Mexico and the Caribbean. Turning to the UK made sense, given the economic and strategic importance of Middle East oil and the Suez, all of which was controlled by the UK. In this context the study of modern Egyptian history became Anglo-American. The book found that, while the missionaries—among whom were a number of Americans—produced sociological insights about Egypt, it was the British colonial administrators who produced most of the historical narratives. This finding explains the focus on the main narrative of the period, Cromer's *Modern Egypt*, which was taken to be the founding work of the field.

What is clear is that no other book in the Anglo-American tradition came as close to synthesizing what was known about modern Egypt at a given moment as did that book, and no other was so well received as an instant classic, nor so often referred to in Anglo-American imperial circles, even long after Cromer himself had left the scene. Reading Cromer's book on Egypt along with some of his other writings makes clear that, for him, the main concern was always how to control subject peoples and, in Egypt, Oriental despotism was what worked. It is also clear that Cromer was writing for the general public and not simply for the Foreign Office. One can infer this not just from the book's reception, but from the kinds of sources on which the author chose to rely: British administrative records from Egypt, the author's own personal impressions of various Egyptians, material about the economy and about the country's solvency bearing on paying back Egypt's debt, and—last but not least—a range of more general observations about Egypt, Islam, and Egyptians from diverse but unnamed sources. As Cromer spoke no Arabic, one infers that his sources must have included accounts by missionaries, since what he wrote echoed what could be found in their writings and the missionaries were among his greatest admirers. If I am correct, it would seem to follow that Cromer's use of missionary perceptions of Egypt and Islam likely accounted for much of the enthusiasm with which his work was received in America. Most Americans were interested in the idea of restoring Egypt to what it once was: it conjured up thoughts of Moses and the flight out of Egypt to the promised land.

While much today has changed since the time of Lord Cromer, the Anglo-American tradition of study has survived. Most American students continue to visit the British Library, going from there to the libraries of Oxford and Cambridge. Many who wrote their PhDs never went further. The UK remained, in effect, the custodian of knowledge about the field, at least into the 1970s, at which point a significant number of scholars learned to read Arabic and discovered the Egyptian archives and scholarly tradition.

Future Directions

Throughout this book I have been suggesting that more work on this field could be undertaken from the vantage point of American history and American studies and that we in Egyptian studies would benefit were other scholars to become more interested in this field. I will conclude with some examples of possible research areas.

It would be useful if there were research allowing the study of the history of this field to fall into some category such as the history of American knowledge production; this would allow scholars to measure the progress of the field by comparing it to others of a similar sort. Is there such a thing as a history of gatekeeping fields—that is, fields whose mandate is to maintain a certain status quo more than to introduce new ideas? The study of Egypt would fit into such a category. In this respect, the study of Egypt is like the study of Palestine: Palestine during the life of Jesus Christ saw the birth of Christianity, and those who study the subject are also obliged to put other details aside—the Palestinians, for example. Other gatekeeping-type subjects seem capable of greater flexibility than do these two. Consider the gatekeeping in the work of scholars who study the "Early Republic," whose function is one of denying that the Iroquois and other First Americans were in any sense a part of a high culture of a sort that could have influenced the Euro-Americans: their task is to keep America from becoming North American. But in this case there is some greater flexibility, and some internal dissent in the field at this point. Another group studies Western civilization, and for them America has no African heritage—we are Westerners. All of these are examples of gatekeeping that serve to preserve the Euro-American identity as Egyptian studies does. Perhaps, given the help of scholars in those fields and others, we could form a more precise understanding of the American study of Egypt.

For those in the field of modern Egyptian history, there are many gaps for a new generation to explore as well. Among them would be an interpretation of the contribution of the Egyptian American scholars as relates to the paradigm issue. I thought about doing this myself, but realized that it could not be encapsulated in a few observations and would have to be done on its own terms. Egyptian Americans come from many different backgrounds in Egypt. Many at this point are second-generation Egyptian Americans, or simply Americans. Thus, one could not very well argue, for example, that because some brought knowledge and technical skills this was automatically going to have a predictable impact on the issue of the dominant paradigm here.

Another gap is a lack of the history of language acquisition as a possible barometer of de-Orientalization. Since the start of the Title 6 Program, is there evidence that students studying Arabic are coming closer to reaching a level that allows them to participate in conferences? My impression is that students generally learn Arabic as a dead language with a few spoken words useful in restaurants. I hope there is evidence to the contrary.

Other gaps I encountered were of both an empirical and a theoretical nature. The contribution of the missionary to the emergence of modern secular knowledge, the role of sectionalism in the history of this field, and the contribution of what has been termed the "amateur" to professional knowledge, as a part of women's history, African American history, or history more generally, stand out as subjects yet to be developed.

Glossary

Notes

Selected Bibliography

Index

Glossary

'Ali Bey al-Kabir (1728–63). For a brief time the ruler of Egypt. Known for declaring its independence.

capitulation agreements. Agreements wherein a state ceded sovereignty over citizens of another country resident in its borders. The Ottomans signed capitulation agreements with various European nations.

Copts. The main Egyptian Christian community.

dialectical materialism. The systematic working out of communist theory as knowledge and as a research agenda.

faute de mieux. "For want of anything better."

Hanafi Code. The Sunni Islamic legal tradition with the largest following in the Ottoman Empire and successor states, at least among officials.

Iltizam system. Tax farming system used in early modern times (e.g., in the Ottoman Empire).

Kuttab system. Elementary schools, most of which are Muslim; some are Coptic.

Deborah Manley. American author, known for a number of books on travel and Egypt.

Milner Commission (also Milner Mission). A commission of inquiry led by Alfred Milner, colonial secretary, sent to Egypt in 1919 to ascertain the political goals of the Egyptians.

Moustafa M. Mosharrafa. Egyptian literature professor, author of one of the first works on Egyptian cultural history written by an Egyptian, published in the UK.

Multazims. Tax farmers.

Napoleonic Code. Legal code introduced in Egypt in 1798, which became, along with Shari'ah law, the basis of Egyptian jurisprudence. Noted for increasing male power over women.

Salafism. A trend in Sunni Islam associated currently with violent jihadism. In previous generations, Salafi implied a reverence for the great exemplars of faith from early Islam.

savants. The 160 or so civilian scholars accompanying the French invasion of Egypt, 1798–1801.

sectionalism. Trend in US political history dividing the country between the East Coast supporters of the gold standard and international trade and the Middle West supporters of bimetallism and tariffs.

Zamindars. Wealthy landowners of South Asia, sometimes aristocrats, or tax farmers controlling tenant farmers.

Notes

Introduction

1. In Anglo-American scholarship, the study of modern Egypt has typically been included as a part of Middle East studies. It has never stood on its own, in contrast to the situation in Egypt, where Egyptian historical scholarship has been the theme of many books. The main contours of the Anglo-American field of modern Middle East studies can be identified from the following works: Osamah Khalil, *America's Dream Palace* (Cambridge, MA: Harvard Univ. Press, 2016); Irene Gendzier, *Dying to Forget: Oil, Power, Palestine, and the Foundations of US Policy in the Middle East* (New York: Columbia Univ. Press, 2015); and Zachary Lockman, *Contending Visions of the Middle East* (Cambridge: Cambridge Univ. Press, 2009) and *Field Notes* (Stanford, CA: Stanford Univ. Press, 2015). As this should suggest, there are gaps in knowledge about much of the subject matter involved, and uncertainty at least about how the field arose in the United States and how it functioned thereafter.

As regards the origins of Middle East studies in the United States, there is a difference of opinion. Zachary Lockman finds little evidence of sustained work on the Middle East until after World War II; see *Contending Visions of the Middle East*, 279n8. He criticizes Robert Vitalis, who finds Middle East studies embedded in American racial discourse going back to the social science of the World War I period; see Vitalis, "International Studies in America," *Ideas and Issues* 3 (2002): 1–12. In this, Lockman is closer to Timothy Mitchell, "The Middle East in the Past and Future of Social Science" (http://blogs.cuit.columbia.edu/tm2421/files/2018/01/Szanton-ed-Middle-East-in-Soc-Sci.pdf, accessed March 24, 2020). Mitchell grapples with the question of when the professional field arose and decides that the evidence of the existence of professionalization is the existence of professional institutions. He begins his account with the formation of the Middle East Institute in 1947 and notes the government funding of various programs and centers in the years to follow. The text is closer to Vitalis and to Osamah Khalil, "At the Crossroads of Empire: The United States, the Middle East, and the Politics of Knowledge, 1902–2002" (PhD diss., Univ. of California, Berkeley, 2011).

The decision to characterize this work as a study of modern scholarship alerts us to yet another problem: the highly ambiguous nature of the term "modern." The approach to the solution adopted here is often used by historians of academic disciplines, accentuating the aspects of the term that connect us to our origins—in this case, of this particular contemporary academic field. The reader familiar either with social theory or with Egyptian studies will see the price being paid. Given this approach, no mention is made of a standard work such as E. W. Lane's *Manner and Customs of the Modern Egyptians*, because it was published back in 1836 and the modern structure of knowledge as defined here only begins in the very late nineteenth century.

2. Siep Stuurman, "Cosmopolitan Egalitarianism in the Enlightenment: Anquetil Duperron on India and America," *Journal of the History of Ideas* 68, no. 2 (2007): 255–78. See 256n4 and 256n5 for a review of writings on the eighteenth-century critique of European justifications for colonial conquest.

3. Cenk Aygul, "Asiatic Mode of Production and the Ottoman Empire," *Journal of Social Sciences* 4, no. 2 (2011): 2–33 reviews the literature, taking a similar line to the one in this book about the recent relative decline of a still-hegemonic paradigm. As for the early stages of the modern Egyptian adoption of the Oriental despotism paradigm prior to the age of Isma'il, we remain uncertain. For an account of a panegyric history written for Muhammad 'Ali but then never published by Khalil al-Rajabi, see Dyala Hamzah, "Nineteenth-Century Egypt as Dynastic Locus of Universality: The History of Muhammad 'Ali by Khalil Ibn Ahmad al-Rajabi," *Comparative Studies of South Asia, Africa, and the Middle East* 27, no. 1 (2007): 62–82. There is also unpublished historical work of this sort by Shaykh Hasan al-'Attar. These works, however, do not make use of the Oriental despotism paradigm.

4. No doubt for some readers, it may suffice simply to note that Herodotus saw Egypt as the Oriental antithesis of the Greek polis and that Cromer and his contemporaries were steeped in such works. See Kostas Vlassopoulos, *Unthinking the Greek Polis: Ancient Greek History beyond Eurocentrism* (Cambridge: Cambridge Univ. Press, 2007). However, for other readers, it may seem more appropriate to note the more recent usages of the term and, in particular, the importance of India to the Oriental despotism model, especially considering that Cromer and many others had their training in India. A specialized study on the model as applied to India is Brendan O'Leary, *The Asiatic Mode of Production: Oriental Despotism, Historical Materialism, and Indian History* (Oxford: Basil Blackwell, 1989).

Other works include the classic text by Karl Wittfogel, *Oriental Despotism: A Comparative Study of Total Power* (New Haven, CT: Yale Univ. Press, 1957). See also the survey by Michael Curtis, *Orientalism and Islam: European Thinkers on Oriental Despotism in the Middle East and India* (Cambridge: Cambridge Univ. Press, 2009);

for information about the history of AMP, see Stephen Dunn, *The Fall and Rise of the Asiatic Mode of Production* (Boston: Routledge & Kegan Paul, 1982).

5. The prestige of Cromer in American eyes may be inferred from the *New York Times Book Review* editor C. R. Miller's review of *Modern Egypt*, which begins, "A book by 'the greatest living Englishman' ought to engage the attention of the enlightened world. . . . the writer is the highest living authority on the subject" ("Lord Cromer's Work in Egypt," May 21, 1908, 149). The *American Historical Review* turned to James Bryce, the British legal historian then serving as ambassador to Washington, for its review. Bryce begins by arguing that historical works written by the great figures of their time are of inestimable value, and he compares the present work to that of Thucydides, Julius Caesar, and a number of others (*American Historical Review* 14, no. 2 [January 1909]: 357–62). The American scholar and white supremacist Lothrop Stoddard (1883–1950), who received a PhD in history from Harvard University in 1914, used Cromer as his main source on Egypt in his 1921 *New World of Islam*. For the way Cromer became a part of American colonial thought, see Patrick M. Kirkwood, "'Lord Cromer's Shadow': Political Anglo-Saxonism and the Egyptian Protectorate as a Model in the American Philippines," *Journal of World History* 27, no. 1 (2016): 1–26. For further commentary on Cromer, one could look at the writings of the secretary of war Elihu Root and the correspondence of Theodore Roosevelt. For Cromer's continuing presence in American thought as in Iraq War discourse, see Harvey Sicherman, "Adventures in State-Building: Bremer's Iraq and Cromer's Egypt," *American Interest* 2, no. 5 (2007): 28–41; more recently, see the commentary around Bruce Gilley's attempt to rehabilitate the image of British colonialism.

6. Wilfrid Scawen Blunt and Ahmad 'Urabi, *Secret History of the English Occupation of Egypt* (New York: Knopf, 1922) contains 'Urabi's autobiography; Theodor Rothstein, *Egypt's Ruin: A Financial and Administrative Record* (London: Fifield, 1910).

7. A classic analysis of Egyptian history along these lines was written by Shuhdi 'Atiyyah al-Shafi'i (1912–60): *Tatawwur al-haraka al-wataniya al-Misriya, 1882–1956* (Cairo: Dar al-Shuhdi, 1957). By way of contrast, the more elite-oriented communist leader—the one following AMP analysis—was Henri Curiel, *Awraq Hinri Kuryil wa-al-harakah al-shuyu'iyah al-Misriyah* (Cairo: Sina lil-nashr, 1988). See also the work of Ahmad Sadiq Sa'd, *Ta'rikh al-'Arab al-ijtima'i: Tahawwul al-takwin al-Misri min al-namat al-Asiyawi ilá al-namat al-ra'smali* (Beirut: N.p., 1981).

Not surprisingly, best known to the Anglo-American scholarly world are Henri Curiel, Anouar Abdel-Malek, and Ahmad Sadiq Sa'd, all of whom took up variants of AMP analysis in their work. See Anouar Abdel-Malek, *Egypt Military Society* (New York: Random House, 1968); Henri Curiel, *Inventory of the Papers of the*

Egyptian Communists in Exile (Rome Group) Including the Papers of Henri Curiel (1914–78), ed. Marianne Wigboldus and Jaap Haag (Amsterdam: Stichting Beheer IISG, 1997); and Ahmad Sadiq Saʻd, *L'Égypte pharaonique* (Paris: CERM, 1975).

8. Amin ʻIzz al-Din, *Ta'rikh al-tabaqah al-ʻamilah al-Misriyah: Mundhu nush-uiha hattá sanat 1970* (Cairo: Dar al-Ghad al-ʻArabi, 1987), 1035.

9. Raʼuf ʻAbbas Hamid and ʻAsim al-Disuqi, *Kibar al-mullak wa-l-fallahun fi Misr 1837–1952* (Cairo: Dar al-Qiba, 1998).

10. Joel Beinin and Zachary Lockman, *Workers on the Nile* (Princeton, NJ: Princeton Univ. Press, 1987).

11. For a recent view of ancient Egypt, see June Ambridge Lindsay, "Search-ing History: The Non-elite in Ancient Egypt," *History Compass* 2 (2007): 1–11. So "revisionist" is contemporary scholarship that a recent commentator felt obliged to point to times when the state asserted itself: Brendan Haug, "Water and Power: Reintegrating the State into the Study of Egyptian Irrigation," *History Compass* (2017): 1–9.

12. Clayton R. Koppes, "Captain Mahan, General Gordon, and the Origins of the Term 'Middle East,'" *Middle East Studies* 12 (1976): 95–98.

13. Khalil, *America's Dream Palace*.

14. This view is disputed by Sir Ronald Storrs, *Orientations* (London: Readers Union, 1939), 155, where the author, the British governor of Palestine, states that the Mandate existed to help protect the Suez Canal, which was the center of the empire.

15. To my knowledge, the idea of linking oil and Palestine has not been es-tablished for this period, but only as regards the later 1948 Partition period. See Gendzier, *Dying to Forget*.

16. There is a vast body of writing on the Arab–Middle Eastern nature of Egypt. Recent works include Michael Doran, *Pan-Arabism before Nasser* (New York: Ox-ford Univ. Press, 1999); and Adam Mestyan, *Arab Patriotism: The Ideology and Cul-ture of Power in Late Ottoman Egypt* (Princeton, NJ: Princeton Univ. Press, 2017).

17. See, for example, J. (John) Kent, "The Egyptian Base and the Defence of the Middle East," *Journal of Commonwealth and Imperial History* 21 (1993): 45–65; see also the statement by Philip Baram, a historian of the State Department, that the British made Cairo the center of the Middle East by World War II, as did the Ameri-cans. Baram, *The Department of State in the Middle East, 1919–45* (Philadelphia: Univ. of Pennsylvania Press, 1978), 185, 187.

18. For the latter perspective, one can go back all the way to the "rise of global-ism." The diplomatic record reveals plenty of tensions, such as rivalries between the United States and the UK. For example, Woodrow Wilson with his Fourteen Points was interpreted by British imperialists, doubtless incorrectly, as being an agent bent on destabilizing the British Empire. Erez Manela, *The Wilsonian Moment:*

Self-Determination and the International Origins of Anticolonial Nationalism (Oxford: Oxford Univ. Press, 2007), 247, footnotes correspondence between Sa'd Zaghlul and Wilson during World War I.

19. On the Cromer model, see Kirkwood, "Lord Cromer's Shadow."

20. Among reference works useful here are Julie Des Jardins, *Women and the Historical Enterprise in America* (Chapel Hill: Univ. of North Carolina Press, 2003), one of the main works showing how women have heretofore been written out of the history of the history profession. Another is Jennifer Scanlon and Shaaron Cosner, *American Women Historians, 1700s–1990s* (Westport, CT: Greenwood, 1996). A standard work on the history of the professions, and a useful one, that covers the period of concern here is Dorothy Ross, *The Origins of American Social Science* (Cambridge: Cambridge Univ. Press, 1991). The idea that subfields of knowledge are parts of the larger move toward professionalization even before they manifest themselves as full-blown entities on their own, if that is what happens, is obviously an assumption that not everyone would share, as the above makes clear. Still, it is tempting to suggest that when American Egyptology became a professional field, thanks to James Breasted and George Reisner, an indirect effect might have been to stimulate the development of a more autonomous modern field. John A. Wilson, *A History of American Egyptology* (Chicago: Univ. of Chicago Press, 1964).

21. A study of the origins of African American women's scholarship in the United States by Pero Gaglo Dagbovie, "Black Women Historians from the Late Nineteenth Century to the Dawning of the Civil Rights Movement," *Journal of African American History* 89, no. 3 (2004): 241–61, argues that in practice the field progressed thanks to the inclusion of writings of educated individuals, whether they were academics or not.

22. Billie Melman, *Women's Orients: English Women and the Middle East, 1718–1918* (Ann Arbor: Univ. of Michigan Press, 1992), 4–5.

23. Deborah Manley, ed., *Women Travelers in Egypt* (Cairo: American Univ. in Cairo Press, 2012), 3.

24. Other scholars go further; some argue that one should take it for granted that women as scholars are usually more progressive than men. Elisabeth Israel Perry, "Men Are from the Gilded Age, Women are from the Progressive Era," *Journal of the Gilded Age and the Progressive Era* 1 (2002): 25–48.

25. Melissa Lee Miller, "The Imperial Feminine: Victorian Women Travelers in Late Nineteenth-Century Egypt" (PhD diss., Kent State Univ., 2000), 1; this is reinforced in Jeanne-Marie Warzeski, "Mapping the Unknown: Gendered Spaces and the Oriental Other in Travelogues of Egypt by US Women, 1854–1914," *History and Anthropology* 13 (2002): 301–17. A well-known writer in the feminist tradition taking the race line is Ruth Frankenberg, *White Women, Race Matters: The Social*

Construction of Whiteness (Minneapolis: Univ. of Minnesota Press, 1993); race was apparent in the work of one of the best-known American writers on Egypt, Elizabeth Cooper (1877–1945), *The Women of Egypt* (London: Hurst & Blackett, 1914).

26. Scanlon and Cosner's *American Women Historians* includes, for Middle East studies, Christina P. Harris, *The Anglo-American Peace Movement in the Mid-nineteenth Century* (New York: Columbia Univ. Press, 1930) and *Nationalism and Revolution in Egypt: The Role of the Muslim Brotherhood* (Stanford, CA: Hoover Institute, 1964). Looking a bit further, however, one notes what may be a few other exceptions as well: Alda Belle Atchison (1886–1972), "The Study of the Development of Education in Modern Egypt" (MA thesis, Univ. of Southern California, 1926). Atchison taught at the American Girl's College in Cairo and was thereafter active in missionary circles. Her argument was that, in the British period, it was missionaries who led the way in Egyptian education. Helena Reimer (1905–93), "The Role of Women and the Development of Nursing Education in Modern Egypt" (MA thesis, Univ. of Chicago, 1957); Des Jardins's *Women and the American Historical Enterprise* is one of the main general reference works of women scholars in the United States and shows a number of recognized historians in the nineteenth and twentieth centuries, many of whom studied US history. As regards Ella Torrey, see Jane Lenel, "She Was an Aide to Eleanor Roosevelt," *Chestnut Hill Local*, March 24, 2011, https://www.chestnuthilllocal.com/2011/03/24/she-was-an-aide-to-eleanor-rooseelt-ella-torrey-50-years-working-for-international-peace (accessed July 29, 2018). Torrey worked in Egypt for an Egyptian newspaper. As regards Egyptian studies before the 1960s, one basically finds mention of Christina Phelps Harris and a few Egyptologists. For the British women, access to Egypt was a lot easier, but not free from constraints. For example, the women of ancient Egypt may have functioned in writing by women travelers as symbols in the writers' own struggles during the Victorian period, but contemporary Egyptian women apparently did not play a role, as they were not well thought of as a result of their characterizations by earlier travelers, such as Edward W. Lane. See Molly Youngkin, *British Women Writers and the Reception of Ancient Egypt, 1840–1910* (New York: Palgrave, 2016). While travel literature is of some importance, doubtless it would also be fruitful to search through the writings of critical women intellectuals to see whether they ever visited Egypt, or to look for their reflections about women and about the paradigm more generally.

27. Cited in Lisa Pollard, "Amateur Historians, the 'Woman Question,' and the Production of Modern History in Turn-of-the-Twentieth-Century Egypt," in *Making Women's Histories: Beyond National Perspectives*, ed. Pamela Nadell (New York: New York Univ. Press, 2013), 137–60, especially 137–38; Cynthia Nelson, *Doriya Shafiq: Egyptian Feminist, a Woman Apart* (Gainesville: Univ. of Florida Press, 1996); and Margot Badran, *Feminists, Islam, and Nation* (Princeton, NJ: Princeton Univ. Press, 1996).

28. For reading on Egypt as a subject with a racial tinge, see Scott Trafton, *Egypt Land: Race and Nineteenth-Century Egyptomania* (Durham, NC: Duke Univ. Press, 2004); and, most famously, Martin Delany, *Principia of Ethnology* (Philadelphia: Harper & Brothers, 1879).

29. William Jennings Bryan, *The Old World and Its Ways* (St. Louis: Thompson, 1907), 126–28, went out of its way to criticize Cromer's policies in Egypt.

30. Conflicts over the Middle East Supply Center and the failure of the United States to support Great Britain during the Suez War have been written about extensively. See, for example, John A. DeNovo, "The Culbertson Economic Mission and Anglo-American Tensions in the Middle East, 1944–45," *Journal of American History* 63, no. 4 (1977): 913–36, especially from 915. In diplomatic history, there is a vast literature on Anglo-American relations; it is somewhat divided between those stressing the special relationship tying the United States to the UK and those stressing the competitive nature of the relationship. The present work begins in the special-relationship mode but tries to modify it, never claiming that the Middle East defined the relationship.

31. Georgia Duerst-Lahti, "The Government's Role in Building the Women's Movement," *Political Science Quarterly* 104, no. 2 (1989): 249–68.

32. Ian Almond, *The New Orientalists: Postmodern Representations of Islam from Foucault to Baudrillard* (London: I. B. Tauris, 2007), especially 7–22.

33. Kelly Oliver and Marilyn Pearsall, eds., *Feminist Interpretations of Friedrich Nietzsche* (Univ. Park: Penn State Univ. Press, 1998).

34. Donald Reid, *Contesting Antiquity in Egypt* (Cairo: American Univ. in Cairo Press, 2015), especially 112–13, shows how early one can date the beginning of professional Egyptian archaeology. It was only later, in the 1930s, that professional history began. Eric Goldstein, *The Price of Whiteness* (Princeton, NJ: Princeton Univ. Press, 2008).

35. This speaks to one side of whiteness theory. See also Sacvan Bercovich, who was a major scholar in the American character literature tradition: *The Puritan Origins of the American Self* (New Haven, CT: Yale Univ. Press, 1975).

36. Francis Jennings, *The Invasion of America: Colonialism and the Cant of Conquest* (Chapel Hill: Univ. of North Carolina Press, 2010) argues that the First Americans in North America were largely engaged in commerce, as were the Europeans who killed them. One cannot claim therefore that the First Americans were a part of the Fourth World that unfortunately simply was dying off. Donald Grinde, *Exemplars of Liberty* (Los Angeles: UCLA/Native American Political Series, 1991) deals with the American elite and the influence of the Iroquois on the US Constitution and on US democracy.

37. A protagonist of the ethnicity school interpretation is Eric P. Kaufmann, *The Rise and Fall of Anglo-America* (Cambridge, MA: Harvard Univ. Press, 2004),

which sees Anglo-Saxon solidarity in a state of decline in the years leading up to World War II and thereafter in collapse. For the ethnic school critique of whiteness theory, see Eric Kaufmann, "The Dominant Ethnic Moment: Towards the Abolition of 'Whiteness,'" *Ethnicities* 6, no. 2 (2006): 231–53.

38. In US cultural history, if one were to risk a huge generalization, the idea of the prehistory of modern fields of knowledge—be it the short- or the long-term prehistory—has yet to receive the attention it deserves. A glance at the short-term prehistory of modern Egyptian studies alerts us to the role played by race, region, and gender; the long-term prehistory alerts us to issues in American identity. The fact that the study of modern Egypt emerged as a subfield adds to the challenges of the undertaking.

39. Russell Jacoby, *Social Amnesia: A Critique of Contemporary Psychology* (Piscataway, NJ: Transaction Press, 1997). This work opened the door to the idea of blind spots, of the unsaid, and of repressed knowledge.

40. The accuracy of the scholarship is not in question.

1. The History of Anglo-American Scholarly Writing on Modern Egypt from the Late Nineteenth Century until Today

1. Heather Sharkey, whom I here wish to thank, sent me in March 2018 the following examples of missionary scholarship from Egypt: W. H. T. Gairdner, a CMS missionary, wrote *Egyptian Colloquial Arabic: A Conversation Grammar*, a work prefiguring the development of AUC's Arabic program, leading eventually to the development of CASA. The earliest version was coauthored with Shaykh Kurayyim Sallam (Cambridge: W. Heffer & Sons, 1917), then reprinted. For his theology, see Michael T. Shelley, "Temple Gairdner of Cairo Revisited," *Islam and Christian-Muslim Relations* 110, no. 3 (1999): 261–78. Other works include Constance Padwick, *Muslim Devotions* (London: Society for Promoting Christian Knowledge, 1961); and C. C. Adams, *Islam and Modernism in Egypt* (London: Oxford University Press, 1968).

2. Lord Cromer, *Modern Egypt* (London: Macmillan, 1908). See also the heavily documented work of Roger Owen, *Lord Cromer: Victorian Imperialist, Edwardian Proconsul* (Oxford: Oxford Univ. Press, 2004). For statistics of the considerable sales and reviews of *Modern Egypt* in the United States and the UK, see Owen, *Lord Cromer*, 359–62. In choosing Cromer over Alfred Milner or other knowledgeable British colonial writers of the period on Egypt, the deciding factor was Cromer's being well known in the United States and not simply in the UK.

3. The influence of British India on British Egypt is another early strand of some importance. See Roger Owen, "The Influence of Lord Cromer's Indian Experience on British Policy in Egypt, 1883–1907," in *St. Antony's Papers* no. 17, ed. Albert Habib Hourani (Oxford: Oxford Univ. Press, 1965, 109–39); and Robert L.

Tignor, "The Indianization of the Egyptian Administration under British Rule," *American Historical Review* 68 (1963): 636–61.

4. Some scholars even doubt how much the Egyptian economy rested on agriculture. The export-oriented monoculture that we find in the nineteenth century we now believe to be unprecedented. As research shows, Egypt may have been a breadbasket or a granary at different times, but it was always also more than that. For example, the medievalist Gladys Frantz-Murphy, drawing on a range of primary sources and somewhat supported by the work of Egyptian scholars such as Yusuf Raghib, argues that the economic prosperity of medieval Egypt hinged on the textile industry ("A New Interpretation of the Economic History of Medieval Egypt: The Role of the Textile Industry 254–567/868–1171," *Journal of the Economic and Social History of the Orient* 24, no. 3 [October 1981]: 274–97). Her argument about the country's economic decline in later centuries is that it was not simply external competition but also change in the policy of the elite toward its investments. In A. L. Udovitch, "International Trade and the Medieval Egyptian Countryside," in *Agriculture in Egypt from Pharaonic to Modern Times*, ed. Alan K. Bowman and Eugene Rogan (Oxford: Oxford Univ. Press, 1999), 267–86, the author also writes that the main source of revenue of the state came from the urban economy from the production and sale of textiles and from port taxes. Agriculture was not intensive, and the production of food for the local area was definitely a preoccupation. Egypt sometimes supplied some food as tribute to the Ottomans and Holy Cities.

Beginning in the 1960s, studies of the Ottoman period (1517–1798) underwent a major transformation with the work of André Raymond. Raymond concluded from a range of archival sources that the bulk of the state revenue did not come from agriculture but from port taxes and from the urban economy more generally (*Artisans et commerçants au Caire au XVIIIᵉ siècle* [Damascus: IFAO, 1973/74]). Subsequently, Nelly Hanna showed how the artisan Abu Taqiyya amassed wealth and was able to place his men inside the military political elite (*Making Big Money in 1600* [Syracuse, NY: Syracuse Univ. Press, 1998]). This finding challenged the older view that had a purely Turkic military ruling class supported by the land tax. In my own earlier work, I found an eighteenth-century cultural revival supportive of capitalism where the Oriental despotism paradigm predicted decline and stagnation. See Peter Gran, *Islamic Roots of Capitalism: Egypt, 1760–1840* (Syracuse, NY: Syracuse Univ. Press, 1998).

5. Michael Kalin, "Hidden Pharaohs: Egypt, Engineers, and the Modern Hydraulic" (MA thesis, Trinity College, Oxford, 2006). Most recently, Alan Mikhail, in *Nature and Empire in Ottoman Egypt: An Environmental History* (Cambridge: Cambridge Univ. Press, 2012), supplies more detail supporting these contentions.

6. Jennifer Kernaghan, "Lord Cromer as Orientalist and Social Engineer in Egypt, 1882–1907" (MA thesis, Univ. of British Columbia, 1993), 118, 168.

Influenced by Edward Said and Timothy Mitchell, Kernaghan's reading of Cromer's writings ferrets out his actual motives for what he was doing in Egypt.

7. Owen, *Lord Cromer*, 391–404.

8. As an aside, it is important to acknowledge that other scholarly work was being produced in this period. Several American works of scholarship on modern Egypt appeared but, given that they dealt with demography, as in the case of W. Wendell Cleland's *The Population Problem in Egypt* (Lancaster, PA: Science Press, 1936), and educational reform, as in the case of Russell Galt's *The Effects of Centralization on Education in Modern Egypt* (Cairo: American Univ. in Cairo Press, 1936), and not with the inner workings of government, which the Oriental despotism paradigm prioritized, they are made to seem more peripheral.

9. Lord George Lloyd, *Egypt since Cromer* (London: Macmillan, 1933).

10. Henry Dodwell, *The Founder of Modern Egypt: A Study of Muhammad Ali* (Cambridge: Cambridge Univ. Press, 1931).

11. Valentine Chirol, *The Egyptian Problem* (London: Macmillan, 1921); Clayton R. Koppes, "Captain Mahan, General Gordon, and the Origins of the Term 'Middle East,'" *Middle East Studies* 12 (1976): 95–98. Koppes believes the term "Middle East" was being used before Chirol. One could look at Chirol's writing as punditry, but scholars continue to echo his justification for England's role in Egypt and for the Empire in general, suggesting a kind of influence exceeding that of other writers—for example, George Young, *Egypt* (New York: Scribner's, 1927); and P. G. Elgood, *The Transit of Egypt* (London: Edward Arnold, 1928). For these references I am indebted to the useful collection edited by Arthur Goldschmidt, Amy Johnson, and Barak Salmoni, *Re-Envisioning Egypt, 1919–1952* (Cairo: American Univ. in Cairo Press, 2005), 467.

12. Walter Laqueur, *Nasser's Egypt* (London: Weidenfeld & Nicolson, 1956), 34. For the eventual British recovery from the debacle of the Suez War, one may turn to the somewhat optimistic account of Noel Brehony and Ayman El-Desouky, eds., *British-Egyptian Relations from Suez to the Present Day* (London: Saqi, 2007); or to a more sobering account, stressing how Eden's secret and illegal collaboration and the documents surrounding what happened have been buried by the British state, from Peter J. Beck, "'The Less Said about Suez the Better': British Governments and the Politics of Suez's History, 1956–1967," *English Historical Review* 127, no. 508 (June 2009): 605–40.

13. P. J. Vatikiotis, *Nasser and His Generation* (London: Croom Helm, 1978). To document the breakdown of British control of the modern field, another approach would be to look at Bernard Lewis and P. M. Holt, eds., *Historians of the Middle East* (London: Oxford Univ. Press, 1962). This work is largely devoted to the study of European specialists in medieval Islamic subjects. Specialists in the modern period, by way of contrast, appear almost as an afterthought.

14. Not only was there the work of the Irish critic and literary figure W. S. Blunt on 'Urabi (see above), but there was the Pan-African anticolonialism of Duse Mohamed's *In the Land of the Pharaohs* (London: Stanley Paul, 1911). This writer of Egyptian Sudanese background lived from 1866 to 1945. He was an important journalist in the UK.

15. H. A. R. Gibb, *Modern Trends in Islam* (Chicago: Univ. of Chicago Press, 1947), 1–2, 55–56, and *Mohammedanism* (London: Oxford Univ. Press, 1949).

16. Mark Curtis, *Secret Affairs: Britain's Collusion with Radical Islam* (London: Serpent's Tail, 2012), 24, gives basic data on the UK and the Muslim Brotherhood, but does not name many names; see James (Jamal-Addin) Heyworth Dunne, *Religious and Political Trends in Modern Egypt* (Washington, DC: N.p., 1950), which suggests the author's very close relations with the MB; see also his book *Land Tenure in Islam* (Cairo: Misr, 1950), which could be read the same way. In the latter book, the author opposes the idea of a state program of land reform (termed "land fragmentation") as being against Islam. Two other books of note on the Muslim Brotherhood written by American scholars with government ties appeared in the 1960s: Christina P. Harris, *Nationalism and Revolution in Egypt: The Role of the Muslim Brotherhood* (Stanford, CA: Hoover Institute, 1964); and Richard P. Mitchell, *The Society of the Muslim Brothers* (London: Oxford Univ. Press, 1969).

17. Moustafa M. Mosharrafa, *Cultural Survey of Modern Egypt*, vol. 1 (London: Longmans, 1947/48), 5; vol. 2, 55, 69; Mohamed Rifaat, *The Awakening of Modern Egypt* (London: Longmans, 1947), v–vi, 234.

18. One of the best-known works of the Pharaonic School tradition in the UK was on the Copts in modern times: S. H. Leeder, *Modern Sons of the Pharaohs* (London: Hodder & Stoughton, 1918).

19. Samuel Zwemer, "The Earl of Cromer on Islam," *Missionary Review of the World* 31 (1908): 649–54; Duncan Black Macdonald, *The Religious Attitude and Life in Islam* (London: Darf, 1909). A general overview on the history of the Hartford Seminary can be found in Willem Bijlefeld, "A Century of Arabic and Islamic Studies at Hartford Seminary," *Muslim World* 83 (1993): 103–17.

20. Doubtless the single most famous attack on Cromer by name by an Egyptian author was the one by Shaykh 'Ali Yusuf, the editor of the newspaper *Al-Mu'ayyad*, a publication combining religious and national elements. See *Rudd Sa'adat al-Shaykh 'Ali Yusuf 'ala Khutbat al-Lurd Krumir* (Cairo: al-Wa'iz, 1907). As regards the countering of missionary activity on a more ongoing basis, see Umar Ryad, "Muslim Response to Missionary Activities in Egypt: With a Special Reference to the al-Azhar High Corps of 'Ulama' (1925–1935)," in *New Faith in Ancient Lands: Western Missions in the Middle East in the Nineteenth and Early Twentieth Centuries*, ed. Heleen Murre-van den Berg (Leiden, Netherlands: Brill, 2006), 281–307; but, equally, secular writers such as the early Mahmud 'Abbas al-'Aqqad also weighed in (287). Beth

Baron, *The Orphan Scandal and the Rise of the Muslim Brotherhood* (Stanford, CA: Stanford Univ. Press, 2014). The missionary tradition adjusted, however, by adopting dialogue and some idea of Islamic modernism; see Heather Sharkey, *American Evangelicals in Egypt: Missionary Encounters in an Age of Empire* (Princeton, NJ: Princeton Univ. Press, 2008); and Ryad, "Muslim Response to Missionary Activities." See also C. C. Adams, *Islam and Modernism in Egypt: A Study of the Modern Reform Movement Initiated by Muhammad Abduh* (Oxford: Oxford Univ. Press, 1933).

21. Lord Cromer, "The Government of Subject Races," *Edinburgh Review* (January 1908): 3–53; Donald M. Reid, "Cromer and the Classics: Imperialism, Nationalism, and the Greco-Roman Past in Modern Egypt," *Middle Eastern Studies* 12, no. 1 (1992): 1–29. The memory of Cromer has not gone away. In more recent years, Cromer's career, and that of several of his contemporaries, found their way into the research of Hannah Arendt in *The Origins of Totalitarianism* as well as that of other writers concerned with the origins of the Final Solution. See Yehouda Shenhav, "Beyond 'Instrumental Rationality': Lord Cromer and the Imperial Roots of Eichmann's Bureaucracy," *Journal of Genocide Research* 15 (2013): 379–99.

22. This last view was common among economic historians—for example, Charles Issawi, "Egypt since 1800: A Study in Lopsided Development," *Journal of Economic History* 21 (1961): 1–25; and A. E. Crouchley, *The Economic Development of Modern Egypt* (London: Longmans, Green, 1938).

23. To repeat a point made earlier, in approaching the US study of the Middle East in this period in terms of the Cold War, the Development Revolution, and the Puritan tradition instead of simply oil and Palestine, this book is trying to explain the development of American studies of Egypt and not American Middle East studies as a whole. For the latter, see Zachary Lockman, *Field Notes: The Making of Middle East Studies in the United States* (Stanford, CA: Stanford Univ. Press, 2016); and Osamah Khalil, *America's Dream Palaces* (Cambridge, MA: Harvard Univ. Press, 2016).

24. Morroe Berger, *Islam in Egypt Today* (Cambridge: Cambridge Univ. Press, 1970); Nadav Safran, *Egypt in Search of Political Community* (Cambridge, MA: Harvard Univ. Press, 1961).

25. Take, for example, Aziz Suryal 'Atiya, founder of the Middle East Center in Utah (1960–) and editor of the *Coptic Encyclopedia*.

26. Afaf Marsot, *Egypt in the Reign of Muhammad 'Ali* (Cambridge: Cambridge Univ. Press, 1984), and *Egypt and Cromer* (New York: Frederick A. Praeger, 1969).

27. More recent work such as Leslie Peirce's *The Imperial Harem* (New York: Oxford Univ. Press, 1993) views this as the period of the Queen Mother. Challenging the idea of decline, see Rifa'at Abou-El-Haj, *Formation of the Modern State* (Albany: State Univ. of New York Press, 1991).

28. Lockman, *Field Notes*, 187.

29. This last is spelled out in works such as John Perkins, *Confessions of an Economic Hit Man* (New York: Plume, 2005) or in movies such as *Syriana* (Stephen Gaghan, 2005).

30. Margot Badran, *Feminists, Islam, and Nation: Gender and the Making of Modern Egypt* (Princeton, NJ: Princeton Univ. Press, 1995) provides an institutional history of the woman's movement in Egypt.

31. Beth Baron, *Egypt as a Woman: Nationalism, Gender, and Politics* (Berkeley: Univ. of California Press, 2005).

32. Judith Tucker, *Women in Nineteenth-Century Egypt* (Cambridge: Cambridge Univ. Press, 1985); see also Judith Gran, "Impact of the World Market on Egyptian Women," *Middle East Report*, no. 58 (1977): 3–7.

33. Cathlyn Mariscotti, *Gender and Class in the Egyptian Women's Movement, 1929–1935* (Syracuse, NY: Syracuse Univ. Press, 2008).

34. Will Hanley, "Grieving Cosmopolitanism in Middle East Studies," *History Compass* 6, no. 5 (2008): 1346–67.

35. Salah Haridi, *Al-Jaliyat fi madinat al-Iskandariyah fi al-ʿAsr al-ʿUthmani, 923–1213 H/1517–1798 M: Dirasah watha'iqiyah min sijillat al-Mahkamah al-Sharʿiyah* (Giza: Ayn, 2004).

36. Deborah A. Starr, "Recuperating Cosmopolitan Alexandria: Circulation of Narratives and Narratives of Circulation," *Cities* 22, no. 3 (2005): 217–28.

37. Bruce Stanley, "Middle East City Networks and the 'New Urbanism,'" *Cities* 22, no. 3 (2005): 189–99.

38. Stanley, "Middle East City Networks," 196.

39. Umar Ryad, *Islamic Reformism and Christianity: A Critical Reading of the Works of Muhammad Rashid Rida* (Leiden: Brill, 2009); a serious attempt to get at the cultural impact of the missionaries in Lebanon is Ussama Makdisi, *Artillery of Heaven* (Ithaca, NY: Cornell Univ. Press, 2008).

40. Roxanne Euben, *Enemy in the Mirror: Islamic Fundamentalism and the Limits of Modern Rationalism* (Princeton, NJ: Princeton Univ. Press, 1999).

41. Marilyn Booth, *May Her Likes Be Multiplied: Biography and Gender Politics in Modern Egypt* (Berkeley: Univ. of California Press, 2001).

42. In Europe, see *La Nahda: Réveils de la pensée en langue arabe, Approches, perspectives*, ed. Karam Rizq and Dominique Avon (Jounieh, Lebanon, 2009); and, in the United States, Samah Selim, "The Nahda, Popular Fiction, and the Politics of Translation," *MIT-EJMES* 4 (2004): 71–90; and Bernard Lewis, *Land of Enchanters: Egyptian Short Stories from the Earliest Times to the Present Day* (Princeton, NJ: Princeton Univ. Press, 1948, 2001).

43. Indira Falk Gesink, "'Chaos on the Earth': Subjective Truths versus Communal Unity in Islamic Law and the Rise of Militant Islam," *American Historical Review* 108, no. 3 (2003): 710–33.

44. Gran, *Islamic Roots of Capitalism*, 139–43; Peter Gran, "Quest for a Historical Interpretation of the Life of Shaykh al-Azhar Ibrahim al-Bajuri," in *Reform or Modernization?*, ed. Ra'uf 'Abbas Hamid (Cairo: Al-Majlis al-A'la lil-Thaqafah, 1999), 59–92.

45. Irfan Ahmad, "Genealogy of the Islamic State: Reflections on Maududi's Political Thought and Islamism," *JRAI* (2009): S145–62.

46. Amira El-Azhary Sonbol, "A History of Marriage Contracts in Egypt," in *The Islamic Marriage Contract*, ed. Asifa Quraishi and Frank E. Vogel (Cambridge, MA: Harvard Univ. Press, 2008), 87–122.

47. Examples include Diane Singerman, *Avenues of Participation: Family, Politics, and Networks in Urban Quarters of Cairo* (Princeton, NJ: Princeton Univ. Press, 1995); and Lila Abu-Lughod, "Zones of Theory in the Anthropology of the Arab World," *Annual Review of Anthropology* 18 (1989): 267–306.

48. Lila Abu-Lughod, "The Romance of Resistance: Tracing Transformations of Power through Bedouin Women," *American Ethnologist* 17, no. 1 (1990): 41–55, and "Modest Women, Subversive Poems: The Politics of Love in an Egyptian Bedouin Society," *Bulletin British Society for Middle Eastern Studies* 13, no. 2 (1986): 159–68.

49. Lila Abu-Lughod, *Dramas of Nationhood: The Politics of Television in Egypt* (Chicago: Univ. of Chicago Press, 2005).

50. Timothy Mitchell, *Colonizing Egypt* (Berkeley: Univ. of California Press, 1988).

51. Timothy Mitchell, *Rule of Experts* (Berkeley: Univ. of California Press, 2002). A more recent work also emphasizing the serendipitous character of history and the role of ordinary people is Asef Bayat, *Life as Politics: How Ordinary People Change the Middle East* (Stanford, CA: Stanford Univ. Press, 2010). See also works by Khaled Fahmy, Mervat Hatem, and Talal Asad, each of whom picked up on Foucault's characterizations of the state as inspector, measurer, and coercer and took these insights in different directions, bringing them to the idea of dystopia. And why not? Dystopia is the order of the day. Anyone might be struck by the similarity of Foucault's master concept of governmentality to the idea of the total power of the Oriental despot; there are some interesting parallels.

52. Zeinab Abul-Magd, *Imagined Empires* (Berkeley: Univ. of California Press, 2013); Mitchell, *Colonizing Egypt*; Timothy Mitchell, "America's Egypt: Discourse of the Development Industry," *Middle East Report*, no. 169 (March–April 1991): 18–34, 36.

53. Vickie Langohr, "Too Much Civil Society, Too Little Politics? Egypt and Other Liberalizing Arab Regimes," *Comparative Politics* 36, no. 2 (January 2004): 181–204; Jason Brownlee, *Authoritarianism in an Age of Democratization* (Cambridge: Cambridge Univ. Press, 2007). An essay critiquing the policy studies of the

period is Ali Ahmida's "Inventing or Recovering 'Civil Society' in the Middle East," *Critique: Journal of Critical Studies of the Middle East* 6 (1997): 127–34.

54. Robert Springborg, "Patrimonialism and Policy-Making in Egypt: Nasser and Sadat and the Tenure Policy for Reclaimed Lands," *Middle Eastern Studies* 15, no. 1 (1979): 49–69.

55. Yahya Sadowski, *Political Vegetables: Businessman and Bureaucrat in the Development of Egyptian Agriculture* (Washington, DC: Brookings Institute, 1991), 312–22.

56. Yoav Di Capua, *Gatekeepers of the Arab Past: Historians and History Writing in Twentieth-Century Egypt* (Berkeley: Univ. of California Press, 2009), 337–43.

57. Recent overviews of knowledge trends in Egyptian history writing and in scholarship in the Middle East more generally suggest the emergence of a recognition that the field's center of gravity is much more Egyptian than was previously thought. See Di Capua, *Gatekeepers of the Arab Past*; and Anthony Gorman, *Historians, State, and Politics in Twentieth-Century Egypt: Contesting the Nation* (London: Routledge Curzon, 2003). Even more recently, in the collection *Middle East Studies for the New Millennium*, ed. Seteney Shami and Cynthia Miller-Idriss (New York: New York Univ. Press, 2016), a group of area specialists pore over the recent trajectory of the field by discipline with a concluding section on the politics of knowledge. The tone throughout is critical of the censorship surrounding controversial issues, the dependence on the government for funding, imbalances, and sundry other topics.

2. The Orthodox Narrative

1. M. W. Daly, ed., *The Cambridge History of Egypt, Vol. 2: Modern Egypt from 1517 to the End of the Twentieth Century* (Cambridge: Cambridge Univ. Press, 1988).

2. For a recent French work on 1798 with fewer expressions of doubt, see Patrice Bret, *L'expédition d'Égypte, une entreprise des lumières 1798–1801* (Cachan: Technique et documentation, 1999).

3. Daly, *Cambridge History of Egypt*, 1–33.

4. Daly, 34–58.

5. Daly, 59–86. More recent work, bearing out the pioneering studies of Nelly Hanna, has been showing that, while such ideas as Mamluk misrule causing decline are no longer tenable, there certainly are historical conjunctures to be explained. According to one scholar, the guilds controlled the textile workshops during the sixteenth and seventeenth centuries, but, with the coming of the eighteenth century, the control of the guilds began to decline. Merchants gained the upper hand over the guilds and, by extension, over the workers. As was the case in other countries, like Egypt, the last century in which the worker could be said to have power in the workplace in modern history was the seventeenth. Thereafter, the worker's power declined, and we enter into the all-too-familiar history of

contemporary capitalism, in which the worker has little power; Nasir 'Uthman, "La Production Textile: Rosette au XVIIIᵉ siècle," *Revue Méditerranéenne*, no. 29 (2008): 25–36. Majdi Jirjis makes an analogous argument about Coptic freedom and its decline. While acknowledging the cultural patronage of the Coptic notables of the eighteenth century, he notes how they smothered both the Church and the rest of the laity, who could do little in the face of their power. "Athar al-arakhina' 'ala awda' al-qibti fi-l-qarn al-thamin 'ashar," *Annales Islamologiques* 34 (2000): 23–44. It appears that the relative freedom of the Coptic masses reached its high point in the later seventeenth century, when the power of the Church and notables was more balanced; the eighteenth century marked the beginning of the modern, lopsided distribution of power, favoring the Church or the merchant class or some alliance of the two against the rest. M. Girguis, "The Coptic Community in the Ottoman Period," in *Society and Economy in Egypt and the Eastern Mediterranean, 1600–1900*, ed. Nelly Hanna and Ra'uf Abbas Hamid (Cairo: American Univ. in Cairo Press, 2005), 201–16. A third historian, Husam 'Abd al-Mu'ti, whose career has long been focused on trade and production in Ottoman Egypt, also cuts across the supposed 1798 watershed in his interpretation. In one of his books, he argues that in the Ottoman period the North African merchant community in Cairo was more or less completely integrated into the affairs of Egypt. *Al-'A'ilah wa-l-tharwa* (Cairo: GEBO, 2008). And, while doubtless more work is needed to fully understand this, this earlier integration may help explain how speedily the Maghariba melted into Egyptian society and disappeared when the trade route economy they had been sustaining declined in the early nineteenth century. Reading this work, one wonders about the general assumption of Egyptian isolation found in the Oriental despotism paradigm. If the merchants of Fez were active in Cairo at the time the United States signed a treaty with the King of Morocco and at a time when the King had ambassadors in Europe, where is the isolation? What difference, then, does 1798 make? A similar critique of the theme of isolation can also be found in 'Abd al-Mu'ti's first book, where we learn how deeply the Egyptian mercantile and 'ulama' world was tied into the affairs of the Hidjaz, so much so that it was not uncommon for Egyptian merchants and 'ulama' to leave Egypt to make their career there, so that when the French invaded Egypt it was not surprising to find contingents from the Hidjaz joining the Egyptians in Egypt in their fight. *Al-'Alaqat al-Misriya al-Hijaziya fi'l-qarn al-thamin 'ashar* (Cairo: GEBO, 1999), 315ff. Of these merchants, the one who has been studied in the most detail is Muhammad al-Mahruqi, a dynamic figure who began his career in Qina in the Qusayr trade but later followed certain members of his family to Cairo, where he continued to be involved in trade—as, for example, in the Hidjaz, still later collaborating with Muhammad 'Ali in the Wahhabi campaign. See Pascale Ghazaleh, *Fortunes urbaines et strategies sociales* (Cairo: IFAO, 2010), vol. 1, 162ff. I would hypothesize that it is the weight of this growing body of scholarship that has made the maintenance of the dominant paradigm more and more difficult, especially in Egypt, where many scholars are aware of these newer findings.

6. Ghazaleh, *Fortunes urbaines et strategies sociales*, 113–38.

7. Ghazaleh, 139–79.

8. Jean Batou, "Nineteenth-Century Attempted Escapes from the Periphery: The Cases of Egypt and Paraguay," *Review* 16, no. 3 (1993): 279–95. This is drawn from his larger study of attempted escapes from underdevelopment.

9. Daly, *Cambridge History of Egypt*, 180–97.

10. Daly, 198–216.

11. Daly, 217–38.

12. Daly, 239–51.

13. Daly, 252–84.

14. Daly, 285–308.

15. Daly, 309–33.

16. Daly, 334–93.

17. Daly, 394–426; Ahmad Hamid Hijazi, *Izdihar al-adab al-ʿArabi fi al-ʿasr al-ʿuthmani* (Cairo: Dar al-Misriya li-l-ʿUlum, 2012).

18. Daly, *Cambridge History of Egypt*, 87–112.

19. Rethinking the Napoleonic legacy from within its sources has also occupied some Anglo-American scholars—for example, Juan Cole, *Napoleon's Egypt: Invading the Middle East* (New York: St. Martin's, 2007).

20. Ibrahim and ʿAbbas Hamid, *Miʾatay ʿam*, 29–55; Vivant Denon, *Voyage dans la basse et la haute Égypte pendant les campagnes du Général Bonaparte* (Paris: P. Didot, 1802).

21. Ibrahim and ʿAbbas Hamid, *Miʾatay ʿam*, 56–106.

22. Ibrahim and ʿAbbas Hamid, 107–46.

23. Ibrahim and ʿAbbas Hamid, 147–75. This is a continuation of the author's earlier work, "The Study of Astronomy According to the Chronicle of al-Jabarti," in *Society and Economy in Egypt and the Eastern Mediterranean, 1600–1900*, ed. Nelly Hanna and Raʾuf Abbas Hamid (Cairo: AUC Press, 2005), 181–200. Jane H. Murphy corroborates al-ʿAdl's point about the large number of individuals studying sciences about whom we know little or nothing. As she points out, al-Muradi identified 114 such figures; see "Ahmad al-Damanhuri (1689–1778) and the Utility of Expertise," *Osiris* 25 (2010): 85–103, especially 90.

24. Ibrahim and ʿAbbas Hamid, *Miʾatay ʿam*, 176–93.

25. Ibrahim and ʿAbbas Hamid, 195–213.

26. Ibrahim and ʿAbbas Hamid, 214–55.

27. Ibrahim and ʿAbbas Hamid, 256–82.

28. Ibrahim and ʿAbbas Hamid, 285–325.

29. Ibrahim and ʿAbbas Hamid, 326–58. The methodology of Maha Jad al-Haqq of looking at how closed or open the room in which an ʿAlim is pictured serves to identify 10A (358ff). It is clearly Shaykh Hasan al-ʿAttar, as he was the only one a French painter would think would be looking observantly out at the world. I am sorry to say I misled my CEDEJ colleagues of the 1990s on this. At the time, they thought the ʿAlim in this picture was known as the poet, and I told them that if that was the case, it was a picture of Ismaʿil al-Khashshab, who was then the recognized poet. But this methodology makes it much more likely to be al-ʿAttar, who was also a poet, albeit not such a well-known one.

30. Ibrahim and ʿAbbas Hamid, *Miʾatay ʿam*, 378–90.

31. Ibrahim and ʿAbbas Hamid, 359–77. Moiret's work has been translated into English and edited by Rosemary Brindle (London: Greenhill, 2001) as *Memoirs of Napoleon's Egyptian Expedition, 1798–1801*.

32. Ibrahim and ʿAbbas Hamid, *Miʾatay ʿam*, 391–410.

33. Ibrahim and ʿAbbas Hamid, 413–33.

34. Ibrahim and ʿAbbas Hamid, 434–56.

35. Ibrahim and ʿAbbas Hamid, 459–80. For Madiha Doss's overview of the history of French language pedagogy in Egypt up until today, see "Le français en Égypte: Histoire et présence actuelle," *Cahiers de l'association international des études françaises* 56 (2004): 75–98.

36. Ibrahim and ʿAbbas Hamid, *Miʾatay ʿam*, 481–540.

37. Samir Amin made an effort to have *Islamic Roots* read by the Left by writing a review essay about it for *Monthly Review* (September 1984): 13–21, and then by spelling out a theoretical basis for it through the idea of mercantilism in eighteenth-century Egypt in his book *Eurocentrism* (1988), however, to no apparent avail.

38. Ibrahim and ʿAbbas Hamid, *Miʾatay ʿam*, 541–69.

39. It would be useful to have a study based on the documents of the ministry of education from around 1923 dealing with what the orthodox line for modern history ought to be and why. As the paper discussed above on French influence in Egyptian history suggests, perhaps French experts had some influence in this period.

40. Ibrahim and ʿAbbas Hamid, *Miʾatay ʿam*, 570–617.

41. Ibrahim and ʿAbbas Hamid, 619–28.

42. Ibrahim and ʿAbbas Hamid, 629–36.

43. Ibrahim and ʿAbbas Hamid, 637–46.

44. Ibrahim and ʿAbbas Hamid, 648–65.

45. Ibrahim and ʿAbbas Hamid, 666–74.

46. Ibrahim and 'Abbas Hamid, 675–96.

47. Ibrahim and 'Abbas Hamid, 677–706.

48. Alan Mikhail, "Labor and Environment in Egypt since 1500," *International Labor and Working Class History*, no. 85 (Spring 2014): 10–32.

3. The Orthodox Narrative's Blind Spots

1. Matthew Restall, *Seven Myths of the Spanish Conquest* (New York: Oxford Univ. Press, 2003).

2. Thomas C. Smith, *The Agrarian Origins of Modern Japan* (Stanford, CA: Stanford Univ. Press, 1959); Andrew Gordon, *A Modern History of Japan* (New York: Oxford Univ. Press, 2014).

3. Muhammad al-Arna'ut, "Sanawat Shaykh al-Azhar Hasan al-'Attar fi-l-Albania," *Al-Wafd*, February 25, 2012; *Al-Hayat* (London), February 2, 2012.

4. Peter Gran, "Hasan al-'Attar," in *Essays in Arabic Literary Biography, 1350–1850*, ed. Joseph Lowry and Devin Stewart (Wiesbaden: Harrassowitz, 2009), 56–69.

5. Mahmud Tanahi, *Madkhal ila ta'rikh nashr al-turath al-'Arabi* (Cairo: Maktabah al-Khanji, 1984); *Al-Kitab al-matbu' bi-Misr fi al-qarn al-tasi' 'ashar* (Cairo: Dar al-Hilal, 1996).

6. Sources for the study of al-Tahtawi include his "secular" library in 'Ayn Shams University. His Arabic and Islamic books are in his library in Suhaj; Yusuf Zaydan, *Fihris Makhtutat maktabat Rifa'ah al-Tahtawi*, 3 vols. (Cairo: ALECSO, 1996). For the attempt to consolidate his more secular and more religious works, see Muhammad 'Imarah, *Al-A'mal al-kamilah li Rifa'ah al-Tahtawi*, 5 vols. (Beirut: Muassasah al-'Arabiyah lil-Dirasat wa al-Nashr , 1973).

7. Al-Arna'ut, "Sanawat Shaykh al-Azhar Hasan al-'Attar fi-l-Albania."

8. Perhaps al-'Attar wrote the unlocated "Al-Risala fi hall lughz ba'd al-'ulama' min Latbalun" manuscript while he was there, the title presumably referring to the South Albanian town of Tepelene.

9. Heath Lowery and Ismail Erunsel, *Remembering One's Roots: Mehmed Ali Pasha's Links to the Macedonian Town of Kavala* (Istanbul: Bahja Shahir Univ. and the Mohamed Ali Institute of Kavala, Greece, 2011).

10. Afaf Marsot, *Egypt in the Age of Muhammad 'Ali* (Cambridge: Cambridge Univ. Press, 1984).

11. Rainer Broemer, "Kulturgeschichte der Osmanischen Medizin: Anatomie von Ibn al-Nafīs und Vesal zu Şanizade und Hasan al-'Attār," in *Medizingeschichte im Rheinland: Beiträge des Rheinischen Kreises der Medizinhistoriker (Schriften des Rheinischen Kreises der Medizinhistoriker 1)*, ed. Dominik Groß and Axel Karenberg (Kassel: Kassel Univ. Press, 2009), 267–76.

4. Hypothesizing the Ottoman-Egyptian Roots of Modern Egypt

1. Samir Amin, *Eurocentrism*, 2nd ed. (New York: Monthly Review, 2009), introduces the idea of Ottoman Egyptian mercantilism. See also Peter Gran, *Rise of the Rich* (Syracuse, NY: Syracuse Univ. Press, 2010), 60–147; and Nelly Hanna, *Ottoman Egypt and the Emergence of the Modern World* (Cairo: American Univ. in Cairo Press, 2014). For a general bibliography, see I. Wallerstein, *Modern World System, Vol. 2: Mercantilism and the Consolidation of the European World Economy* (Berkeley: Univ. of California Press, 2011). For the historiographical issues arising from the study of the transition of Egypt from the Mamluks to the Ottomans, see ʿImad Abu-Ghazi, *Al-Ihtilal al-ʿUthmani li-Misr wa suqut dawlah al-mamalik* (Cairo: Mirit, 2019).

2. A model for this chapter is Barrington Moore, *Social Origins of Dictatorship and Democracy: Lord and Peasant in the Making of the Modern World* (Boston: Beacon Press, 1966), a pioneering work attempting to clarify the nature of and development of modern power structures. I benefited from this in working out the four basic hegemonies of modern world capitalism in *Beyond Eurocentrism: A New View of Modern World History* (Syracuse, NY: Syracuse Univ. Press, 1996); see, especially, 88–192 on the "Italian Road."

3. Nelly Hanna, *Making Big Money in 1600* (Syracuse, NY: Syracuse Univ. Press, 1998).

4. Among the features of a country entering the modern market was the rise in the number of destitute people, who in some instances experienced near starvation due to inadequate access to food. This was explained (and explained away) in various famous works of the eighteenth and nineteenth centuries—for example, Robert Malthus, *An Essay on the Principle of Population* (1798). Malthus focused on how population growth would lead to food scarcity.

5. Antonio Gramsci's various writings on hegemony remain the principal source for this type of analysis. See *Prison Notebooks*, 3 vols. (New York: Columbia Univ. Press, 2011), all annotated by Joseph Buttigieg.

6. Silvia Federici, *Caliban and the Witch* (New York: Automedia, 2009); Friedrich Engels, *Origins of the Family, Private Property, and the State* (Chicago: Charles H. Kerr, 1909); Maria Mies, *Patriarchy and Accumulation on a World Scale* (London: Zed, 1986); Amira El-Azhary Sonbol, "A History of Marriage Contracts in Egypt," in *The Islamic Marriage Contract*, ed. Asifa Quraishi and Frank E. Vogel (Cambridge: Harvard Univ. Press, 2008), 87–122. For general reference, see Afaf Marsot, *Women and Men in Late Eighteenth-Century Egypt* (Austin: Univ. of Texas Press, 2008); for Mamluk women, see Ahmed Abd al-Raziq, *La Femme au temps des Mamluks en Égypte* (Cairo: IFAO, 1973). Studies of women in what appears to be a comparable context (e.g., seventeenth- to eighteenth-century Italy, Spain, and

Mexico) show a women's literary culture—for example, Catherine Marie Jaffe, *Eve's Enlightenment* (Baton Rouge: Louisiana State Univ. Press, 2009). In Nasir 'Uthman, *Qabla ma ya'ti al-gharb* (Cairo: Dar al-Kutub, 2006), 125–26, examples of learned women appear, but Egyptian women's culture remains to be studied.

Another major theme of early modern history yet to be explored in the case of Egypt is that of the dynastic marriage; dynastic marriages sometimes gave certain women considerable power. See, as a general reference, Joan Palos and Magdalena Sanchez, eds., *Early Modern Dynastic Marriages and Cultural Transfer* (London: Routledge, 2016). For the last female lawmaker in the Ottoman-Arab world of the early sixteenth century, see Emil Homerin, "'A'ishah al-Ba'uniyah," in *Essays in Arabic Literary Biography, 1350–1850*, ed. Joseph E. Lowry and Devin J. Stewart (Wiesbaden: Harrassowitz, 2009), 21–26.

7. Zeinab Abul-Magd, *Imagined Empires: A History of Revolt in Egypt* (Berkeley: Univ. of California Press, 2013); Peter Gran, "Upper Egypt in Modern History: A Southern Question," in *Upper Egypt: Identity and Change*, ed. Nicholas Hopkins and Reem Saad (Cairo: American Univ. in Cairo Press, 2004), 79–96.

8. Caste is most clearly seen as a tool of stratification in studies of India. Two recent books on caste as a strategy in the case of early modern India seem useful for Egypt: Susan Bayly, *Caste, Society, and Politics in India from the Eighteenth Century to the Modern Age* (Cambridge: Cambridge Univ. Press, 1999); and Audrey Truschke, *Culture of Encounters: Sanskrit at the Mughal Court* (New York: Columbia Univ. Press, 2016) both note the collaboration of Hindu and Muslim elites in the years before British colonialism. Truschke points out how nonetheless the British played one group against the other thereafter.

9. Doris Behrens-Abouseif, *Egypt's Adjustment to Ottoman Rule* (Leiden: Brill, 1994), 75; Muhammad al-Dali, *Al-Khitab al-siyasi al-sufi fi Misr* (Cairo: Dar al-Kutub, 2004). Despite the Ottoman patronage of Sufism, one also finds secular poetry continuing; see Ahmad Hijazi, *Izdihar al-adab al-'Arabi fi-l-'asr al-'Uthmani* (Cairo: N.p., 2012). With the decline of Ottoman influence in the eighteenth century, one encounters the beginning of a more general resecularization. With this there appears to have been a sort of appreciation of the Cartesian worldview of the value of practical science; see Jane H. Murphy, "Ahmad al-Damanhuri (1689–1778) and the Utility of Expertise in Early Modern Ottoman Egypt," *Osiris* 25 (2010): 85–103. And, from the eighteenth century onward, one finds praise for practical science but also criticism. Taha Hussein, the dean of Arabic letters, embraced it but looked at it as too spiritually impoverished to be the basis of philosophy. Here the parallels to Italy stand out. For Italy, the philosophical critique of worshipping science began with Giambattista Vico, *On the Study Methods of Our Times (1708–9)*, continuing on to Croce in the twentieth century. For the widening use of the idea of the Enlightenment, see Richard Butterwick-Pawlikowski, Simon Davies, and Gabriel Sanchez

Espinosa, eds., *Peripheries of the Enlightenment* (Oxford: Oxford Univ. Press, 2008). For the Egyptian enlightenment, see Peter Gran, *Islamic Roots of Capitalism: Egypt, 1760–1840* (Syracuse, NY: Syracuse Univ. Press, 1998), 35–91.

   10. Hossam M. Issa, *Capitalisme et sociétés anonymes en Égypte* (Paris: CNRS, 1970).

Selected Bibliography

The material listed below served as a basis for the research, to be distinguished from many other works alluded to in passing in the notes, which were intended as illustrative material.

Arabic Language

'Abd al-Mu'ti, Husam. *Al-'Alaqat al-Misriya al-Hijaziya fi'l-qarn al-thamin 'ashar*. Cairo: GEBO, 1999.

———. *Al-'A'ilah wa-l-tharwa*. Cairo: GEBO, 2008.

Abu-Ghazi, 'Imad. *Al-Ihtilal al-'Uthmani li-Misr wa suqut dawlah al-mamalik*. Cairo: Mirit, 2019.

al-Arna'ut, Muhammad. *Al-Jaliyah al-Makhfiyah: Fusul min ta'rikh al-Alban fi Misr*. Cairo: Shuruq, 2018.

———. "Sanawat Shaykh al-Azhar Hasan al-'Attar fi-l-Albania." *Al-Wafd*, February 25, 2012; *Al-Hayat* (London), February 2, 2012.

'Atiyyah al-Shafi'i, Shuhdi. *Tatawwur al-haraka al-wataniya al-Misriya, 1882–1956*. Cairo: Dar al-Shuhdi, 1957.

al-'Attar, Hasan. "Al-Risala fi hall lughz ba'd al-'ulama' min Latbalun." Unlocated manuscript.

Curiel, Henri. *Awraq Hinri Kuryil wa-al-harakah al-shuyu'iyah al-Misriyah*. Cairo: Sina lil-nashr, 1988.

Haridi, Salah. *Al-Jaliyat fi madinat al-Iskandariyah fi al-'Asr al-'Uthmani, 923–1213 H/1517–1798 M: Dirasah watha'iqiyah min sijillat al-Mahkamah al-Shar'iyah*. Giza: 'Ayn, 2004.

Hijazi, Ahmad Hamid. *Izdihar al-adab al-'Arabi fi al-'asr al-'uthmani*. Cairo: Dar al-Misriya li-l-'Ulum, 2012.

Ibrahim, Nasir A. *Al-Azamat al-ijtima'iyya fi Misr fi-l-qarn al-sabi' 'ashar*. Cairo: Dar al-Afaq al-'Arabiyya, 1998.

Ibrahim, Nasir A., and 'Abbas Hamid, Ra'uf, eds. *Mi'atay 'am 'ala al-hamlah al-firansiya (Ru'ya Misriyah)*. Cairo: Maktabat al-Dar al-'Arabiyyah li-l-Kitab, 2008.

'Imarah, Muhammad. *Al-A'mal al-kamilah li-Rifa'ah al-Tahtawi*. 5 vols. Beirut: Muassasah al-'Arabiyah li-l-Dirasat wa al-Nashr, 1973.

'Izz al-Din, Amin. *Ta'rikh al-tabaqah al-'amilah al-Misriyah: Mundhu nush-uiha hattá sanat 1970*. Cairo: Dar al-Ghad al-'Arabi, 1987.

Jirjis, Majdi. "Athar al-arakhina' 'ala awda' al-qibti fi-l-qarn al-thamin 'ashar." *Annales Islamologiques* 34 (2000): 23–44.

Mahmud, Yahya' Muhammad. *Al-Dayyun al-'amm*. Cairo: N.p., 1998.

Mitwalli, Mahmud. *Al-Usul al-ta'rikhiyya li-l ra'smaliyya al-misriyya wa ta-tawwuruha*. Cairo: N.p., 1974.

Sadiq Sa'd, Ahmad. *Ta'rikh al-'Arab al-ijtima'i: Tahawwul al-takwin al-Misri min al-namat al-Asiyawi ilá al-namat al-ra'smali*. Beirut: N.p., 1981.

Tanahi, Mahmud. *Al-Kitab al-matbu' bi-Misr fi al-qarn al-tasi' 'ashar*. Cairo: Dar al-Hilal, 1996.

———. *Madkhal ila ta'rikh nashr al-turath al-'Arabi*. Cairo: Maktabah al-Khanji, 1984.

Yusuf, Shaykh 'Ali. *Rudd Sa'adat al-Shaykh 'Ali Yusuf 'ala Khutbat al-Lurd Krumir*. Cairo: al-Wa'iz, 1907.

Zaydan, Yusuf. *Fihris Makhtutat maktabat Rifa'ah al-Tahtawi*. 3 vols. Cairo: ALECSO, 1996.

European Languages

Abdel-Malek, Anouar. *Egypt Military Society*. New York: Random House, 1968.

Abou-El-Haj, Rifa'at. *Formation of the Modern State*. Albany: State Univ. of New York Press, 1991.

Abul-Magd, Zeinab. *Imagined Empires: A History of Revolt in Egypt*. Berkeley: Univ. of California Press, 2013.

Abu-Lughod, Lila. *Dramas of Nationhood: The Politics of Television in Egypt*. Chicago: Univ. of Chicago Press, 2005.

———. "Modest Women, Subversive Poems: The Politics of Love in an Egyptian Bedouin Society." *Bulletin British Society for Middle East Studies* 13, no. 2. (1987): 159–68.

———. "The Romance of Resistance: Tracing Transformations of Power Through Bedouin Women." *American Ethnologist* 17, no. 1 (1990): 41–55.

————. "Zones of Theory in the Anthropology of the Arab World." *Annual Review of Anthropology* 18 (1989): 267–306.

Adams, C. C. *Islam and Modernism in Egypt: A Study of the Modern Reform Movement Initiated by Muhammad Abduh.* Oxford: Oxford Univ. Press, 1933.

Afary, Janet. *Foucault and the Iranian Revolution: Gender and the Seductions of Islamism.* Chicago: Univ. of Chicago Press, 2005.

Ahmad, Irfan. "Genealogy of the Islamic State: Reflections on Maududi's Political Thought and Modernism." *Journal of the Royal Anthropological Institute* 16 (2009): 145–62.

Ahmida, Ali. "Inventing or Recovering 'Civil Society' in the Middle East." *Critique: Journal of Critical Studies of the Middle East* 6 (1997): 127–34.

Almond, Ian. *The New Orientalists: Postmodern Representations of Islam from Foucault to Baudrillard.* London: I. B. Tauris, 2007.

Amin, Samir. *Eurocentrism.* 2nd ed. New York: Monthly Review, 1988.

Aygul, Cenk. "Asiatic Mode of Production and the Ottoman Empire." *Journal of Social Sciences* 4, no. 2 (2011): 2–33.

Badran, Margot. *Feminists, Islam, and Nation: Gender and the Making of Modern Egypt.* Princeton, NJ: Princeton Univ. Press, 1995.

Baram, Phillip. *The Department of State in the Middle East, 1919–1945.* Philadelphia: Univ. of Pennsylvania Press, 1978.

Baron, Beth. *Egypt as a Woman: Nationalism, Gender, and Politics.* Berkeley: Univ. of California Press, 2005.

————. *The Orphan Scandal and the Rise of the Muslim Brotherhood.* Stanford, CA: Stanford Univ. Press, 2014.

Bayat, Asef. *Life as Politics: How Ordinary People Change the Middle East.* Stanford, CA: Stanford Univ. Press, 2010.

Beck, Peter J. "'The Less Said about Suez the Better': British Governments and the Politics of Suez's History, 1956–1967." *English Historical Review* 127, no. 508 (June 2009): 605–40.

Beinin, Joel, and Zachary Lockman. *Workers on the Nile.* Princeton, NJ: Princeton Univ. Press, 1987.

Bercovich, Sacvan. *The Puritan Origins of the American Self.* New Haven, CT: Yale Univ. Press, 1975.

Berger, Morroe. *Islam in Egypt Today.* Cambridge: Cambridge Univ. Press, 1970.

Bijlefeld, Willem. "A Century of Arabic and Islamic Studies at Hartford Seminary." *Muslim World* 83 (1993): 103–17.

Blunt, Wilfrid Scawen, and Ahmad Urabi. *Secret History of the English Occupation of Egypt*. New York: Knopf, 1922.

Booth, Marilyn. *May Her Likes Be Multiplied: Biography and Gender in Modern Egypt*. Berkeley: Univ. of California Press, 2001.

Brandis, Royall. "Cotton Competition: US and Egypt, 1929–1948." *Southern Economic Journal* 19, no. 3 (1953): 339–52.

Brehony, Noel, and Ayman El-Desouky. *British-Egyptian Relations from Suez to the Present Day*. London: Saqi, 2007.

Bret, Patrice. *L'expédition d'Égypte, une entreprise des lumières 1798–1801*. Cachan: Technique et documentation, 1999.

Bryan, William Jennings. *The Old World and Its Ways*. St. Louis: Thompson, 1907.

Chirol, Valentine. *The Egyptian Problem*. London: Macmillan, 1920.

Cole, Juan. *Napoleon's Egypt: Invading the Middle East*. New York: St. Martin's, 2007.

Cooper, Elizabeth. *The Women of Egypt*. London: Hurst & Blackett, 1914.

Cromer, Lord Baring. "The Government of Subject Races." *Edinburgh Review* (January 1908): 3–53.

———. *Modern Egypt*. London: Macmillan, 1908.

Curiel, Henri. *Inventory of the Papers of the Egyptian Communists in Exile (Rome Group) Including the Papers of Henri Curiel (1914–1978)*. Edited by Marianne Wigboldus and Jaap Haag. Amsterdam: Stichting Beheer IISG, 1997.

Curtis, Mark. *Secret Affairs: Britain's Collusion with Radical Islam*. London: Serpent's Tail, 2012.

Curtis, Michael. *Orientalism and Islam: European Thinkers on Oriental Despotism in the Middle East and India*. Cambridge: Cambridge Univ. Press, 2009.

Dagbovie, Pero Gaglo. "Black Women Historians from the Late Nineteenth Century to the Dawning of the Civil Rights Movement". *Journal of African American History* 89, no. 3 (2004): 241–61.

Daly, M. W., ed. *The Cambridge History of Egypt, Vol. 2: Modern Egypt from 1517 to the End of the Twentieth Century*. Cambridge: Cambridge Univ. Press, 1988.

Delany, Martin Robinson. *Principia of Ethnology*. Philadelphia: Harper & Brothers, 1879.

Denon, Vivant. *Voyage dans la basse et la haute Égypte pendant les campagnes du Général Bonaparte*. Paris: P. Didot, 1802.

DeNovo, John A. "The Culbertson Economic Mission and Anglo-American Tensions in the Middle East, 1944–55." *Journal of American History* 63 (1977): 913–36.

Des Jardins, Julie. *Women and Historical Enterprise in America*. Chapel Hill: Univ. of North Carolina Press, 2004.

Di Capua, Yoav. *Gatekeepers of the Arab Past: Historians and History Writing in Twentieth-Century Egypt*. Berkeley: Univ. of California Press, 2009.

Dodwell, Henry. *The Founder of Modern Egypt: A Study of Muhammad 'Ali*. Cambridge: Cambridge Univ. Press, 1931.

Doss, Madiha. "Le français en Égypte: Histoire et présence actuelle." *Cahiers de l'association international des études françaises* 56 (2004): 75–98.

Duerst-Lahti, Georgia. "The Government's Role in Building the Women's Movement." *Political Science Quarterly* 104 (1989): 249–68.

Dunn, Stephen. *The Fall and Rise of the Asiatic Mode of Production*. Boston: Routledge & Kegan Paul, 1982.

Elgood, P. G. *The Transit of Egypt*. London: Edward Arnold, 1928.

Euben, Roxanne. *Enemy in the Mirror: Islamic Fundamentalism and the Limits of Modern Rationalism*. Princeton, NJ: Princeton Univ. Press, 1999.

Frankenberg, Ruth. *White Women, Race Matters: The Social Construction of Whiteness*. Minneapolis: Univ. of Minnesota Press, 1993.

Frantz-Murphy, Gladys. "A New Interpretation of the Economic History of Medieval Egypt: The Role of the Textile Industry." *Journal of the Economic and Social History of the Orient* 24, no. 3 (1981): 254–567, 868–1171.

Gairdner, W. H. T., and Sheikh Kurayyim Sallam. *Egyptian Colloquial Arabic: A Conversation Grammar*. Cambridge: W. Heffer & Sons, 1917.

Gallagher, John, and Ronald Robinson. *Africa and the Victorians: The Official Mind of Imperialism*. London: Macmillan, 1965.

Gendzier, Irene. *Dying to Forget: Oil, Power, Palestine, and the Foundations of US Policy in the Middle East*. New York: Columbia Univ. Press, 2015.

Gershoni, Israel, and James P. Jankowski. *Redefining the Egyptian Nation, 1930–1945*. Cambridge: Cambridge Univ. Press, 1995.

Gesink, Indira Falk. "Chaos on the Earth: Subjective Truths versus Communal Unity in Islamic Law and the Rise of Militant Islam." *American Historical Review* 108, no. 3 (2003): 710–33.

Gibb, H. A. R. *Modern Trends in Islam*. Chicago: Univ. of Chicago Press, 1945.

———. *Mohammedanism: A Historical Survey*. London: Oxford Univ. Press, 1949.

Goldschmidt, Arthur, Amy Johnson, and Barak Salmoni, eds. *Re-Envisioning Egypt, 1919–1952*. Cairo: American Univ. in Cairo Press, 2005.

Goldstein, Eric. *The Price of Whiteness*. Princeton, NJ: Princeton Univ. Press, 2008.

Gorman, Anthony. *Historians, State, and Politics in Twentieth-Century Egypt: Contesting the Nation*. London: Routledge Curzon, 2003.

Gran, Judith. "Impact of the World Market on Egyptian Women." *Middle East Report* 58 (1977): 3–7.

Gran, Peter. *Beyond Eurocentrism: A New View of Modern World History*. Syracuse, NY: Syracuse Univ. Press, 1996.

———. "Contesting Hegel and Exceptionalism in a Middle Eastern Context: The Experiences of an American Specialist on Modern Egypt (1970–2011)." In *Getting the Question Right*, edited by Mahmood Mamdani, 113–30. Makerere: Misr, 2013.

———. *Islamic Roots of Capitalism: Egypt, 1760–1840*. Syracuse, NY: Syracuse Univ. Press, 1998.

———. "Quest for a Historical Interpretation of the Life of Shaykh al-Azhar Ibrahim al-Bajuri." In *Reform or Modernization?*, edited by Ra'uf 'Abbas Hamid, 59–92. Cairo: Al-Majlis al-A'la li-l-Thaqafah, 1999.

———. *Rise of the Rich*. Syracuse, NY: Syracuse Univ. Press, 2010.

———. "Upper Egypt in Modern History: A Southern Question." In *Upper Egypt: Identity and Change*, edited by Nicholas Hopkins and Reem Saad, 79–96. Cairo: American Univ. in Cairo Press, 2004.

Grinde, Donald. *Exemplars of Liberty*. Native American Political Series no. 3.3. Los Angeles: Univ. of California Press, 1991.

Hamzah, Dyala. "Nineteenth-Century Egypt as Dynastic Locus of Universality: The History of Muhammad 'Ali by Khalil Ibn Ahmad al-Rajabi." *Comparative Studies of South Asia, Africa and the Middle East* 27, no. 1 (2007): 62–82.

Hanley, Will. "Grieving Cosmopolitanism in Middle East Studies." *History Compass* 6, no. 5 (2008): 1346–67.

Hanna, Nelly. *Making Big Money in 1600*. Syracuse, NY: Syracuse Univ. Press, 1998.

Harris, Christina P. *The Anglo-American Peace Movement in the Mid-nineteenth Century*. New York: Columbia Univ. Press, 1930.

———. *Nationalism and Revolution in Egypt: The Role of the Muslim Brotherhood*. Stanford, CA: Hoover Institute, 1964.

Hashimoto, C[hikara]. "Fighting the Cold War or Post-Colonialism." *International History Review* 36 (2014): 19–44.

Haug, Brendan. "Water and Power: Reintegrating the State into the Study of Egyptian Irrigation." *History Compass* 15 (2017): 1–9.

Heyworth Dunne, James (Jamal-Addin). *Land Tenure in Islam*. Cairo: Nahda, 1950.

———. *Religious and Political Trends in Modern Egypt*. Washington, DC: N.p., 1950.

Howell, J. Morton. *Egypt's Past, Present, and Future*. Dayton, OH: Service, 1929.

Irwin, Robert. *Dangerous Knowledge: Orientalism and Its Discontents*. Woodstock, NY: Overlook, 2006.

Jacoby, Russell. *Social Amnesia: A Critique of Contemporary Psychology*. Piscataway, NJ: Transaction Press, 1997.

Jennings, Francis. *The Invasion of America: Colonialism and the Cant of Conquest*. Chapel Hill: Univ. of North Carolina Press, 2010.

Kalin, Michael. "Hidden Pharaohs: Egypt, Engineers, and the Modern Hydraulic." MA thesis, Oxford Univ., Trinity College, 2006.

Kaufmann, Eric. "The Dominant Ethnic Moment: Towards the Abolition of 'Whiteness.'" *Ethnicities* 6, no. 2 (2006): 231–53.

———. *The Rise and Fall of Anglo-America*. Cambridge, MA: Harvard Univ. Press, 2004.

Kent, J[ohn]. "The Egyptian Base and the Defence of the Middle East, 1945–1954." *Journal of Imperial and Commonwealth History* 21 (1993): 45–56.

Kernaghan, Jennifer. "Lord Cromer as Orientalist and Social Engineer in Egypt, 1882–1907." MA thesis, Univ. of British Columbia, 1993.

Khalil, Osamah. *America's Dream Palace*. Cambridge, MA: Harvard Univ. Press, 2016.

————. "At the Crossroads of Empire: The United States, the Middle East, and the Politics of Knowledge, 1902–2002." PhD diss., Univ. of California, Berkeley, 2011.

Kirkwood, Patrick M. "'Lord Cromer's Shadow': Political Anglo-Saxonism and the Egyptian Protectorate as a Model in the American Philippines." *Journal of World History* 27, no. 1 (2016): 1–26.

Koppes, Clayton R. "Captain Mahan, General Gordon, and the Origins of the Term 'Middle East.'" *Middle East Studies* 12 (1976): 95–98.

Langohr, Vickie. "Too Much Civil Society, Too Little Politics? Egypt and Other Liberalizing Arab Regimes." *Comparative Politics* 36, no. 2. (January 2004): 181–204.

Laqueur, Walter. *Nasser's Egypt*. London: Weidenfeld & Nicolson, 1956.

Leeder, S. H. *Modern Sons of the Pharaohs*. London: Hodder & Stoughton, 1918.

Lewis, Bernard. *Land of Enchanters: Egyptian Short Stories from the Earliest Times to the Present Day*. Princeton, NJ: Princeton Univ. Press, [1948] 2001.

Lewis, Bernard, and P. M. Holt. *Historians of the Middle East*. London: Oxford Univ. Press, 1962.

Lindsay, June Ambridge. "Searching History: The Non-elite in Ancient Egypt." *History Compass* 2 (2007): 1–11.

Lloyd, George (Lord). *Egypt since Cromer*. London: Macmillan, 1933.

Lockman, Zachary. *Contending Visions of the Middle East*. Cambridge: Cambridge Univ. Press, 2009.

————. *Field Notes*. Stanford, CA: Stanford Univ. Press, 2015.

Macdonald, Duncan Black. *The Religious Attitude and Life in Islam*. London: Darf, 1909.

Makdisi, Ussama. *Artillery of Heaven*. Ithaca, NY: Cornell Univ. Press, 2008.

Manela, Erez. *The Wilsonian Moment: Self-Determination and the International Origins of Anticolonial Nationalism*. Oxford: Oxford Univ. Press, 2007.

Manley, Deborah, ed. *Women Travelers in Egypt*. Cairo: American Univ. in Cairo Press, 2012.

Mariscotti, Cathlyn. *Gender and Class in the Egyptian Women's Movement, 1929–1935*. Syracuse, NY: Syracuse Univ. Press, 2008.

Marsot, Afaf Lutfi al-Sayyid. *Egypt and Cromer*. New York: Frederick A. Praeger, 1969.

————. *Egypt in the Reign of Muhammad 'Ali*. Cambridge: Cambridge Univ. Press, 1984.

Melman, Billie. *Women's Orients: English Women and the Middle East, 1718–1918*. Ann Arbor: Univ. of Michigan Press, 1992.

Mikhail, Alan. "Labor and Environment in Egypt since 1500." *International Labor and Working Class History*, no. 85 (Spring 2014): 10–32.

————. *Nature and Empire in Ottoman Egypt: An Environmental History*. Cambridge: Cambridge Univ. Press, 2012.

Miller, Melissa Lee. "The Imperial Feminine: Victorian Women Travelers in Late Nineteenth-Century Egypt." PhD diss., Kent State Univ., 2000.

Mitchell, Timothy. "America's Egypt: Discourse of the Development Industry." *Middle East Report* (March–April 1991): 18–34, 36.

————. *Colonizing Egypt*. Berkeley: Univ. of California Press, 1988.

————. "The Middle East in the Past and Future of Social Science." Univ. of California International and Area Studies (UCIAS) digital collection, 2013. Accessed March 24, 2020. http://repositories.cdlib.org/uciaspubs/editedvolumes/3/3.

————. *Rule of Experts*. Berkeley: Univ. of California Press, 2002.

Mohamed, Duse. *In the Land of the Pharaohs*. London: Stanley Paul, 1911.

Mosharrafa, Moustafa M. *Cultural Survey of Modern Egypt*. 2 vols. London: Longmans, 1947–48.

Murphy, Jane H. "Ahmad al-Damanhuri (1689–1778) and the Utility of Expertise." *Osiris* 25 (2010): 85–103.

Nelson, Cynthia. *Doriya Shafiq: Egyptian Feminist, a Woman Apart*. Gainesville: Univ. of Florida Press, 1996.

O'Leary, Brendan. *The Asiatic Mode of Production: Oriental Despotism, Historical Materialism, and Indian History*. Cambridge, MA: Basil Blackwell, 1989.

Oliver, Kelly, and Marilyn Pearsall, eds. *Feminist Interpretations of Friedrich Nietzsche*. Univ. Park: Penn State Univ. Press, 1998.

Owen, Roger. "The Influence of Lord Cromer's Indian Experience on British Policy in Egypt, 1883–1907." In *St. Antony's Papers*, no. 17, 109–39. Oxford: Oxford Univ. Press, 1965.

————. *Lord Cromer: Victorian Imperialist, Edwardian Proconsul*. Oxford: Oxford Univ. Press, 2004.

Peirce, Leslie. *The Imperial Harem*. New York: Oxford Univ. Press, 1993.

Perkins, John. *Confessions of an Economic Hit Man*. New York: Plume, 2005.

Perry, Elizabeth Israel. "Men Are from the Gilded Age, Women Are from the Progressive Era." *Journal of the Gilded Age and the Progressive Era* 1 (2002): 25–48.

Pollard, Lisa. "Amateur Historians, the 'Woman Question,' and the Production of Modern History in Turn-of-the-Twentieth-Century Egypt." In *Making Women's Histories: Beyond National Perspectives*, edited by Pamela Nadell, 137–60. New York: New York Univ. Press, 2013.

Raymond, André. *Artisans et commerçants au Caire au XVIII*e *siècle*. Damascus: IFAO, 1973–74.

Reid, Donald M. *Contesting Antiquity in Egypt*. Cairo: American Univ. in Cairo Press, 2015.

———. "Cromer and the Classics: Imperialism, Nationalism, and the Greco-Roman Past in Modern Egypt." *Middle Eastern Studies* 12, no. 1 (1992): 1–29.

Rifaat, Mohamed. *The Awakening of Modern Egypt*. London: Longmans, 1947.

Rizq, Karam, and Dominique Avon. *La Nahda: Réveils de la pensée en langue arabe, Approches, perspectives*. Jounieh, Lebanon: Presses de l'USEK, 2009.

Ross, Dorothy. *The Origins of American Social Science*. Cambridge: Cambridge Univ. Press, 1991.

Rothstein, Theodor. *Egypt's Ruin: A Financial and Administrative Record*. London: Fifield, 1910.

Ryad, Umar. *Islamic Reformism and Christianity: A Critical Reading of the Works of Muhammad Rashid Rida*. Leiden: Brill, 2009.

———. "Muslim Response to Missionary Activities in Egypt: With a Special Reference to the al-Azhar High Corps of 'Ulama' (1925–1935)." In *New Faith in Ancient Lands: Western Missions in the Middle East in the Nineteenth and Early Twentieth Centuries*, edited by Heleen Murre-van den Berg, 281–307. Leiden, Netherlands: Brill, 2006.

Sadiq Sa'd, Ahmad. *L'Égypte pharaonique*. Paris: CERM, 1975.

Sadowski, Yahya. *Political Vegetables: Businessman and Bureaucrat in the Development of Egyptian Agriculture*. Washington, DC: Brookings Institute, 1991.

Scanlon, Jennifer, and Shaaron Cosner. *American Women Historians, 1700s–1990s*. Westport, CT: Greenwood, 1996.

Selim, Samah. "Languages of Civilizations." *Translator* 15 (2009): 39–56.

———. "The Nahda, Popular Fiction, and the Politics of Translation." *MIT-EJMES* 4, no. 3 (2004): 71–90.

Shami, Seteney, and Cynthia Miller-Idriss. *Middle East Studies for the New Millennium*. New York: New York Univ. Press, 2016.

Sharkey, Heather. *American Evangelicals in Egypt: Missionary Encounters in an Age of Empire*. Princeton, NJ: Princeton Univ. Press, 2008.

Shelley, Michael T. "Temple Gairdner of Cairo Revisited." *Islam and Christian-Muslim Relations* 110, no. 3 (1999): 261–78.

Shenhav, Yehouda. "Beyond 'Instrumental Rationality': Lord Cromer and the Imperial Roots of Eichmann's Bureaucracy." *Journal of Genocide Research* 15 (2013): 379–99.

Sicherman, Harvey. "Adventures in State-Building: Bremer's Iraq and Cromer's Egypt." *American Interest* 2, no. 5 (2007): 28–41.

Singerman, Diane. *Avenues of Participation: Family, Politics, and Networks in Urban Quarters of Cairo*. Princeton, NJ: Princeton Univ. Press, 1995.

Sirrs, Owen L. *A History of the Egyptian Intelligence Service, 1910–2009*. London: Routledge, 2010.

Sonbol, Amira El-Azhary. "A History of Marriage Contracts in Egypt." In *The Islamic Marriage Contract*, edited by Asifa Quraishi and Frank E. Vogel, 87–122. Cambridge, MA: Harvard Univ. Press, 2008.

Springborg, Robert. "Patrimonialism and Policy-Making in Egypt: Nasser and Sadat and the Tenure Policy for Reclaimed Lands." *Middle Eastern Studies* 15, no. 1 (1979): 49–69.

Stanley, Bruce. "Middle East City Networks and the 'New Urbanism.'" *Cities* 22, no. 3 (2005): 189–99.

Stanton, Elizabeth Cady. *The Woman's Bible*. North Chelmsford, MA: Courier, 1895.

Starr, Deborah A. "Recuperating Cosmopolitan Alexandria: Circulation of Narratives and Narratives of Circulation." *Cities* 22, no. 3 (2005): 217–28.

Stoddard, Lothrop. *New World of Islam*. New York: C. Scribner's Sons, 1921.

Storrs, Sir Ronald. *Orientations*. London: Readers Union, 1939.

Stuurman, Siep. "Cosmopolitan Egalitarianism in the Enlightenment: Anquetil Duperron on India and America." *Journal of the History of Ideas* 68, no. 2 (2007): 255–78.

Tibebu, Teshale. *Hegel and the Third World: The Making of Eurocentrism in World History*. Syracuse, NY: Syracuse Univ. Press, 2010.

Tignor, Robert L. "The Indianization of the Egyptian Administration under British Rule." *American Historical Review* 68 (1963): 636–61.

Trafton, Scott. *Egypt: Land, Race, and Nineteenth-Century Egyptomania.* Durham, NC: Duke Univ. Press, 2004.

Tucker, Judith. *Women in Nineteenth-Century Egypt.* Cambridge: Cambridge Univ. Press, 1985.

Udovitch, A. L. "International Trade and the Medieval Egyptian Countryside." In *Agriculture in Egypt from Pharaonic to Modern Times*, edited by Alan K. Bowman and Eugene Rogan, 27–86. Oxford: Oxford Univ. Press, 1999.

Vatikiotis, P. J. *Nasser and His Generation.* London: Palgrave Macmillan, 1978.

Vitalis, Robert. "International Studies in America." *Ideas and Issues* 3 (2002).

———. "The New Deal in Egypt: The Rise of Anglo-American Commercial Competition in World War II." *Diplomatic History* 20, no. 2 (1996): 211–40.

Vlassopoulos, Kostas. *Unthinking the Greek Polis: Ancient Greek History beyond Eurocentrism.* Cambridge: Cambridge Univ. Press, 2007.

Warzeski, Jeanne-Marie. "Mapping the Unknown: Gendered Spaces and the Oriental Other in Travelogues of Egypt by US Women, 1854–1914." *History and Anthropology* 13 (2002): 301–17.

Watson, Andrew. *The American Mission in Egypt, 1854–1896.* Pittsburgh: United Presbyterian Board, 1898.

Watson, Charles R. *Egypt and the Christian Crusade.* Philadelphia: Board of Foreign Missions of the United Presbyterian Church of NA, 1907.

Welch, William M. "British Attitudes to the Administration of Egypt under Lord Cromer, 1892–1907." PhD diss., Oxford Univ., 1978.

Wilford, Hugh. *America's Great Game.* New York: Basic Books, 2013.

Wilson, John A. *A History of American Egyptology.* Chicago: Univ. of Chicago Press, 1964.

Wittfogel, Karl. *Oriental Despotism: A Comparative Study of Total Power.* New Haven, CT: Yale Univ. Press, 1957.

Young, George. *Egypt.* New York: Scribner's, 1927.

Zwemer, Samuel. "The Earl of Cromer on Islam." *Missionary Review of the World* 31 (1908): 649–54.

Index

'Abbas Hamid, Ra'uf, 9–10
'Abbas Hilmi Pasha, 116, 117
'Abd al-Hafiz, Magdi, 106, 107
'Abd al-Mu'ti, Husam, 165–67n5
'Abd al-Rahman al-Rafi'i, 103–4
Abd al-Rahman Sami Bey, 112–13, 122
'Abd al-Raziq, Muhammad Hasanayn,
    47
'Abd al-Raziq 'Isa, 46, 105, 108–9
'Abduh, Ibrahim, 18
'Abduh, Muhammad, 46, 68, 72
Abou el-Haj, Rifa'at, 60
absolutism, 6, 125, 127, 128
abstract science, 76–77
Abu'l-Futuh, Raghda, 102
Abul-Magd, Zeinab, 77
Abu-Lughod, Lila, 74–76
Abu Taqiyya, 159n4
academia: American identity and, 31;
    Egyptian scholars and, 49; global-
    ization and, 23; Hegelian tradition
    in, 25, 80; hierarchy of, 29; middle
    class and, 33, 52; professionaliza-
    tion and, x, 14, 15; women in,
    24, 140. *See also* Anglo-American
    scholarship; scholars
'Adl, Sabri al-, 98–99, 167n23
Afandiyya, 94. *See also* middle class
Africa, 18–19, 45, 129
African Americans, 18, 24, 32, 146

agriculture: economy and, 37–38,
    140, 159n4; grain trade and, 85,
    87, 134; irrigation system and, xiii,
    10–11, 38, 140, 154n11
Ahmad, Irfan, 72–73
Akbar, 43
Albania: Egyptian royal family and,
    122; Hasan al-'Attar and, 118–19,
    169n8; Muhammad 'Ali and, 112,
    120–21, 122, 142
Alexandria, 63, 64–65, 68, 90, 142
Algeria, 6, 100, 106
'Alim, 168n28
Alleaume, Ghislaine, 108
Al-Misri (newspaper), 18
amateurs, 13, 16, 146
American character literature, 31, 32
American Historical Association, 20
American Historical Review, 153n5
American identity: ethnicity and, 32;
    as national identity, xiii; Oriental
    despotism paradigm and, xiii–xiv,
    28, 32–33, 140–43; scholarship
    and, viii, xiii–xiv, 33
American missionaries. *See*
    missionaries
*American Mission in Egypt, 1854–
    1896, The* (Watson), ix
American Research Center in Egypt,
    22

185

marriage, 73–74, 133, 170–71n6

Marsot, Afaf, 54, 56–57, 122

Marxism, 7–8, 60–61

masculinism, 17, 60, 63

materialism, dialectical, xii, 8, 9, 149

Mawdudi, 73

McKinley, William, 19

medicine, 98–99, 123, 136, 167n23

medieval studies, x, 10, 27, 159n4

Meguid, Ibrahim Abdel, 65

Melman, Billie, 17

Memoires (Moiret), 101–2

mercantilism: birth and development
    of, 84, 125; *The Cambridge History
    of Egypt* on, 85–86; European, 5,
    127; French Occupation and, 89;
    legal system and, 135; Muhammad
    'Ali period and, 89; in Ottoman
    period, 127–30; women and, 132,
    133

merchants: vs. Church, 165–67n5;
    class divisions and, 131; Dutch,
    129; Egyptian, 129, 166n5;
    French, 85–86, 142; guilds and,
    10, 165n5; Ladino, 129; Ottoman
    period and, 5; Shaykh Hummam
    and, 88; Venetian, 129

MESA (Middle East Studies Associa-
    tions), 22, 23

*Mi'atay 'am 'ala al-hamlah al-
    firansiya (R'ya Misriyah)* (Ibrahim
    and Hamid), 82–83

middle class: academia and, 33, 52; *The
    Cambridge History of Egypt* on, 94;
    indigenous, 90; narcotics and, 51;
    Nietzschean thought and, 24–25;
    scholars from, 52–53; wealth of, 23,
    25; working women, 133

Middle East, terminology of, 43,
    160n11

Middle East Centers, 53, 139, 162n25

Middle East Institute, 151–52n1

Middle East studies: Cold War and,
    162n23; Development Revolution
    period and, 139; emergence of,
    ix, 14, 151–52n1; gender in, 140;
    modern Egypt studies and, 51n1;
    New Urbanism and, 66; oil indus-
    try and, 3, 12; policy associations
    for, 138; Saidian tradition and, xii;
    subfields of, 11–12, 138, 154n14;
    women and, 27; Zachary Lockman
    on, 53

Middle East Studies Associations
    (MESA), 22, 23

Middle East Supply Center, 21,
    157n30

military technology, 86, 142

Milla, 134

Miller, C. R., 153n5

Miller, Melissa Lee, 17

Milner Commission, 44, 149

Ministry of Education, 103

Ministry of Social Affairs, 56

Ministry of the Interior, 56

missionaries: colonial officials and, 37;
    contributions of, ix–x, 146; decline
    of, 52; Development Revolution
    period and, 52; formative period
    and, 36, 51, 52, 138, 158n1, 161–
    62n20; on Islam, 1, 51, 144–45;
    Nahda and, 68; Oriental despotism
    model and, 7; as sources, 144–45

mission civilatrice (civilizing mission),
    97–98

Mitchell, Timothy, 76–77, 151–52n1,
    159–60n5

mode of production: Asiatic, 8–9,
    152n3; capitalism as, 126; coming
    of the West change in, 104

postracial society, 32
post–World War II era, 1, 2, 50, 55.
    See also Cold War; Development
    Revolution period
poverty, 74, 131–32, 170n4
power structures, 125, 170n2. See also
    political structures
presentism, vs. historicism, 140
professionalization: academia and, x,
    14, 15; of archaeology, 157n34;
    civil society and, viii–ix; develop-
    ment of, 23; of Egyptian studies,
    ix, 14, 35; of knowledge, vii, viii–x,
    13–14; prehistory of, 14; sectional-
    ism and, 19–20; the state and, ix;
    women and, 24, 155n20
progressives, women as, 17, 155n24
property rights, 4, 6, 10
Protestant missionaries. See
    missionaries
Ptolemaic worldview, 109
public debt, 90–91, 144
Puritan tradition, xiii, 162n23

Qadi, Jihan al-, 103–4
Qazdogli Mamluks, 85
Qutb, Sayyid, 73

race/racism: Anglo-American scholar-
    ship and, 18–19; ethnicity school
    and, 32; gender and, 17; global-
    ization and, 23; Lord Cromer
    and, 52; Middle East studies and,
    151n1; professional women and, 24
racial myths, 31, 157n35
radicalization, 24, 50
Rafi'i, al-, 105
Raghib, Yusuf, 159n4

Rawdat al-Madaris (journal), 117
Raymond, André, 104, 108, 159n4
Razi, al-, 123
Reagan, Ronald, 26
regional stratification, 133–34
Reid, Donald, 91–92
Reimer, Helena, 156n26
Reisner, George, 155n20
religion, 55–56, 71–74, 134. *See also*
    Christians and Christianity; Islam
*Religious and Political Trends in
    Modern Egypt* (Heyworth-Dunne),
    47–48, 161n16
*Remembering One's Roots: Mehmed
    Ali Pasha's Links to the Macedonian
    Town of Kavala* (Lowery), 121–22
repressed knowledge, 158n39
revisionist scholarship, 154n11
Revolution of 1919, 62, 92
Revolution of 1952, 55, 69, 94
Rida, Rashid, 68–69
Rifaat, Mohamed, 49–50
"Risala fi hall lughz ba'd al-'ulama'
    min Latbalun, Al-," 169n8
rise of the West, xii, 25, 30, 31, 89
Rivlin, Helen, 104
Roosevelt, Eleanor, 18
Roosevelt, Theodore, 13
Rothstein, Theodor, 7
Roussillon, Alain, 94–95
Roux, Charles, 103
royal family, 3, 7, 37, 122
Rule of Experts (Mitchell), 76–77
ruling elites: dynastic marriage and,
    170–71n6; globalization and, 25;
    Liberal Age and, 93; mercantil-
    ism and, 128; Oriental despotism
    model and, 3, 4; vs. the ruled, xii,
    4; scholars' deference to, 29
Russia, 26, 119

Peter Gran is professor of history at Temple University. He is the author of *The Rise of the Rich: A New View of Modern World History*, *Islamic Roots of Capitalism: Egypt, 1760–1840*, and *Beyond Eurocentrism: A New View of Modern World History*, all published by Syracuse University Press.